Witness the Madness of Man
in the History of

THE KISS

CANNIBALISM

HEAD-SHRINKING

HARI-KARI

CHINESE FOOT BINDING

TATTOOS

MUMMIES

THE SACRIFICE OF THE MERIAH

CIRCUMCISION

THE MURDEROUS BROTHERHOOD OF THE THUGS

AND MANY MORE....

D1097174

THE STRANGE WAYS OF MAN
was originally published by Hart Publishing Company, Inc.

THE
STRANGE WAYS
OF
MAN

RITES AND RITUALS
AND THEIR INCREDIBLE ORIGINS

E. ROYSTON PIKE

 A POCKET BOOK EDITION published by
Simon & Schuster of Canada, Ltd. ○ Richmond Hill, Ontario, Canada
Registered User of the Trademark

THE STRANGE WAYS OF MAN

Hart edition published May, 1967

Pocket Book edition published February, **1970**

2nd printing . . . . December, 1969

Contents

Introduction

MEN ARE STRANGE CREATURES, and, so most men would probably agree, women are stranger. And what strange things they have been up to, since they first came down from the trees and started to move around on their own two feet!

Some of the strangest things they have been responsible for are described in the pages that follow. But only some, for great libraries would be needed to hold all the books that have been written on this most fascinating subject. This is a selection, and of course a personal one. Every connoisseur of human oddities keeps his own notebook, and what its pages report is what has struck most powerfully on his individual fancy.

All the same, there is something here that should appeal to readers of widely different tastes. There is a drama, plenty of it—"strong" drama, and tender love-making. Stories of murder and sudden death that put into the shade anything you may read in the Sunday newspapers. Travellers' tales from distant places. Exhibitions of religious ecstasy, and mysterious revelations of the artistic impulse. Freaks of outrageous fashion. Bodily mutilations and mental aberrations, and uninhibited displays of the most wayward of human inclinations.

Whenever possible, the narrative is that of an eye-witness, so in effect we are indeed "there". We may join a gang of Thugs that is following hard upon the footsteps of an unsuspecting traveller, and may stay with them until we hear the whistling of the fatal noose and see the victim brought down in a scurry of blood and dust. We may take a trip to the lairs of the head-hunters in Borneo or the Amazonian jungles, observe at close quarters the technique of the blowpipe, and note how a human head can be shrivelled into a pocket-sized memento. If our nerves are strong enough, we may sit within a few feet of a Japanese officer who is performing on himself the time-honoured ritual of hara-kiri; and our stomach as well as our nerves must be strong when, stumbling up the beach on one of the idyllic isles of the South Seas, we come across the grisly preparations for a cannibal banquet.

Perhaps you have a bent towards travel in the more out-of-the-way places of the world? Then here are the stately Toda tribesfolk waiting to make you welcome. Seat yourself in the porch of one of their huts of cane and thatch, and try to make out the shockingly complicated marriage arrangements of a society in which as a rule a girl marries all her husband's brothers. Or you may ride across the great open spaces of southern Africa, catch up with some of the little, pot-bellied and big-bottomed Bushmen, and wonder whether those drawings and carvings with which they have covered every convenient rock face are indeed an indication of their descent from the highly gifted cave-artists of the Old Stone Age in Europe. Or again, with Miss Margaret Mead and David Attenborough as guides, you may stand on the beaches of the Pacific and look out across the ocean for the coming of the mysterious vessels bearing "cargo", on receipt of which the natives (so they hold with the completest confidence) will enter upon a blessed time of peace and plenty and endless joy.

Now in conclusion, a word of warning. Don't let us fall into the vulgar error of supposing that we are such fine fellows, and that those who think and act differently are nothing better than benighted savages. True enough we do not dine off the man next door (although our remote ancestors may have done). But there are other things that we do that some people think almost equally strange and abhorrent. Kissing, for instance. . . . When Winwood Reade tried to kiss his pretty little savage in the heart of Africa, she made a bolt for the bush; and Savage Landor's "Ainu belle" didn't kiss: she used to bite instead! If you want to know more, read on, as they used to say in the old novelettes. You can meet both these young ladies in the first chapter. . . .

August, 1966   E. ROYSTON PIKE

Chapter 1

The Natural History of a Kiss

WHAT'S so strange about a kiss? Surely kissing is one of the most natural things in the world, so natural indeed that we might almost ask, what are lips for if not for kissing? But this is what *we* think, and a whole lot of people think very differently. To them kissing is not at all natural. It is not something that everybody does, or would like to do. On the contrary, it is a deplorable habit, unnatural, unhygienic, bordering on the nasty and even definitely repulsive.

When we come to look into the matter, we shall find that there is a geographical distribution of kissing; and if some enterprising ethnologist were to prepare a "map of kissing" it would show a surprisingly large amount of blank space. Most of the so-called primitive races of mankind, such as the New Zealanders (Maoris), the Australian aborigines, the Papuans, Tahitians, and other South Sea Islanders, and the Esquimaux of the frozen north, were ignorant of kissing until they were taught the technique by the white men who appeared among them as voyagers and explorers, traders and missionaries. The

Chinese have been wont to consider kissing as vulgar and all too suggestive of cannibalism, and, as we shall see in a moment, they have not been alone in this. The Japanese have no word for it in their vocabulary, and the practice is tabooed as utterly immodest and revolting, except of course among those who have made a point of adopting Western ways. But it is Africa which "has the sad distinction of being the largest non-kissing area in the world".

Such at least was the conclusion of the young English traveller Winwood Reade, and (to meet the objections of those who speak out of present-day experience) it should be explained that he was writing of a time when the natives of Equatorial Africa were still savages. The words are taken from his book *Savage Africa* (1863), in which he describes his travels in the then unknown "Gorilla country" of the Upper Gaboon in West Africa. Alone save for a few native attendants, he penetrated farther up-country than a white man had ever been before, and for some time he remained in a kind of honourable captivity as the guest of Quenqueza, the "king" of the Rembo tribesfolk. It was then that he met Ananga. She was beautiful—"full and finely moulded, hands and feet exquisitely small, complexion a deep warm colour, her eyes large and filled with a melancholy expression"—no wonder that, in one of those unguarded moments "in which the heart rises to the lips, and makes them do all sorts of silly things", he made to kiss her. . . .

Not on first meeting, of course, but when for weeks they had been for hours each day in one another's company. He had gone to Africa to study the gorilla in his native haunts, but he found "this pretty savage" a much more delicious study. At first she was timid, very timid, for she had never seen a white man before, but she tried to keep this from him lest she should hurt his feelings, "and I could read it only in her fluttering eyes and in her poor little heart, which used to throb so loudly when we were alone. I found her as chaste, as coquettish, and as full of innocent mischief, as a girl of sixteen would have been in England. In a little while I found myself becoming fond of her". So the thought came to him of a "new and innocent pleasure". To bestow a kiss upon lips which tremble with love for the first time—that (he reflected) was certainly an epoch in a man's existence; but just imagine what it must be to kiss one who has never conceived the possibility of such a thing, who has never dreamt that human lips could be applied to such a purpose! "And so, I kissed Ananga, the daughter of the king." And what happened? "She gave a shriek, and bounded from the house like a frightened fawn." What Winwood Reade had forgotten, or perhaps he had never realized, was that "this mode of salutation is utterly unknown in Western Africa. Ananga knew that the serpent moistens its victim with its lips before it begins its repast. All the tales of white cannibals which she had heard from infancy had returned to her. The poor child had thought that I was going to dine off her, and she had run for her life!"

Soon, however, it was "all's well that ends well". Ananga was pursued and brought back by Winwood Reade's native interpreter. She was "panting and trembling, and her cheeks were wet with tears; but I explained to her that this was only a fashion of my country, and she offered her pouting lips in atonement of her folly".

Why was it, the young man mused, that these "poor benighted creatures", as he half-humorously calls them, "had never discovered our civilized method of endearment?" It was certainly not through any deficiency in their affection, or in their ability to show it. He had seen many a time the hunters returning to their village in the late afternoon, bringing with them the food they had gathered in the bush, and their womenfolk had hurried out to meet them and welcomed them as though they had been away for years, murmuring to them in baby language, calling them by their names of love, patting their breasts and laying arm upon arm, shaking their hands, caressing their faces and embracing them in every possible way—except with the lips. He sought an explanation, and all he could think of was that perhaps it was because African women have black lips ("though sometimes, but rarely, the under lip is red"), which hardly sounded very convincing.

Then like the cheerful young Englishman that he was, he went on to urge his lady-readers not "to despise the poor untutored African, or judge him too severely on account of an ignorance for which he is not to blame. He is ever willing to adopt the customs of a higher race". One day he had met a Negro in the Gaboon who had been converted to Christianity, and this man had assured him with honest pride that though the heathen did not know how to kiss, the Christians were becoming quite proficient in the art. Then on another occasion when visiting a village on the Grain Coast, a young Kruman, sitting with his wife in front of his hut, had called out to him as he went by, "Lookee, Massa, I sabby kiss!", and forthwith had suited the action to the word. But the lady "seemed to be much amused, and not altogether pleased with this novel application of the lips".

Dr. Johnson in his Dictionary defines a kiss as "a salute given by joining the lips", which may be accepted as the minimum of definition; a more intimate one is, "a prolonged pressing of mouth against mouth with slight intermittent movements". How and when did it all begin? In dictionaries of quotations we may find the pious wish, "May his soul be in heaven—he deserves it, I'm sure—who was first the inventor of kissing." But there is no knowing who that man was, and it may well be (as naturalists have suggested) that kissing was not a human invention at all, but derives from such animal practices as a dog or cat rubbing its head against its master's knee, the intertwining of elephant trunks, the billing of birds, and the "caressing" strokes of insects' antennae. But if there *was* a man who first tried the experiment of pressing his lips against those of a pretty woman, we may be sure that he belonged to the Indo-European stream of race and culture.

In tracing the history of the kiss we are led back to ancient India. In the period of the Vedas, round about 2000 B.C., the Indians seem to have practised what is called the nose or sniff kiss, of which more later; but by about the time of the great Mahabharata epic (500 B.C.?) the salutation with the lips had become general. It was certainly well established when the ancient sage Vatsyayana composed his *Aphorisms on Love (Kama Sutra)*, for amongst its twelve hundred and fifty verses are a number concerned with the technique of kissing with the lips. The best places for kissing are indicated, viz., the forehead, the eyes, the cheeks, the throat, the bosom, the breasts, the lips, and inside the mouth; and the different kinds of kiss are analysed according to their intensity and method of application, and it is further explained that there are different kinds of kisses for different parts of the body.

From India the practice is supposed to have spread westwards to Persia, Assyria, Syria, Greece, Italy, and by way of the channels of Roman influence throughout most of

Europe. The Teutonic tribes on the borderlands of the Empire practised the mouth kiss, but it has been pointed out that there is no word for "kiss" in the Celtic tongues.

The Romans had different words for different kinds of which the primary meaning was "a little mouth" or "a sweet mouth". The osculum was not applied to the lips but to the face or cheek, and it came to be established as the kiss of friendship; in direct descent from it is the public embrace performed by French generals and politicians. Was this the kind of kiss that (so we are told by Plutarch) the Roman women, after they had burnt the ships which brought them from distant Troy, turned away the anger of their menfolk? We can hardly suppose so. Surely their endearments took the form of the mouth-to-mouth application, which is so much more tender and satisfying. But it would seem that a special word for this species of kiss did not make its appearance in the vocabulary until the last century B.C.

This was *basium*, and we are told that the young poet Catullus was the first and for some time the only writer to employ it to indicate something much more passionate than the osculum. This was, we may be sure, the kind of kiss that he applied to the lips of his beautiful but notoriously flighty mistress whom he calls Lesbia, although her name in real life was Clodia. Nor is there any reason to doubt that she liked them, if not quite so much as he did. "You ask how many kissings of you, Lesbia, are enough for me, and more than enough? As many as the grains of sand in the Libyan deserts, or as the stars that look down, in the silent watches of the night, on the stolen loves of men. If your Catullus, your mad Catullus, could kiss you with as many kisses as that, then perhaps this might be enough." Or as he put it in his most famous poem, that has been many times rendered into English, as by the young Coleridge:

> A thousand kisses take and give!
> Another thousand!—to the store
> Add hundreds—then a thousand more!
> And when they to a million mount,
> Let confusion take the account—

That you, the number never knowing,
May continue, still bestowing. . .

From *basium* is derived the French *baiser*, as also the words for "kiss" in Italian, Spanish, and Portuguese. Some etymologists hold that it was also the parent of the old English word "buss", defined as a rude or playful kiss, a smack on the lips.

The Romans had a third kind of kiss, one that was given between the lips with the assistance of the tongue. This was *savium*, which meant originally "a mouth, or lips, puckered up to kiss". A diminutive of this was *saviolum*, "a sweet kiss", a word which Catullus employed in his verses; the transition from this to the kiss of passion was easy. Although Ovid seldom used the word, he was well acquainted with this sort of kiss, as every reader of his amatory poems will not need to be told; thus in Christopher Marlowe's translation of the *Amores* we read of a girl "who eagerly kissed me with her tongue", and another who "in my lips her whole tongue hid, mine in hers she dips".

From the Romans the custom of kissing with the lips or mouth passed into the Middle Ages, when to be able to kiss nicely was a required accomplishment of a knight in the Courts of Love. Dante's description of the rapturous kissing of Paola and Francesca leads up to the Renaissance, when poet and playwright surrounded the kiss with all that speaks of romantic ecstasy. Nor were all the great practitioners of the art drawn from the warmer south; the custom was highly developed in England, so that we find Erasmus, the great Dutch humanist, expressing himself most favourably concerning the kissing powers and propensities of English womanhood. "The English girls are divinely pretty," he wrote in a letter to a friend on the Continent; "soft, pleasant, gentle, and charming as the Muses. They have one custom which cannot be too much admired. When you go anywhere on a visit all the girls kiss you. They kiss you when you arrive, they kiss you when you go away, and they kiss you again when you return. Go where you will, it is all kisses; and, my dear Faustus, if you had once tasted how soft and fragrant those lips are, you would wish to spend your whole life here."

One of the most persistent notes in the music of English poetry is the sound of the intimate contact of lips on lips, of mouth on mouth. Looking at it from the physiological angle, a kiss is what has been described as "a special case of tactile sensory pleasure". Of the senses involved (and there is more than one) the most important is touch. Nowhere is the sense of touch more highly developed than where the outer skin meets the inner skin or mucous membrane, and it is for this reason that the lips are one of the most erogenic areas in the body.

Another of the senses that may play a part is taste. The pioneer English anthropologist E. B. Tylor described a kiss as "salute by tasting", and it is on record that the lovers of Poppaea, the beautiful but licentious consort of the Emperor Nero, declared that her kisses had the flavour of wild berries. Closely connected with tasting is biting, and that refinement of it, suction with the closed lips. In one of his love-letters to Sophie de Monnier, Mirabeau writes, "I am kissing you and biting you all over: so enamoured am I of your creamy skin that I would cover it with bruises." In Italian there is an expression, "kissing with the teeth", which is a synonym for love-making. This form of kissing (if, indeed, it may be called that) is frequently met with in the literature of eroticism, but a specially charming illustration may be found in the "tender little idyll" that the young A. H. Savage Landor described in his book *Alone with the Hairy Ainu*.

In the course of his wanderings, on foot and on horseback, among these primitive people of the far north of Japan, he encountered many personable specimens, but there was one girl in particular, "the most lovely Ainu girl I had ever come across, and not nearly so hairy as most of them". When they sat together in the twilight she was a "perfect dream". He asked her to let him see the tattooing on her arm, and, rather to his surprise, the pretty maid took his hand in hers, clasped it tightly, and pressed it to her chest. "Then we wandered and wandered till it grew dark; we sat down, we chattered, we made love to each other." He would not have mentioned this small episode, he tells us, "if her ways of flirting had not been so extraordinary and funny. Loving and biting went together with her. She could not do the one without doing the other. As we sat on a stone in the semi-darkness she began by gently biting my fingers, without hurting me, as affectionate dogs often do their masters; she then bit my arms, then my shoulder, and when she had worked herself up into a passion she put her arms round my neck and bit my cheeks. It was undoubtedly a curious way of making love", and it was not until he "had been bitten all over, and was pretty tired of the new sensation", that she accompanied him back to the village. Kissing, as he understood the word, was apparently an unknown art to her.

Much more important than the gustatory is the olfactory element in kissing, even though there is next to nothing of it in the kisses given and taken in the Western world—probably because, as has been suggested, the sense of smell with us has become atrophied for want of use. Only rarely do we come across such a tribute as that of the old Roman poet Martial, here very prettily translated by an anonymous writer of the sixteenth century:

> In winter chests like apples ripening. . .
> As broken jars of Falerna wines to smell
> Far off: or flowery gardens where bees dwell:
> Perfumers' pots, burnt incense tossed on the air,
> Chaplets new-fallen from rich perfumed hair. . .

Among primitive peoples, including all those mentioned above who do not kiss with the lips, the so-called "nose kiss" is the common form. Charles Darwin came across it among the Maoris of New Zealand. "The women on our first approach," he wrote, "began uttering something in a most dolorous voice; they then squatted themselves down and held up their faces; my companion (Mr. Bushby, the British Resident at Waimate) standing over them, one after another, placed the bridge of his nose at right angles to theirs, and commenced pressing. This lasted rather longer than a cordial handshake of the hand with us; and as we vary the force of the grasp of the hand in shaking, so do they in pressing. During the process they uttered comfortable little grunts, very much in the same manner as two pigs do, when rubbing against each other."

"Grunts", like a pair of affectionate pigs! "Comfortable" perhaps, but surely this is not the kind of thing that the Rose of Sharon burningly longed for when she implored her lover to "kiss me with the kisses of his mouth, for thy love is better than wine", or what Romeo proffered Juliet with the "two blushing pilgrims" of his lips, or what made Gretchen cling to Faust and ask for nothing better than that she, "faint with his kisses, should swoon and die!", or what Rabbie Burns bestowed on one of his Annies "that happy night Amang the rigs o' barley". No, not piggy grunts, not pressed noses, not amorous sniffings, but what Byron (who knew more than most men about this particular subject) described in a famous stanza of *Don Juan* as the action—

Where heart, and soul, and sense, in concert move,
And the blood's lava, and the pulse a blaze,
Each kiss a heart-quake. . .

Chapter 2

A Taste of Cannibalism

WHITE man's flesh does not taste so good as coloured man's. This was the decided opinion of the cannibals of the South Sea Islands, who had the opportunity of tasting both. The most savage tribes among the Australian aborigines thought the same, and so did the fierce Maoris whom the early voyagers discovered in New Zealand.

So repugnant is the very idea of human man-eaters that when the first reports reached Europe they were found hard to believe, and this although students of history were aware that even in Europe, as during the Thirty Years' War, there had been cases of cannibalism in a population reduced to the last degree of starvation. But the cannibalism reported by such explorers as Captain Cook was of a different character. In his account of his first voyage to the South Seas, Cook said that in 1770 they had come across cannibals among the natives of the northern part of New Zealand who had made no secret of this "fearful custom", but had assured him, through his native interpreter, that they thought human flesh most delicious food. Men who devoured their fellows just because they liked the taste: that was something that the sophisticated reader found it hard to swallow.

Three years later when Cook was on the second of his great voyages of exploration he found abundant confirmation. Again they were in New Zealand waters, and one afternoon some of the ship's officers who had gone ashore to amuse themselves came across the head and bowels of a native youth who had lately been killed, lying on the beach, and the head was stuck on a forked stick fixed to the prow of a large canoe. One of the officers bought the head and took it back to the ship, where a native, one of a number who had been allowed to come on board, was permitted to broil a piece of the flesh and then eat it, while the ship's company looked on with fascinated disgust. Cook was on shore at the time, and when on his return he was informed of what had happened he was filled with horror. But soon curiosity got the better of his indignation, especially when he considered that the victim was dead any way; and, since he was desirous of becoming an eye-witness of a fact which many had doubted, even when *he* had related it, he ordered that another piece of the flesh should be broiled and brought to the quarter-deck, where one of the assembled cannibals ate it with what was described as "surprising avidity". This had such an effect on the sailors that some of them were sick.

A short time after, there was confirmation of an even more horribly convincing kind. A violent storm separated Cook's ship, the *Resolution*, from her companion vessel, the *Adventure*, commanded by Captain Furneaux. While the *Adventure* was undergoing some repairs, her commander sent a cutter ashore to gather wild greens for the mess-table. The men did not return that evening as had been expected, nor the next morning, and Furneaux then despatched a launch with a boat's crew and ten marines under Lieutenant Burney (brother of the subsequently famous woman novelist Fanny Burney) to look for them. Burney and his party did not return until late that night, and then they had a horrible tale to tell, as these extracts from Burney's own story will show. "In a small beach we saw a very large double canoe just hauled up, with two men and a dog. The men, on seeing us, left their canoe, and ran up into the woods. We went ashore, and searched the canoe, where we found one of the rullock-ports of the cutter, and some shoes, one of which was known to belong to Mr. Woodhouse, one of our midshipmen. One of the people, at the same time, brought me a piece of meat, which he took to be some of the salt meat belonging to the cutter's crew. On examining this, and smelling it, I found it was fresh. Mr. Fannin (the master), who was with me, supposed it was dog's flesh, and I was of the same opinion; for I still doubted their being cannibals. But we were soon convinced by the most horrid and undeniable proof. A great many baskets (about twenty) lying on the beach, tied up, we cut them open. Some were full of roasted flesh, and some of fern-root, which serves them for bread. On further search we found more shoes, and a hand, which we immediately knew to have belonged to Thomas Hill, one of our forecastlemen, it being marked T.H. with an Otaheite tattoo-instrument."

A little farther along the beach they found a broken oar stuck upright in the ground, to which the natives had tied their canoes. "I then searched all along at the back of the beach, to see if the cutter was there. We found no boat, but instead of her, such a shocking scene of carnage and barbarity, as can never be mentioned or thought of but with horror; for the heads, hearts, and lungs of several of our people were seen lying on the beach; and at a little distance, the dogs gnawing their entrails." A few of these pitiful fragments of humanity were taken back by Burney's party to their ship, tied in a hammock, and thrown overboard, with ballast and shot sufficient to sink it.

After this there could be no longer any doubt that the natives of New Zealand were cannibals; for many years every ship that touched at the islands found confirmation of the fact, and it is not too much to say that the country was a terror to sailors. Then in 1814 the first Christian missionary (Rev. Samuel Marsden, colonial chaplain to the Government of New South Wales) established a church at the Bay of Islands, on the east coast of North Island, and he was followed by others, both Protestant and Roman Catholic, with the result that in the next thirty years or so practically the whole native population was converted to Christianity. But it was with the utmost reluctance that many of them abandoned a custom which only the white man found so horrifying.

As late as 1827 cannibalism in New Zealand was still rife,

as may be learnt from the narrative of young Augustus Earle, who spent nine months in the country in that year. Earle had gone to sea at an early age, tempted by "a love of roving and adventure"—it is worth mentioning that some years later he was appointed draughtsman to H.M.S. *Beagle,* and was thus a shipmate of Charles Darwin—and he joined a passenger-ship proceeding to New Zealand with a band of Wesleyan missionaries. On his first trip on shore, he had not rambled far when he was "appalled by the sight of remains of a human body which had been roasted, and a number of hogs and dogs were snarling and feasting upon it". It turned out that a chief had just killed one of his *kookies* (or slaves), a poor lad who had been so excited by the sight of the ship's arrival that he had suffered the hogs to wander at will through his master's plantation of sweet potatoes; whereupon his master had knocked him on the head with his stone hatchet, and ordered a fire to be lit and the body dragged to it, where it was roasted and consumed. This was bad enough, but much worse was to follow.

One morning, when he had just returned from a long walk, Earle was informed by Captain Duke that he had heard, on very good authority (though the natives wished it to be kept a profound secret), that in the adjoining village a female slave named Matowe had been put to death, and that the people were at that very moment preparing her flesh for cooking. At the same time Duke reminded him of something which had taken place the evening before. A young native chieftain named Atoi had been paying them a visit, and on leaving he had recognized a girl whom he declared was a runaway slave of his, and had forthwith given her in charge to some of his people.

"The girl had been employed in carrying wood for us; Atoi's laying claim to her had caused us no alarm for her life, and we had thought no more on the subject; but now, to my surprise and horror, I heard that this poor girl was the victim they were preparing for the oven! Captain Duke and myself were resolved to witness this dreadful scene. . . ."

Taking every precaution not to be observed, they took a circuitous route to the village, where on a spot of rising ground they came upon a man preparing a native oven "in the following simple manner: a hole is made in the ground, and hot stones are put within it, and then all is covered up close". Then in the village itself they found bloody mats strewn around, "and a boy was standing by them, actually laughing! He put his finger to his head, and then pointed towards a bush. I approached the bush, and there discovered a human head. My feelings of horror may be imagined as I recognized the features of the unfortunate girl I had seen forced from our village the preceding evening!"

Running towards the fire, they surprised a man "occupied in a way that few would wish to see. He was preparing the four quarters of a human body for a feast; the large bones, having been taken out, were thrown aside, and the flesh being compressed, he was in the act of forcing it into the oven. While we stood transfixed by this terrible sight, a large dog, which lay before the fire, rose up, seized the bloody head, and walked off with it into the bushes! The man completed his task with the most perfect composure, telling us at the same time that the repast would not be ready for some hours!"

So there the two Englishmen stood, witnessing "a scene which many travellers have related, and their relations have invariably been treated with contempt". And what was the excuse that might be put forward? In this instance it was no warrior's flesh that was to be eaten; there was no enemy's blood to drink, in order to infuriate them. They had no revenge to gratify; no plea could they make of their passions having been roused by battle, nor the excuse that they ate their enemies to perfect their triumph. Nor could it be said that they were in want of food, since the night before Atoi had sold them four pigs for a few pounds of gunpowder.

Filled with disgust and indignation, the two hurried off to charge Atoi with his brutality. He received them in his usual manner, and it was hard to believe that his handsome open countenance could belong to the savage monster he had proved himself to be. Earle "shuddered at beholding the unusual quantity of potatoes his slaves were preparing to eat with this infernal banquet". Atoi at first tried to convince them that he knew nothing about it, but at length he frankly owned that he was only waiting till the cooking was completed to partake of it. He added that, "knowing the horror we Europeans held these feasts in, the natives were always most anxious to conceal them from us, and he was very angry that it had come to our knowledge; but, as he had acknowledged the fact, he had no objection to talk about it". He told them that human flesh required a longer time to cook than any other; that if not done enough, it was very tough, but when sufficiently cooked was as tender as paper—and he tore a piece of paper that he held in his hand by way of demonstration. He said that the flesh that was then cooking would not be ready till next morning—but one of his sisters whispered in Earle's ear that her brother was deceiving them, and that they intended to feast at sunset.

Then they inquired why and how he had murdered the poor girl? He replied, that running away from him to her relations had been her only crime. He then took them outside the village and showed them a post to which she had been tied, "and laughed to think how he had cheated her. 'For,' said he, 'I told her I only intended to give her a flogging; but I fired, and shot her through the head!' My blood ran cold on this relation, and I looked with feelings of horror at the savage while he related it. Shall I be credited when I again affirm, that he was not only a handsome young man, but mild and genteel in his demeanour? He was a man we had admitted to our table, and was a general favourite with us all; and the poor victim to his bloody cruelty was a pretty girl of about sixteen years of age!"

Sick almost to fainting, the two Englishmen left Atoi and again went to where the "disgusting mess" was cooking. Not a native was now to be seen near it, but the dog was still sneaking around, and on their approach a large hawk rose heavily from the spot. "It was a lowering, grisly day, and the moaning of the wind through the bushes seemed in unison with our feelings." They contemplated the miserable scene for some time, and then took a sudden resolve to spoil the intended feast. Earle ran down to the beach, collected all the white men there, informed them of what was afoot, and urged them to assist in destroying the oven and burying the remains of the girl. They needed little prompting, but snatched up shovels and pickaxes and hurried to the spot. Atoi protested, but since none of his followers seemed ready to come to blows, the English sailors were able to dig a tolerably deep grave. Then they attacked the oven, and retrieved the mangled pieces of human flesh and buried them, after which they filled in the grave as well as they could and broke and scattered the oven. Such a scene had never been witnessed before in New Zealand. "Six unarmed men had attacked and destroyed all the preparations of the natives for what they considered a national feast, and this was done in the presence of a great body of armed chiefs who had gathered to partake of it."

The next day they were gravely reprimanded by a friendly native chieftain called "King George", who a year before had been taken on a visit to England where he had been received in audience by King George IV. He highly disapproved of their conduct. "In the first place," he said, "you did a very foolish thing, which might have cost you your lives; and yet did not accomplish your purpose after all, as you merely succeeded in burying the flesh near the spot where you found it. After you went away, it was again taken up, and every bit was eaten."

Then "King George" impressed upon them that cannibalism was an old custom which their fathers had practised before them, "and you had no right to interfere with their ceremonies. I myself have left off eating human flesh, out of compliment to you white men, but you have no right to expect the same compliance from all the other chiefs." What punishments had they in England, the old man enquired, for thieves and runaways? "We answered, 'After trial, flogging or hanging.' 'Then,' he replied, 'the only difference in our laws is, you flog and hang, but we shoot and eat'."

As exploration of the Pacific proceeded, it was found that cannibalism was an established institution on most of the islands strung across its surface. In some the heart and liver of any prominent warrior slain in battle were devoured by the victor chiefs in the belief that they would thereby inherit the valour of the dead man. This was probably the explanation of the treatment accorded to the body of Captain Cook, after he had been killed on 14 February, 1779, on the beach at Kealakekua Bay, on the west coast of Hawaii. Immediately after he was struck down, his body was dragged away in triumph, dismembered, and portions distributed among chiefs and other notables, while the remainder was burnt. The natives who were induced to return such fragments as could be found indignantly denied that it had been the intention to devour the body after the way of cannibals in general.

Nowhere was cannibalism more rife than in Fiji, as is made abundantly clear in the description of the islands and their inhabitants that was published in 1860 by the Rev. Thomas Williams, who was for thirteen years a Wesleyan Methodist missionary there in the middle of the last century. "Cannibalism among the Fijians," he wrote, "is one of their institutions; it is interwoven in the elements of society; it forms one of their pursuits, and is regarded by the mass as a refinement."

Human bodies were sometimes eaten in connexion with the building of a temple or a canoe, or on the launching of a large canoe, or on taking down the mast of one which had brought some chief on a visit, or on the occasion of the feasting of such as took tribute to a principal place. Mr. Williams had known a chief to kill several men for "rollers", to facilitate the launching of his canoes, the "rollers" being afterwards cooked and eaten.

Formerly a chief would kill a man or men on laying down the keel of a new canoe, and try to add one for each new plank. These were always eaten as "food for the carpenters". This practice had ceased, and it was no longer common to murder men in order that the deck of a new canoe might be washed in human blood. But the latter was still sometimes done, and would be the regular practice if it were not for the opposition of the missionaries. To give an instance, Williams quoted the case of a canoe that had been completed at Somosomo. Vexed that the noble vessel had reached Mbau unstained with blood, the Mbau chieftains attacked a town, and killed fourteen or fifteen men to eat on first taking down the mast. But for Christian influence men would have been killed at every place where the canoe put in for the first time.

If a chief did not lower his mast within a day or two of his arrival at a place, it was the practice for some poor creature to be killed and taken to him at the "lowering of the mast". An enemy was preferred, but when an enemy was not available, the first common man at hand was taken and slaughtered. It was not uncommon to find a "black list" of men in every island, and these were taken first. Names of villages or islands might similarly be put on the "black list".

Captives were sometimes preserved to be killed on special occasions as they might arise. Those who died a natural death were always interred. Those slain in war were not invariably eaten, for persons of high rank were spared this indignity. Occasionally, however, the supply was too great to be all consumed, as was the case once at Mbouma, when the bodies were piled up between two coconut trees, and the cutting up took two days. The *valekarusa*, or trunk, of the bodies was thrown away. This native word (explains Williams) was a creation of cannibalism, and alluded to the practice of eating the trunk first, as it would not keep.

When the slain were not too numerous, it was the general rule for the victors to eat their bodies. As late as 1851, fifty bodies were cooked at one time on Namena. In such cases of plenty, the head, hands, and intestines were thrown away. But when one or two bodies had to be shared among a large party, every part was consumed.

Native warriors carried their revenge beyond death, so that they often mutilated the bodies of slain enemies in a frightful manner, and they considered this treatment neither mean nor brutal.

When the bodies of enemies had been procured for the oven, the event was published by a peculiar beating of the drum, which alarmed Williams even before he had been informed of what it meant. "Soon after hearing it, I saw two canoes steering for the island, while someone on board struck the water, at intervals, with a long pole, to denote that they had killed someone. When sufficiently near, they began their fiendish war-dance, which was answered by the indecent dance of the women. On the boxed end of one of the canoes was a human corpse, which was cut adrift and tumbled into the water soon after the canoe touched land, where it was tossed to and fro by the rising and falling waves until the men had reported their exploit, when it was dragged ashore by a vine tied to the left hand. A crowd, chiefly females, surrounded the dead man, who was above the ordinary size, and expressed most unfeelingly their surprise and delight. 'A man truly! a ship! a land!' The warriors, having rested, put a vine round the other wrist of the *bakolo*—dead body designed for eating—and two of them dragged it, face downwards, to the town, the rest going before and performing the war-dance, which consists in jumping, brandishing of weapons, and two or three, in advance of the main body, running towards the town, throwing their clubs aloft, or firing muskets, while they assured those within of their capability to defend them.

"On reaching the middle of the town, the body was thrown down before the Chief, who directed the priest to offer it in due form to the war-god. Fire had been placed in the great oven, and the smoke arose above the old temple, as the body was again drawn to the shore to be cut up. The carver was a young man, but he seemed skilful. He used a piece of split bamboo, with which, after having washed the body in the sea, he cut off the several members, joint by joint. He first made a long deep gash down the abdomen, and then cut all round the neck down to the bone, and rapidly twisted the head from the axis. The several parts were then wrapped in leaves, and placed in the oven."

On the larger islands the bodies had often to be carried to some distance inland. In these cases a strong stick was lashed down the back at the arms, knees, and sometimes the trunk, and the burden was carried on the shoulders of two men.

"I never saw a body baked whole," continues Williams, "but have most satisfactory testimony that this is really done. The body is first placed in a sitting posture, and, when taken from the oven, is covered with black powder, surmounted with a wig, and paraded about as if possessed of life."

Revenge was undoubtedly the main cause of cannibalism in Fiji, but by no means invariably so. Williams had known many cases in which such a motive could not be present, and he describes one specially horrible case.

"When I first knew Loti, he was living at Na Ruwai. A few years before, he killed his only wife and ate her. She accompanied him to plant taro [a plant of the arum family with an edible root], and when the work was done he sent her to fetch wood, with which he made a fire, while she, at his bidding, collected leaves and grass to line the oven, and procured a bamboo to cut up what was to be cooked. When she had cheerfully obeyed his commands, the monster seized his wife, deliberately dismembered her, and cooked and ate her, calling some to help him in consuming the unnatural feast. The woman was his equal, with whom he had lived comfortably; he had no quarrel with her, or cause of complaint. His only motives could have been a fondness for human flesh, and a hope that he should be spoken of and pointed out as a terrific fellow."

Not all the native chiefs were cannibals. Some of them hated it, and Williams had known several who could never be induced to taste human flesh. But he was obliged to acknowledge that these were rare exceptions. "No one who is

thoroughly acquainted with the Fijians can say that this
vitiated taste is not widely spread, or that there is not a large
number who esteem such food a delicacy, giving it a decided
preference above all other. The heart, the thigh, and the arm
above the elbow are considered the greatest dainties. The
head is the least esteemed.

"Cannibalism does not confine its selection to one sex, or
a particular age. I have seen the grey-headed and children of
both sexes devoted to the oven. I have laboured to make the
murderers of females ashamed of themselves, and have heard
their cowardly cruelty defended by the assertion that such
victims were doubly good—because they ate well, and because
of the distress it caused their husbands and friends. . . .
Women seldom eat *bakolo,* and it is forbidden to some of the
priests. On the island of Moala, graves were not infrequently
opened for the purpose of obtaining the occupant for food.
It is most certainly true, that while the Fijian turns with
disgust from pork, or from his favourite dish if at all tainted,
he will eat *bakolo* when fast approaching putrescence. . . .
Human bodies are generally cooked alone, and generally
ovens and pots in which human flesh is cooked, and dishes
and forks used in eating it, are strictly *tabu* for any other
purpose. . . . Would that this horrible record could be finished
here! But the *vakatotoga,* the 'torture', must be noticed. Nothing short of the most fiendish cruelty could dictate some of
these forms of torture, the worst of which consists in cutting
off parts and even limbs of the victim while still living, and
cooking and eating them before his eyes, sometimes finishing
the brutality by offering him his own cooked flesh to eat. . . ."

In most of the Pacific lands and islands cannibalism was a
thing of the past by the end of the last century, but in New
Guinea the horrible custom continued in full force. In 1901
the world was shocked by the news of the tragic end of the
veteran Scottish missionary James Chalmers and his young
companion Oliver Tomkins at the hands of New Guinea
cannibals. Chalmers had gone out to the South Seas in 1867
under the auspices of the London Missionary Society, and in
1876 had removed to New Guinea, where he carried the
Christian message into numbers of villages where a white man
had never been seen before, besides doing some explorations
of real value. Robert Louis Stevenson came to know him
when he was on a visit to Samoa, and spoke of him in terms

of hero-worship. In April, 1901 Chalmers and Tomkins called at the island of Goaribari. Crowds of savages boarded the vessel, and in order to induce them to leave the two missionaries led the way ashore. There they were attacked, knocked on the head, killed, and eaten. From time to time reports still come to hand of cannibal tribes dwelling in the mountainous and largely unexplored heart of New Guinea.

Chapter 3

Women of the Yoshiwara

FOR generations a visit to the Yoshiwara has been considered as almost a "must" among the tourist attractions of Tokyo. There is nothing quite like it anywhere else, so the guide-books have asserted; nowhere else can you see women put on display in cage-like apartments, to be looked at through the bars, inspected and compared and looked over again and again, until you have made your pick and go to the cash-box to enquire her price. So the foreigners have flocked there, men (and often women too) who would never dream of being seen anywhere near the red-light district in their own town; and they have been amazed, strangely fascinated, perhaps disgusted, by this most open exhibition of commercialized eroticism.

The word Yoshiwara is of uncertain origin. One derivation takes us back to the time, about the beginning of the seventeenth century, when Yedo (as Tokyo was then called) was just rising into prominence as the chief city of the Shogun, the generalissimo who had supplanted the Mikado as the real ruler of the country. People flocked to the city from all parts in the hope of making their fortune, and the courtesans were not behindhand. From Kyoto, from Nara, from Fushimi, they arrived—so the native accounts inform us—in little parties of threes and fours. But a band of some twenty or thirty came from the town of Moto-Yoshiwara, and because they were either the most numerous or the most beautiful, the district where they took up their abode came to be called the Yoshiwara after them.

But some scholars have preferred another derivation. Here again the story begins in Yedo's early days of rapid growth, and we are told that when the young courtesans made their first appearance in the city they were allowed to ply their trade wherever they chose. But this appears to have scandalized a certain reformer named Shoji Jinyemon, and in 1612 he addressed a memorial to the Government, petitioning that the loose women should all be collected in one "Flower Quarter". His petition was granted in 1617, and being asked to fix a place, he chose one called Fukiyacho, which, on account of the quantities of rushes which grew there, was named Yoshi-Wara, or "the rush-moor". Forty years later Yedo had grown to such an extent that the Yoshiwara was in the centre of the city, and it was transferred to the north-western outskirts.

So famous did the Yedo Yoshiwara become, that the name was given to its counterparts in other cities. But this usage is generally confined to foreigners. For Japanese there has generally been only one Yoshiwara: other brothel districts are spoken of as *yujoba* or *kuruwa*.

The Yoshiwara had been in being for rather more than three hundred years when in 1868 Japan opened her doors to foreign visitors. Japanese customs and institutions were so different from anything encountered in the West that they aroused the intensest interest. Naturally enough, the Yoshiwara came in for its full share of attention. One of the first accounts of it to appear in English was included by A. B. Mitford in his *Tales of Old Japan*, published in 1871.

The Official Guide to the Yoshiwara for 1869 (he begins) gave a return of 153 brothels in the establishment, containing 3,289 courtesans of all classes, "from the *Oiran*, or proud beauty, who, dressed up in gorgeous brocade of gold and silver, with painted face and gilded lips, and with her teeth fashionably blacked, has all the young bloods of Yedo at her feet, down to the humble *Shinzo,* or white-toothed woman, who rots away her life in the common stews". He goes on to explain that these figures did not represent the whole of the prostitution in Yedo: the Yoshiwara was the chief, but not the only, abiding-place of the public women. There was another "Flower District" at Fukagawa, built on the same principles, and there were districts in which the hotels contained women who, while nominally only waitresses, were in reality prostitutes. There were also women called *Jigoku-Onna,* or "hell women", who, without being borne on the books of any brothel, lived in their own houses and plied their trade in secret. But there was good reason to believe that, considering the city's vast size, the amount of prostitution in Yedo was wonderfully small.

The best time to see the Yoshiwara was just after nightfall, when the lamps were lighted. "Then it is that the women— who for the last two hours have been engaged in gilding their lips and painting their eyebrows black, and their throats and bosoms a snowy white, carefully leaving three brown Van-dyke-collar points where the back of the head joins the neck, in accordance with one of the strictest rules of Japanese cosmetic science—leave the back rooms, and take their places, side by side, in a kind of long narrow cage, the wooden bars of which open on to the public thoroughfare. Here they sit for hours, gorgeous in dresses of silk and gold and silver embroidery, speechless and motionless as wax figures, until they shall have attracted the attention of some of the passers-by, who begin to throng the place."

On the whole there was little to complain of in their behaviour—so very different were they from the women in the Yoshiwaras at Yokohama and the other ports open to foreign commerce, who "are loud in their invitations to visitors, frequently relieving the monotony of their own language by some blasphemous term of endearment picked up from British and American seamen. But in the Flower District at Yedo, and wherever Japanese customs are untainted, the utmost decorum prevails".

Within the Yoshiwara were also 394 tea-houses. These were not brothels, but they were largely used as places of assignation. It was also the custom to give dinners and drinking-parties at these houses, for which the services of jesters, dancing- and singing-girls were retained. Fifty-five famous singing-girls were listed by name in the Yoshiwara Guide, besides a host of minor stars. These women were not courtesans. Their conduct was closely watched over by their masters, and they always went out in parties or couples, so that they might be a check on one another. "Doubtless, however, in spite of all precautions, the shower of gold does from time to time find its way to Danae's lap; and to be the favoured lover of a fashionable singer or dancer is rather a feather in the cap of a fast young Japanese gentleman."

All the women in the Yoshiwara—courtesans, singers and dancers—were provided by contractors, who bought them from their parents or guardians at an early age. Their engagement was never life-long, for once past the flower of their youth they might be only burdens on their masters. A courtesan was usually bought until she should reach the age of twenty-seven, after which she became her own property. Singing-girls remained longer in harness, but even they rarely worked after the age of thirty, "for Japanese women, like Italians, age quickly, and have none of that intermediate age between youth and old age, which seems to be confined to countries where there is a twilight."

Children destined to be trained as singers (so Mitford was informed) were usually bought when they were five or six years old, a likely child fetching from about thirty-five to fifty shillings; the purchaser undertook the child's education, and brought it up as his own. Girls of fifteen and upwards who were sufficiently accomplished to join a company of singers fetched ten times as much as the children, for in their case there was no risk and no expense of education. Little girls bought for purposes of prostitution at the age of five or six fetched about the same price as those bought to become singers. During their novitiate they were employed to wait upon the *Oiran*, or fashionable courtesans, in the capacity of little female pages. Girls who entered the profession later in life were orphans, or had no other means of earning a livelihood, or they sold their bodies out of filial piety, that they might succour their sick or needy parents. Some were married women, who entered the Yoshiwara to supply the wants of their husbands, and a very small proportion were girls who had been seduced and abandoned, or even perhaps sold, by faithless lovers.

Mitford's account may be supplemented by that of another English writer who reported on the Yoshiwara some twenty years later. This was Henry Norman, who included a chapter on it in his book *The Real Japan*, published in 1893. Norman claimed to be the first foreigner who had been allowed to investigate the establishment on the spot in the company of the chief of the special Yoshiwara police.

An hour's ride in a jinriksha from the centre of the city, on the north-western outskirts, is "a colony apart", as he calls it. You enter it through a wide gate, on one side of which is a weeping willow, the "Willow of Welcome" of Japan, and on the other a police station. Within the walls the streets are wide and long, lined with shops and tea-houses. Down the middle of the street is a flower-garden, six feet across, where a succession of flowers is maintained among pleasant fountains and quaint stone lanterns. In the flower-beds are a number of wax figures, startlingly lifelike, of men and women plucking the blossoms and strolling among the fountains; one is of a man who has just stepped on a toad and is starting back in disgust, another is of a lady who has stopped before a little brook and with her gown gathered up is hesitating to cross when a coolie runs up and, like some Japanese Sir Walter Raleigh, spreads his coat on the mud before her. All day long a crowd of real people gaze with delight on these waxwork representations, or with typically Japanese tenderness and simplicity of feeling find pleasure in admiring the flowers and the butterflies flitting among them.

From this idyllic description we may well wonder where we are, and even suppose that we have come to the wrong address. But that big building at the end of the street, surmounted with a clock-tower that seems to dominate the colony—that is the brothel, or rather, it is one of them, for there are half a dozen of these massive buildings of brick and stone, with pillared verandas and lofty vaulted entrances through which you may get a glimpse of great stairways and columns of polished wood, and cool green gardens extending temptingly beyond. There are no finer buildings in all Tokyo than these, and they cost hundreds of thousands of dollars to erect. They bear no sign to indicate their purpose, though if you should happen to look up you may see a graceful figure or two strolling upon the balcony, or a pair of black eyes will be looking curiously down upon you, or perhaps you may catch sight of a graceful head with monumental coiffure resting upon a tiny hand and bare arm.

This is the Yoshiwara by day, but the time to see it is after dark, when the brilliant red lanterns hanging from the shops and tea-houses and other buildings make the darkness gay with streams of dancing colour. Then the streets are packed with people, both men and women, most of them come for nothing more than a stroll through the pushing, struggling throng, among the bright lights and the strains of lively music.

When Norman was there making his careful notes, there were a hundred *kashi-zashiki*, as the houses of prostitution were called, and these had about 1,850 women on their books. They were classified according to status. The politest name for them was *oiran*, and women in this grade were of the highest class. The most general was *shogi*. The most "animal and severe" term was *joro*, which may be rendered as "whore". The prettiest was *yujo*, which might be taken, perhaps, as more or less equivalent to the French *fille de joie*.

Each *kashi-zashiki* paid a tax of three dollars per month to the Government, and each courtesan one of between half a dollar and three dollars, according to her grade or class.

According to Norman, it was only in the lowest houses that the women sat in the ground-floor room, behind wooden bars and windows of plate glass, where they were exposed to the gaze of all who went past. Some of them, he noted, were "dressed in what passes for European costume", and they were "a sight of indescribable vulgarity and horror".

The Yoshiwara was under strict Government control, exercised through a Bureau of Prostitution, which was a department of the Board of Trade. The special Yoshiwara Police was entrusted with the maintenance of good order and discipline. Official regulation was defended on several grounds. In the first place, the licensed houses of prostitution might be effectively concentrated, and their extension into respectable districts prevented. Next, the system of regular medical inspection was facilitated and made certain. Then the tax imposed on each courtesan and establishment might be more easily collected. The rules laid down for the operation of the establishment might be properly enforced. And finally, the Yoshiwara was a most likely place in which to look for and find swindlers and other persons who were "wanted" by the police.

One morning Norman went along to the Bureau of Prostitution to see how the system of registration worked. In a small room on the ground floor he found two officials sitting behind desks on a platform. Opposite them were sliding doors in the wall, and there entered the girl who was applying to become a licensed *shogi,* her parent or guardian, and the keeper of the *kashi-zashiki.* All three made very low bows, and throughout the proceedings maintained an attitude of the deepest respect.

The girl was questioned first, and replied automatically; the parent next—apologetically; and finally the keeper—profusely, with practised fluency. There was a good deal of talk, and the official made an entry from time to time in the big ledger on the desk in front of him. All the circumstances of the application were noted down—the names of the girl's parents, the name of the keeper of the house to which the girl was to be assigned, and the details of the contract that was to be entered into.

Why had the parents given their consent, and did they fully understand what sort of a life their daughter would have to lead if the application were granted? How much money had the keeper offered to the parents in advance—twenty dollars, fifty, even a hundred? Who was the surety for the bond that would be entered into, that the girl would remain in the keeper's house for three years certain, or until such time as the proportion of her earnings (theoretically a half) was sufficient to recoup him for the sum advanced, together with the cost of her upkeep and education? It was made clear that if the girl should take it into her head to run away before her term had expired, her parents and the surety would be responsible for her "debts".

When her apprenticeship should have expired, the girl would be at liberty to engage herself for a further period of years, or she might prefer to take her departure and perhaps start up on her own, or she might quit the prostitute's life altogether. If, however, she were still in the keeper's debt, she had no option: she stayed, until the sum had been completely worked off. Since the girl was usually uneducated and not too intelligent, whereas the keeper was a clever rogue, it was not difficult to see how the matter would turn out.

Why did parents sign away their daughter's liberty in this fashion? According to some writers—including, as we have seen, Mitford—it was a common act of devotion on the girl's part in order to pay off her parents' debts or to keep a roof over their heads in hard times. But Norman had come to the conclusion that this was just rubbish. True, most of the girls in the Yoshiwara were there because their parents were hard up, but not one in a hundred could be called an unwilling victim. In Japanese society, the will of the parents was accustomed to be taken as law. When a girl was told, "You are to enter the Yoshiwara", she no more dreamed of questioning it than she would have done if she had been told, "You are to marry so-and-so". Of course, when the police officer put the question to her, "Are you doing this of your own free will?", she replied, "Yes, I am," but in fact she was no more of a free agent than the criminal who walks up the steps of the scaffold unaided.

When Norman inquired of the police, what were the determining causes that recruited the ranks of the Yoshiwara, he received the answer, "There are only two: poverty and natural inclination".

Most of the girls came from the poorer classes, and to such the prospect of life in the comparatively luxurious surroundings of the Yoshiwara must have made a strong appeal. Sometimes, however, the daughter of a Samurai, or gentleman, might be found there, as a consequence of the death or utter ruin of her parents; but this was so exceptional that the presence of a young lady in such a place proved an enormous attraction, her superior education and accomplishments shedding a lustre over the house.

Did a Yoshiwara girl ever "make good" and return to respectability in the bosom of her family? Norman had heard this stated, but he found it very hard to believe. Whatever the motives that led her to enter the Yoshiwara in the first place, they were never taken as something to be proud of. Her attitude towards the establishment and her life in it was shown by the fact that as a rule when a girl left she never took away anything that might remind her of her days there— none of her clothes, her furniture, her pictures, even her personal knick-knacks—but left them all behind with the instruction that they were to be sold to her successor for what they might fetch. A few of the women left to get married, possibly to one of their customers in the Yoshiwara. Occasionally a girl committed suicide, having found the conditions unbearable.

Good-hearted prostitutes are to be found in Japanese literature as elsewhere; thus we read in the biography of a beautiful *oiran* named Murasaki that "she defiled her body, but not her heart", and she is prettily described as "a lotus in the mud". But there is a Japanese proverb that runs, "Once get into dirty water, and you will never be washed clean again as long as you live!" While a few of the women managed somehow to return to independence and respectability, the great majority stayed in the Yoshiwara, sinking lower and lower in the scale of employments as they got older and lost their good looks, until they were menials where once they had queened it as *oirans*.

Once a girl had had her name entered on the roll of licensed women and taken her place in the Yoshiwara, she was never allowed to go outside the walls without a police pass, and even then she was generally accompanied by her maid and a male attendant. Every Monday morning she had to submit to a medical examination at the police station, and if a *shogi* were found to have become infected with V.D. she was forthwith conducted to the hospital that was conveniently situated in the grounds. In theory this was supported out of contributions levied on the keepers of the licensed houses, but in practice these fellows recouped themselves out of a tax that they regularly levied on their women for the purpose.

Each woman in the Yoshiwara had her own small room, and her own personal maid or attendant. Her room was often charmingly decorated in accordance with the occupant's taste, and there might be displayed paintings and screens adorned with little carvings or porcelain, bits of silverware or lacquer-work, the gifts of satisfied customers. Nearly always there might be seen hanging on the wall an illuminated scroll, inscribed with some scrap of appropriate poetry. One that Norman made a note of consisted of the four Chinese characters for "pine, chrysanthemum, still, are", which, having in mind that the pine and the chrysanthemum preserve their charm even in winter, might be translated, "My charms are as long-lasting as the pine and the chrysanthemum".

On entering her profession as a public woman or singer, a girl was wont to assume a picturesque name by which she was known as long as her engagement lasted. When Mitford looked down the list in the Yoshiwara Guide he found a number of names so pretty and quaint that he made a note of them, e.g. Little Pine, Little Butterfly, Brightness of the Flowers, Jewel River, Gold Mountain, Pearl Harp, The Stork that Lives a Thousand Years, Village of Flowers, Sea Beach, Little Dragon, Little Purple, Silver, Chrysanthemum, Waterfall, White Brightness, Forest of Cherries, and so on.

Three times a year the Yoshiwara put on a special show— in the spring, when the cherry blossom is in full glory; in the summer at the time of the flowering of the purple iris; and in the autumn when the chrysanthemum, Japan's national flower, displays its hundred shades of colour. This took the form of a procession, known as the *hachimonji*.

From each of the principal houses half a dozen of the most beautiful women were chosen to represent the quality of the place. They were arrayed in the most gorgeous costumes, their hair was arranged in a stately coiffure with immense combs stuck through it from side to side, and their splendid *obi*, or sash, tied with an exaggerated bow in front, this being a distinguishing feature of the courtesan. This done, they were lifted on to huge *geta*, or wooden clogs, a foot high. When all was ready to start, the door was flung open and they emerged on to the street, attended by a number of attendants and servants.

On each side of the *yujo* walked a little girl as a waiting-woman, painted and bedizened like her, and holding with her finger-tips one of the long embroidered sleeves that were outstretched on either side like wings. Behind came five or six men carrying large paper lanterns inscribed with the name of the house, and there might also be a big fellow in livery holding aloft a huge ceremonial umbrella, likewise marked with the house's name.

Solemnly, with slow precision, the procession moved down the street to the gardens, where other similar processions were arriving. Progress was necessarily slow, for the heavy geta clogged the women's steps. In fact, they had to be specially trained for it: one foot forward, just a little way, and planted firmly on the ground; now the other geta, lifted by the toes grasping the strap passed between the first and second, and swung round in front of the first and across it. Now the same thing all over again. . . .

The spectacle was a splendid one, and never to be forgotten.

The *yujo,* dressed in her costly and outrageously flamboyant robes, the brocades blazing with scarlet and gold—the huge bow of the *obi*—and her face powdered a snowy white, her eyebrows and eyelashes deeply black, her lips coloured a glowing vermilion—her toenails stained a bright pink. . . .

Slow and painful was the beauty's passage. She gazed straight before her, with an expression on her face—half-contemptuous perhaps, proud, sometimes timid. Or there might be no expression at all, nothing but a mask of impassiveness. The dense throng through which she moved fell silent, as though they were participating in some religious ritual. Perhaps they were, thought Norman, as he stood among the goggling, gaping, almost breathless crowd. He recalled what he had read about the phallic ceremonials of the Greeks and Romans, and it seemed that the procession was a resuscitation of the worship of Priapus, the ancient divinity of lust and licence.

*   *   *

This was the Yoshiwara of Tokyo, as it was when the curtains were pulled back from Japanese life. And so it remained in its essentials, with the exception that some time before the Second World War it was arranged that the women should no longer be displayed in the windows but photographs of them were put up outside instead. An intending customer glanced at these, made his choice, and then went to the pay-office and bought a ticket for a certain time with the lady he preferred. There was nothing much more to it than buying a ticket for a seat in a cinema or theatre. Then came the War, and in a wave of puritanical patriotism the Yoshiwara was closed. But in 1945 (as had been the case after the great Tokyo earthquake and fire of 1923) the Yoshiwara was among the very first institutions to be granted funds for its restoration and re-opening.

Chapter 4

The Murderous Brotherhood
of the Thugs

I N the records of human villainy there is no set of worse
scoundrels than the Thugs. They were robbers and they
were murderers, and they committed their crimes under the
influence of religion. And yet (so strange is human nature)
these professional stranglers were, on their off days, decent
family men.

"Thug" comes from a Hindustani word meaning "deceiv-
ers", and the name by which the gangsters were known in the
more southern parts of India, Phansigars, comes from the
Hindustani word for a noose. Both names are altogether
appropriate, since the Thugs were adepts in deceiving those
whom they intended to slaughter, and their instrument of
murder was the noose.

For hundreds of years the Thug gangs beset the native
travellers along the paths and trackways of India. There is no
knowing when they took their rise, but they had undoubtedly
been operating a very long time when they attracted the

notice of the French traveller Jean de Thevenot, who was in India in 1666. Although Thevenot does not mention them by name, there is no doubt that he had them in mind when he included organized bands of robbers in his list of dangers to be encountered on the road from Delhi to Agra. "The cunningest robbers in all the world are in that country," he wrote. "They use a certain slip with a running noose, which they cast about a man's neck with such skill that they never fail to strangle him in a trice. They have another clever trick for catching travellers. They send out a handsome woman along the road, who with hair dishevelled and all in tears, complains loudly of some misfortune which she says has befallen her. Soon she falls in with a sympathetic traveller who happens to be going her way. He enters into conversation with her, and, finding her good-looking, offers her his assistance. She accepts, and he takes her up behind him on his horse. But hardly has he done so, when she throws a snare about his neck and strangles him, or at least renders him insensible until the robbers in the gang, who have been lying in hiding, come running up and give the finishing touches to what she has begun."

The Thugs themselves professed to trace their origin back to the time when the gods lived on earth among men, and in proof of their claim to immense antiquity they pointed to the sculptures in the great rock-temples at Ellora which (so they claimed) include among the figures representations of Thug operators going about their business. "Look," they would say, "there is the inveigler sitting on the same mat with the traveller he has designs on, worming out his secrets and trying to gain his confidence; over there stranglers are at their deadly work; and in that corner you may see the corpse being dragged to the grave which is being dug for it by the sexton-Thug with the sacred pickaxe."

What is most surprising is that the British were in India for nearly two hundred years before they even realized that such a race of marauders were in operation in their midst. Up to 1799 they seem to have known nothing of the Thugs, but in that year a number were captured at Bangalore. Even so, however, they were treated as ordinary dacoits or bandits. The first definite information concerning Thuggee was not obtained until 1807, when a Thug gang were arrested near Arcot; and more information came to hand a year later, when the bodies of some thirty Thug victims were recovered from wells into which they had been thrown. But even when the authorities had come to learn of the existence of the Thug organization, it was some time before they were able to bring any of the miscreants to justice, what with the reluctance of witnesses to give evidence for fear of reprisals, and the frequent impossibility of identifying the remains of Thug victims that happened to be recovered from where they had been buried or otherwise got rid of. It was not until Lord William Bentinck became Governor-General of India in 1833 that a really determined effort was launched to suppress the gangs. Bentinck appointed Captain (later Sir) William Sleeman general superintendent of the operations against them, and Sleeman formed a detective force of sepoys (native soldiers) who became expert in the tracking down and capture of Thug operators. Many were induced to become informers in return for their lives being spared, and it is from what these men told Sleeman that much of our information concerning the Thugs was obtained.

Like all callings in India, the trade of a Thug was mainly hereditary, and children, both boys and girls, were initiated into it from a very early age. The greater number were Moslems of a sort, but Hindus, especially Rajputs, were generally associated with them. They managed to escape detection for so long because on the face of it they were peaceable villagers, good husbands, fathers, and neighbours, going about their daily task of cultivating their little patches of crops and tending their cattle. Their villages were often models of cleanliness and neatness. When they went off on one of their expeditions, their womenfolk remained at home and carried on in their stead; very often they were kept in complete ignorance of what it was that took their husbands away. Instances were known of Thugs becoming traders and taking shops in the town bazaar, where they did an extensive business, and this occupation might provide a most satisfactory screen for their real activities. If the Thug were questioned by a neighbour concerning his absence from the village, he would say that he had been on a journey to a distant town to buy fresh stock, and he was careful to point to his purchases to prove it.

But the day would come, or the night rather, when the honest peasant or trader became transformed into the predatory prowler. Choosing a time when his departure would be most likely to go unnoticed, he hurried away to join the gang to which the Thug commander had allotted him. These gangs consisted of between ten and fifty men, but they might be as large as two hundred, in which case they were subdivided into smaller parties which moved along parallel roads, or along the same road at intervals of a mile or two, but always taking care to keep in touch. Contact was maintained by scouts, and a code of signals had been worked out for their guidance. Thus, a line drawn by the feet across a dusty road indicated the way the advance party had taken, and if the dust were heaped up at the end of the line those coming along behind would know that their friends in front were in urgent need of assistance. A long line of leaves placed across the track was also a "hurry up" message. In talking among themselves the Thugs used a language of their own, of which Sleeman later compiled a dictionary.

These expeditions were not a matter of a day or two. Very often journeys extended over many days, even months, if the trail they were following seemed to promise a rich haul at the end of it. For the first six days after setting out, the Thugs were forbidden to eat any food dressed in ghee (buffalo butter), or any meat, although fish was allowed. They might not shave their faces, nor have their clothes washed by a *dhobi* (professional washerman). They were forbidden to give alms to beggars along the road, nor might they throw tit-bits to a dog or a cat. They were not allowed to bathe, or to clean their teeth with a brush. On the seventh day they might partake of a good meal, provided that it included a substantial helping of greens.

When on the road they assumed the guise of traders or inoffensive travellers, proceeding usually on foot but, if their previous expedition had been sufficiently profitable, on horseback, thus giving the appearance of men of wealth and station. As often as not they were accompanied by young children, since this added to their general air of respectability.

Whenever possible they arranged to arrive at a village or town when it was just getting dark. They would straggle in by ones or twos, and make their way to the inn, where they would be careful to give the impression that they had never seen one another before. Then one of the gang would make up to some traveller who was putting up there for the night, engage him in conversation, and try to find out what his route was likely to be in the morning, and whether he was carrying anything on him that might make his murder worth while. If the information wormed out in this way seemed satisfactory, the Thug would then suggest that the two should join forces in the morning, since they would have the pleasure of each other's company and also two were better than one if bandits should happen to put in an appearance. So in the morning the pair would set off together, while the other members of the gang kept them under observation as they followed them up along the road. If, however, the offer of his company were declined, the Thug would take a side road and get ahead of his intended victim. In either case an ambush would be arranged, and they would rush out on the traveller in some lonely spot. Usually three men were engaged in an attack, but there were always others within easy reach, to prevent interruption and to provide reinforcements if needs be.

The instrument of murder was sometimes a short rope with a loop at one end, but more usually a turban or *dothi*, i.e., the long narrow sash or cloth worn by Indian men round the waist. There was a special name for this—the *roomal*. This was thrown adroitly over the victim's head by one of the assassins, a second man seized one end and drew it tight, and a third, running up behind, would lay hold of the victim by the feet and tilt him forwards on to the ground. Then the first Thug would fold the roomal more securely round his neck, and put his foot on it to draw it tight—"in the manner of packing a bundle of straw", was how one of the informers concisely phrased it. The victim was probably already dead when he was flung to the ground, but just to make sure they would kick him as he lay there in the most vulnerable parts.

While every precaution was taken against surprise, it sometimes happened that another traveller put in his appearance at a very inconvenient moment. Then the gang had to think, and act, quickly. A favourite ruse was for one of them to throw himself on the ground in a pretended fit, so as to give his accomplices time to get the tell-tale corpse out of sight. Another dodge was to cover the body with a cloth, and make a great show of mourning a comrade who had been suddenly taken ill and died. Yet another was to erect a tent or screen by the roadside in or behind which the corpse was hidden. Then if someone came up and asked what was going on, they could calmly inform him that they had women with them in their party and they were within the screen.

If a party of travellers was attacked by the gang, it did happen occasionally that one of the intended victims managed to get away, and ran down the road yelling and screaming "murder!" But he would not get far. Scouts were always in the neighbourhood, and they would make short work of him with their swords.

The corpse was got rid of as soon as possible. First, it was horribly mangled—stabbed under the armpits, gashed in the ribs and chest and sides, the belly cut open, and sometimes the limbs disjointed—this with the double purpose of making identification impossible and to hasten the processes of decomposition. While one of the gang was mutilating the corpse, his comrades would be busy digging the grave—a hole in the ground three or four feet deep, into which the corpse was dropped unceremoniously, face downwards, after which the hole was hurriedly filled in and the earth smoothed over. Or it might be dropped down a well if there happened to be one in the vicinity.

Certain classes of travellers were immune from attack, for example, washerwomen, poets, professors of dancing, blacksmiths, carpenters, musicians, oil-vendors, and street-sweepers. Water-carriers likewise, but only if the pots they were carrying were full of water. Fakirs and other "holy men" might also be left alone, as well as the crippled and lepers (in this case for fear of contamination). Dogs, it may be noted, were always killed, since they might watch where their masters were buried and attract attention to the spot.

Women as a rule were not attacked, although, as one of Sleeman's informers told him, "if we come up with a particularly rich old dame we sometimes arrange for one of our number to kill her in consideration of an extra share in the booty". Another informer told of a wealthy lady who would certainly have been strangled but for the fact that she was so very good-looking. "She was the handmaid of the Peishwa Bajee Rao, on her way from Poona to Cawnpore. For three days she and her party were in our hands, but after taking the lac and a half's worth of jewels and other things she had with her we let her and her party go—for she was so very beautiful!"

Not that female beauty was always powerful to save. One

of the most useful of the informers, a young fellow named Feringeea, who happened to be strikingly handsome, told how one day he and his gang captured a young Moslem girl, who was travelling in a palanquin with six bearers, accompanied only by an elderly female servant mounted on a pony and a single armed attendant. She belonged to a family of rank and wealth, it appeared, but had thrown over the traces and was thoroughly enjoying herself in her new-found freedom. Unfortunately for her, she was most strongly attracted by the handsome young Thug; who, however, felt bound to repel her overtures since he was a Hindu and she a Moslem, and if it ever came out that he had had anything to do with a Moslem woman he would inevitably lose caste and face ostracism in his community. But the girl became ever more impassioned, and refused to be shaken off. Several of the gang urged that they should let her go, since she had only a small amount of cash with her; but Feringeea, who perhaps had gone farther with her than he wished it to become known, had resolved on her death. While they were looking for a suitable place for the murder, darkness fell; the girl became desperately frightened, but her complaints and entreaties fell on deaf ears, and she was brutally slaughtered. "It was her fate," remarked Feringeea, at the conclusion of the story, in which he had made no attempt to extenuate his crime; "it was her fate to die by our hands."

What made the Thugs so horribly cruel? There is no doubt that it was their religion. As already mentioned, most of them were Moslems, but while they strictly conformed with the rules laid down in the Koran in matters of marriage, inheritance, eating and drinking, etc.; while they prayed to Allah after the Moslem fashion, and looked forward to a future life in a Paradise full of the sensual delights their Prophet had outlined, the deity who was the chief object of their adoration was Kali, the fierce and bloody consort of Siva, the God of Destruction in the Hindu trinity. The "Great Goddess", as she was styled, was represented as a woman with rounded limbs, swelling breasts and wide hips, and with many arms brandishing weapons; she had a variety of other names, but the Thugs generally worshipped her as Bhowanee. Those of them who were Moslems knew, of course, that in worshipping her they were committing idolatry, and in the Koran this is a most grievous sin, to which the most dreadful punishments are attached, but they do not seem to have been much worried. Their attitude was explained to Sleeman by one of his Moslem prisoners.

"Is there any mention of Bhowanee in the Koran?" he asked the man. "Nowhere is she mentioned," he replied.

"Then has she anything to do with your Paradise?" "Nothing." "She has no influence upon your future state?" "None."

"Does Mohammed, your Prophet, anywhere sanction crimes like yours—the murder in cold blood of your fellow-creatures, for the sake of their booty?" "No."

"Does he not say that such crimes will be punished by Allah in the next world?"

"Yes."

"Then do you never feel any dread of punishment hereafter?" "Never. We never murder unless the omens are favourable, and we consider favourable omens as the mandates of the goddess."

"But you admit that Bhowanee has no influence upon the welfare, or otherwise, of your soul hereafter?" "We believe she has none; but she influences our fates in *this* world; and what she orders us to do in this world, we believe that Allah will not punish in the next."

From what we are told about the omens, it is clear that the goddess had plenty of ways of making her wishes known. To begin with, when they had decided on an expedition, the Thugs gave an entertainment in which the principal feature was the sacrifice of a sheep to Bhowanee. The details were given in a paper contributed in 1820 to the Transactions of the Asiatic Society in Bengal by Dr. Sherwood. A silver or bronze image of the goddess was set up, surrounded by representations of lizards and snakes and the paraphernalia of the Thug's trade, namely, a noose, a knife, and a pickaxe. Flowers were then scattered over the collection, incense burnt, and prayers offered to the goddess for success in the projected enterprise. The sheep was then killed, and its head was cut off and placed on the ground before the image with its right forefoot stuck in its mouth. Bhowanee was now asked to indicate her pleasure. Some liquid was poured on the sheep's mouth and nostrils, and if they twitched it was taken as an indication of her approval; if, however, no such agitations appeared, then it was postponed without hesitation. The ceremony might be repeated two or three weeks later, and perhaps this time the signs were favourable, and plans for the expedition were gone on with.

Now a fresh lot of omens came into play. Before the gang set out they sent some of their number along the high road to observe the flight of crows and other birds, and to listen to the chirping of lizards, for by these things the goddess was supposed to indicate whether or not they were going in the right direction. Then after they had started out, they might be halted and made to turn back by an encounter with a corpse of someone from their own village, or with some of those people who were on the "prohibited list", or by hearing women weeping for someone who had just died. On the other hand, meeting the funeral procession of a man who had died in another village, arriving at a village where a fair was in progress, and overhearing women crying with joy as a young bride left her father's house to go to her husband's—these were all good omens, promising well for the success of the expedition.

If a Thug happened to drop his turban, he had to turn back at once, for this was something which the goddess was believed to be most displeased with. And it was considered dreadfully unlucky to sneeze when about to start out.

Many of the omens that were recognized along the road were drawn from the actions of birds and beasts. An ass's bray, for instance: if this were heard coming from the left, and soon afterwards there came an answering bray from the right, the expedition was bound to be successful, however long they might be on the road. A pair of jackals slinking across the road in front was a bad sign, but a solitary jackal crossing from right to left was an excellent one. A dog shaking his head—a bad sign; jackals howling to one another in the daytime—that was worse still; so bad indeed that the expedition was abandoned forthwith. To quote a paragraph from Dr. Sherwood: "If a party, on leaving home to enter upon an expedition, meet a woman bearing a pitcher full of water on her head, it promises a prosperous journey and a safe return; the omen is still better if the female be in a state of pregnancy; but if the pitcher which she carries be empty, the indication is one of misfortune and calamity. An empty pitcher is regarded by Thugs with as much aversion as it is by tipplers."

While most of the Thug gangs operated along the highways,

there were also "river Thugs" who inveigled travellers on to their boats and murdered them when in mid-stream, throwing the bodies overboard after stripping them of everything of any value.

After the Thugs had completed a strangling they held a feast by way of celebration, and this was also a religious rite. *Goor* or sugar was distributed among those who had graduated, as it were, in the university of murder, and it was commonly agreed that to partake of this under those circumstances gave one an irresistible taste for bloodshed.

A Thug who was reproached by Captain Sleeman for his part in a specially atrocious murder made reply: "We all feel pity sometimes, but the goor changes our nature: it would change the nature of a horse. Let any man once taste of that goor, and he will be a Thug, though he knew all the trades and have all the wealth in the world. I myself was never in want of food; my mother's family were wealthy, and their relations high in office. I have been in high office myself, and became so great a favourite wherever I went that I was sure of promotion; yet I was always miserable when absent from my gang, and was obliged to return to Thuggee. My father made me taste that fatal goor when I was yet a mere boy, and if I were to live a thousand years, I never should be able to follow any other trade."

Another of the men questioned by Sleeman declared that he never felt the least pity or compunction in all the many murders that he had committed.

"But how can you murder old men and young children, without some emotions of pity," Sleeman persisted, "calmly and deliberately as they sit with you and tell you of their private affairs—of their hopes and fears—and of the wives and children they are going to meet, after years of absence, toil, or suffering?"

"From the time that the omens are favourable," the hardened ruffian replied, "we consider them as victims thrown into our hands by the goddess to be killed, and that we are mere instruments in her hands to destroy them—that if we do not kill them, she will never again be propitious to us, and we and our families will be involved in misery and want."

"And you can sleep soundly, by the bodies and over the graves of those you have murdered, and eat your meals with as much appetite as ever?"

"Just the same: we sleep and eat just the same, unless we are afraid of being discovered."

"And when you get or hear a bad omen, you think it is the order of the goddess not to kill the travellers you have with you, or are in pursuit of?"

"Yes; it is the order not to kill them, and we dare not disobey."

Such a state of mind as is indicated here could not be induced all at once. There is no reason to believe that the Thugs were born especially cruel: they had to be educated to it. This fact is well brought out in a story that was related by Feringeea to Captain Sleeman in one of their conversations. It concerned a boy, scarcely fourteen, who was sent on his first expedition without being given an inkling of what his father's trade was.

The boy's name was Kurhoora, and since it was intended that he should be broken in to the trade gradually he was put in charge of an old hand named Hursooka. The expedition set out, and, said Feringeea, "we fell in with five Sikhs, and Hursooka was ordered to take the bridle and keep the boy in the rear, out of sight and hearing. But the boy became alarmed and impatient, and galloped up at the instant the *Ihirnee*, or signal for murder, was given. He heard the men's screams, and saw them all strangled. He was seized with trembling, and fell from his pony; he became delirious, was dreadfully alarmed at the sight of the turbans of the murdered men, and, when anyone touched or spoke to him, talked wildly about the murders, screamed as if in a sleep, and trembled violently. We could not get him forward; and after burying the bodies, I myself and a few others sat by him while the gang went on. We were very fond of him, and tried all we could to tranquillize him, but he never recovered his senses, and before evening he died." The event had an unexpected sequel. The old hand Hursooka took the boy's death so much to heart that he quitted the gang and became an ascetic, spending the remainder of his days in a temple on the Nerbudda.

Operating in this way under the umbrella of religion, the Thugs made an excellent living out of their crimes, what with the jewels and clothes that they stripped from the corpses and the goods that they found in the baggage. Sometimes the swag was divided among the gang on the spot, but more usually the distribution was made later when they had returned home or in one of their hide-outs. Some of the most valuable items —pearls, diamonds and other precious stones, Venetian ducats and Spanish dollars, Cashmere shawls, swords, horses, and the rich products of the Benares looms—might be reserved for the polygar or local chief under whose protection the gang operated. Of the remainder, a portion was always set aside to pay for the religious ceremonies that followed upon each successful foray, and something might also be appropriated for the benefit of widows and orphans of deceased members. Then what was left was divided into a number of equal shares. The leader, or sirdar, received two shares; the men who actually did the strangling and mangled the corpse afterwards and disposed of it received one and a half shares each; and the rest of the gang got a share apiece. If the goods could not be conveniently divided, they were disposed of through receivers of stolen goods in the towns, who paid in cash and asked no questions.

From time to time Sleeman learnt from his informers that caches of stolen goods were in certain villages. Then, so we are told by a certain Dr. Spry, who wrote a book on India that was published in 1837, search parties were at once organized and sent out. "The mounted soldiers and infantry sepoys acquit themselves most ably when on this duty," runs his account. "Marching in disguise, they are never suspected, and, as soon as they arrive in sight of the village inhabited by the stranglers, they hide themselves till dark, and then move on. Under cover of the night the village is effectually surrounded by the troopers and a part of the infantry soldiers, while the remainder make the best of their way into the interior. Having by this means made security doubly sure, the head man of the place is called on, and desired to point out the particular houses of the men who are named. This information is no sooner obtained than the buildings are unceremoniously entered, and the Thugs generally secured. Should the Jemadar of the village have pointed out the wrong house, with a view to afford the culprits time to escape, they are sure to fall into the hands of the piquets who are on the watch outside. By the time that these fellows are properly secured, the town or village community is in a pretty general uproar, at the horrifying idea that their next-door neighbours should turn out to be Thugs, and they not know of it."

Very often the Thugs made no attempt to deny the offence, and they seldom showed any signs of remorse. They were guilty, and they were proud of it. Trial and condemnation followed without delay, and the men were led out to execution. Dr. Spry was witness of the scene when he was in residence at Saugur.

"The criminals, drawn up in a semicircle round the bench on which the judge was seated, were surrounded by a strong guard of musketeers and dismounted cavalry. The warrants were placed before them, and each name, as called out, was repeated by the Sheristhadar. At the conclusion of this ceremony Captain Sleeman addressed them in the Hindustani language in a few sentences which may be rendered thus: 'You have been convicted of the crime of blood; the order from the Calcutta Council is, therefore, that at tomorrow's dawn you are all to be hung. If any of you desire to make any further communication, you may now speak.' Few answered; those who did reply merely requested as a dying favour that their bodies on being taken down might be burnt. One hardened villain, however, as he was turning to leave the court, disturbed the solemnity of the scene by muttering, 'Ah, you have got it all your own way now, but let me find you in Paradise, and I will be avenged!'

"The night was passed by these men in displays of coarse and disgusting levity. Trusting in the assurance that, dying in the calling, Bhowanee would provide for them in Paradise, they evinced neither penitence nor remorse. Stifling their alarm with boisterous revelling, they hoped to establish in the minds of their comrades who could hear them through the wall, a reputation for courage which at once proved their insincerity and belied their fortitude. Imagine such men on the last night of their existence on earth, not penitent for their individual errors, or impressed with a sense of the public mischiefs to which they had contributed; not even rendered serious by the dismal ordeal which in a few hours was to usher them into an unseen world; but, singing, singing, in the condemned cell, and repeating their unhallowed carols while jolting along in the carts that conveyed them to their gibbets!"

When morning came, a number of carts drew up to the gaol door, taking five men in each. The men looked dreadfully haggard, noted Dr. Spry, but as he rode past them on the way to the execution-ground some of them called out to him, *"Rooksut, Doctor Sahib; Salaam, Doctor Sahib"* (Adieu, Dr. Sahib, Compliments to you, Doctor). So they were jolted along in their "wretched tumbrils", piercing the air with their "hoarse and hollow shoutings", until they arrived at where temporary gibbets had been erected, forming three sides of a square. There were ten of them, one for each man, and from them nooses were dangling. About five feet from the ground footboards were placed, on which the male-factors stood as they were unloaded from the carts and mounted the ladders that were provided. "Their irons were not removed. Each man as he stepped out on the platform walked at once to the halter and tried its strength by weighing his whole body on it. Then having proved the strength of the rope with his own hands (for they were not handcuffed) each introduced his head into the noose, drew the knot behind the right ear, and amid terrific cheers jumped off the board and launched himself into eternity."

Thus in the moment of death these men, who would not have turned a hair at committing the most atrocious murder, showed a scrupulous concern for the preservation of caste. Explains Dr. Spry: "To wait to be hung by the hands of a *chumar* (hangman) was thought too revolting for endurance. His name would be disgraced for ever; and therefore, rather than submit to this degradation, every man hung himself."

This was at nearly the end of the history of the Thugs. For hundreds of years they had practised their dreadful trade with near impunity, and justice had been long in bringing them to book. It is impossible to determine the number of their victims, but it was estimated that in the early years of the last century Thugs were strangling a thousand or fifteen hundred persons annually. Then Lord William Bentinck came on the scene, and Captain Sleeman. Between 1826 and 1835 more than fifteen hundred Thugs were put on trial, and of these 383 were hanged and most of the rest either transported or imprisoned for life. Even after the stranglers had been suppressed cases were reported of Thugs murdering with poison, but by 1848 Thuggee was extinct.

of the Head-Hunters

...nese invaded Borneo in 1942 they came up
...that was strange, swift, silent, and deadly.
...oldier who had happened to stray from the
...was ambushed by a native armed with a
...a few minutes the poisoned dart had done
...and inert, he sank to the ground, and then
...ed from the jungle growth and with a single
...ng sliced off his head. Very soon this had
...e others in the tribal long-house, where the
...may perhaps see it still today, grinning hor-
...dust and cobwebs.

Among the head-hunting peoples of the world, the natives
of Borneo (which in a geographical sense includes Sarawak)
are beyond a doubt the most celebrated. In days gone by
head-hunting was their national sport, and it was with the
greatest reluctance that they agreed to its suppression when
this was demanded by their British rulers in the last century.
Their women were as keen on it as the men, so much so that
a girl would not dream of marrying a man who had not taken

at least one head. The captured heads were hung up as trophies in the same way as a man in our own civilization will display the cups he has won on the golf-course. When the World War engulfed their territories, the natives jumped at the opportunity of reviving their old skills in this direction, and soon demonstrated their efficacy.

Of the Bornean tribes, the Ibans (or Sea Dayaks as they are often called) were the most warlike and particularly devoted to head-hunting. In the olden days they used to accompany the Malays in their big *prahus*, or sailing-vessels, on piratical raids along the coast and up the rivers. The actual planning of these forays fell to the Malays, who engaged in them for plunder, but the Ibans were induced to join them on being promised that all the heads of the slain should fall to their share. It is uncertain whether the "Land Dayaks" adopted the custom of head-hunting from the Ibans, or whether it was indigenous with them, but they practised it with gusto until Rajah Brooke was able to suppress it in Sarawak in the middle of the last century.

When the English ethnologist A. C. Haddon visited the area (as described in his book *Head-hunters: Black, White, and Brown,* published in 1901) the practice was extinct in Sarawak, but there were plenty of evidences of its having been. Hanging from the rafters in most of the houses were trophies of human skulls. Some were fastened to a circular framework, "looking something like a ghastly parody of the glass chandeliers of our young days", while others were suspended from a long board, which might be decorated with carved images of men who represented captives taken in war. The skulls were smoke-begrimed and otherwise dirty, and interspersed among them were streamers of palm-leaves such as were invariably employed, in all the ceremonies connected with skulls. Below the chandelier of skulls a fire was always kept burning, since it was believed that they liked to be kept warm, and that if they were comfortable and had all their wants supplied they would bring good luck to the house and ensure plentiful harvests.

Dr. Haddon was very anxious to obtain some specimen skulls for the ethnographical collections at Cambridge; but skulls were held to be sacred, and while they were bringers of good luck when kindly treated they were just as likely to turn nasty if they were offended in any way. Under such circumstances it proved no easy matter to persuade a man to part with a skull, as he felt that he would be incurring a great risk and that the price paid him might be wealth bought too dearly. However, a way was at length devised of propitiating the skulls that were included in the deal. A *small* fowl was obtained and waved over the skulls, and these were told that they were going to be taken away and not sold ("for here," remarks Haddon, "as in our folk-tales at home, it is very easy to deceive spirits"), that they would be taken well care of, and they were entreated not to be angry, as everything was "quite correct", and the white man would take full responsibility and bear all the risks. Then the head and wings of the luckless chicken were torn off, and the spurting blood sprinkled on the skulls and the surrounding charms, and even on the notched pole which served as a ladder.

Poor skulls, how they are taken in! This is what happens when a house-moving is contemplated by a community of Kenyahs, and for one reason or another they do not wish to take all the skulls with them. This fact must be kept dark as long as may be, for if the skulls should find out how they are being deceived they might avenge themselves on the people of the house—they might even cause them to go mad. This is how the skulls are tricked.

After the site for a new house has been decided upon—the Dayaks, it may be noted, live in communal long-houses, raised on stilts above the ground, and consisting of one long gallery off which open the rooms which are the "homes" of each family composing the community—and before the actual work of building is commenced, a small hut is built alongside the old long-house; it is well roofed but the walls are made only of leaves, a fireplace is installed, and also a new board or framework from which the skulls are suspended. The fire is lit, the place made warm and snug, and then the skulls which are to be left behind are hung up in their new position. It is customary for a pig or chicken to be killed when a new house is entered upon, and this is now done, with the usual ceremony.

The skulls are left in the hut, and each day a fire is lit beneath them; apparently they are very comfortable and pleased with their new home. But at times suspicious skulls are heard to "*kriak kriak*", and they may even throw themselves on the floor. When this happens, they are carefully put back, for the people dare not run any risk of offending them. By this time work on building the new long-house will be well advanced, but the people are most careful to keep all knowledge of what is going on from the old skulls in the hut.

When the new house is completed, the skulls that remained in the old one are removed and put in position with great ceremony. Fowls are killed, and their blood sprinkled about in the customary manner. Then the people move in. The next morning some of them go to the hut and light a fire as before beneath the skulls that have been abandoned, and then they slink away as though they are afraid. The fire smoulders on, but after three days it has generally burnt itself out. Then the skulls begin to talk and grumble to one another. "Where are the people?" "How is it that no fire has been put in?" "It's fearfully cold." The roof then chimes in; "Oh, they are probably away at their farms; most likely they will be back in a day or two."

But day after day goes by, and no one comes, and the skulls begin to feel that there is something wrong. However, they live in hope for some time. After a month or so the leafy roof begins to leak; and when the skulls feel the rain they say to the roof, "Why do you serve us so badly? Why do you allow the rain to fall on us? Why don't you make the people come and mend you?" Then the roof replies: "Don't you know that you have been left? The people have gone long ago." On hearing this, the skulls begin to hustle around and seek to revenge themselves on the people who have deceived them. They look up river and down river and along the banks, but rain has obliterated all the tracks the people made when they flitted. At length, finding it hopeless to think of following them, the skulls give themselves up to their fate, and gradually become bleached by the rain and the heat of the sun. Their ratan-lashing rots, and they fall to the ground. And this is the way in which the people are saved from any serious harm coming to them.

Why (it may be asked) do the natives ever leave skulls behind? It is because they are very old, and the people who obtained them and benefitted thereby are long since dead and buried. And yet these old skulls, as long as they share a house with the living, have to receive the same care and attention as the more recent additions. They have to be fed with pork and refreshed with drink, and the fire has to be attended to daily—otherwise the skulls will be unhappy and bring bad luck. Nothing is to be gained by keeping them. Why, then, should the community be put to all this trouble and expense in keeping them? The natives are sharp enough to appreciate that this is not good business, and so they take steps to rid themselves of the tiresome obligation—but always in such a way as not to bring any unpleasant consequences on themselves.

When he inquired into the reason for head-hunting as it had been practised for generations in Borneo and Sarawak, Dr. Haddon concluded that one of the chief incentives was undoubtedly to please the women. Among some tribes it was said to be an indispensable necessity for a young man to procure a skull before he could marry: the fact that a man was brave enough to go head-hunting spoke well for his ability to protect and provide for a wife and family. Some tribes believed that the persons whose heads they had taken would become their slaves in the after-life: head-hunting was thus a wise precaution for the future. A vendetta or blood-feud was a very common reason for going on the head-hunting war-path. Then among the Kayans and Kenyahs the people could not go out of mourning for their late chief until a new head had been taken—or perhaps an old one, for this might serve the purpose equally well.

Rajah Brooke was well acquainted with this practice in Sarawak, and realized how greatly the people were convinced of its necessity. He would not permit them to take a fresh head, but in order to enable a community to go out of mourning he established a sort of skull-bank, from which skulls might be borrowed as required, and then, when the ceremony was over, returned into stock. He found it worked very well; everybody was satisfied, including (we may assume) the skulls, since they were kept nice and warm when not in use. . . .

While in that part of the world, Dr. Haddon also visited the islands in the Torres Straits where the people had only lately given up head-hunting. From them he got some first-hand details of the procedure. When an enemy was killed, his head was cut off with a bamboo knife, and carried home by the victor on a ratan-sling inserted under the jawbone. It was then hung over a fire and the hair singed off, and while this was being done all the young girls of the village danced and sang in a ring near, but not round, the fire. The head was now taken away and all the flesh was removed, after which it was washed, a carved wooden peg stuck in it, and then it was hung up on the main post of the house.

Sometimes there might be particular difficulty in getting a fresh skull. In this case a young man who was in great need of one would betake himself to some neighbouring island, buy a skull that happened to be on offer, and take it back home with him. Some of his friends might have been told in confidence of the transaction, but it was considered bad form to ask too many questions. Of course, scarcity was reflected in the price, and a canoe might have to be given for a single skull.

Among the other head-hunting peoples the Jivaros of South America occupy a very special place. They are specialists. They kill for heads, and when they have slashed them off they *shrink* them until they are no bigger than an orange.

Few travellers have penetrated to the Jivaro country, situated as it is in the almost inaccessible borderlands of Ecuador and Peru. Furthermore, the Jivaros have let it be known in no uncertain fashion that they do not take kindly to strangers. The Spaniards tried to subjugate them in the early days of the conquest, centuries ago, but they soon had to desist. In those days the Jivaros could send twenty thousand braves on the war-path, but their numbers have so shrunk that they are now not more than four or five thousand all told. Among the causes that have contributed to this decline in numbers is no doubt their relentless pursuit of human heads. For generations they have practised it, until no man can have felt safe. Even now the murders go on. A Jivaro will not, as a rule, seek to kill a near relative, and women are generally thought not worth the killing, but everybody else is fair game; he keeps on, taking more heads, more and more, until his own is taken by someone stronger or cleverer, and is slung round the victor's neck on a string.

What is it that drives him on in this horrid chase? Not blood lust, not excitement, not even the desire to prove himself a man. In part it is the operation of the old law of an eye for an eye, a tooth for a tooth, the law of vengeance. But most important is the belief that in acquiring a man's head there is acquired a measure of magical power, since it is in the head that a man's soul has its dwelling. And when you have got the head you must *shrink* it, for this is the final and most complete demonstration of mastery and possession.

Planning a raid requires a deal of thought. The first thing is to decide on a victim, and here resort may be had to drugs. A glassful of the juice of the rind of one of the Datura plants—and the most powerful hallucinations are induced, in which the person of the man to be slaughtered may make its appearance. Not at once, perhaps, but years hence, when the chances are favourable. Then, one dark night, the destined victim is walking home down a jungle path, when, suddenly, without the least warning, a spear strikes him in the throat and he falls dead. Then the murderer, alone or with an accomplice, rushes up and with a few strokes of his stone axe or bamboo knife gets the head away from the body and carries it off in triumph.

In his home settlement his family and friends will be waiting, or perhaps the place of meeting agreed upon is a glade in the forest. All the necessary preparations will have been made. A pot of water almost on the boil over the fire—a few smooth round stones for pounding—a number of pins made of the black chonta wood—a pile of sand kept hot on the hearth: the headman, witch-doctor or medicine-man runs his eye over the lot and makes sure that nothing is missing.

Now for the first stage of the head-shrinking process. The chief operator—it may be the murderer himself—takes hold of the head, carefully slits the skin just below the ears, and peels it off. The nose and ears require special care, and the eyes are gouged out. Then the bloody scalp is held up on a spear, while the bones of the face and skull are unceremoniously thrown into the river, the Jivaro equivalent of a dustbin.

Meanwhile the pot has been brought to boil, and the scalp is now dropped into the water and allowed to stew for two hours or thereabouts, by which time it has become soft, thick, and looking like a piece of yellow rubber. The operator reaches into the pot with a stick and fishes out the scalp, which is now hung up to dry.

This may conclude the first day's work, and the men involved retire to rest after a meal. But with first light they are at the task again, for until the head is properly shrunk they have not got full possession of the soul within, and the former owner will still be in a position to work evil on his murderers. To ward off the threatened danger the men may now engage in the "rite of tobacco", and a disgustingly messy and nasty business it is. The headman or master of ceremonies chews a number of tobacco leaves, spits them into a shallow dish or gourd, and then crushes and rubs them so as to extract a thick liquid. This he sucks up into his mouth, and then, bending over each participant in the rite in turn, ejects into each man's nostrils a dose of tobacco juice. This rite is repeated several times.

Now the scalp is taken down and its neck ringed with a vine tendril, after which it is sewn up into a kind of pocket. Two or three sharp pieces of wood are passed through the lips, which, so the participants believe, has the effect of preventing speech for good and all. "No fear of being cursed now," they reflect with a grim satisfaction. After this the inside of the skin is rubbed with the stones which have been heated in readiness, and then the scalp is half filled with hot sand which is rolled round and round, pushed into every crevice, and often replenished. Every now and again the face is carefully moulded, so as to retain its shape and appearance. A good deal of the hair is removed, and the eyebrows are plucked. The cheeks are hollowed out, the nose is stiffened, the ears (lobes pierced as in life) are given their proper shape. Perhaps two days are given to this treatment, until the scalp is rendered smooth and polished like fine leather. When all is done, it will be about a quarter of its original size, a miniature human head perfect in all its details. To use the Indian term, it is a *tsantsa*.

Now the trophy is stuck on a spear and held aloft, while the Indians dance and sing round it by way of prelude to an orgy of feasting and sexual licence and drunkenness. Great is their rejoicing, for have they not won a man's soul and added it to their stock of spiritual material? They will be the better men for it, and their women will be more fruitful. For the moment their fear has left them, and they are conscious only of their bravery and the magical power they have acquired. But before long the fear will be back again, and with it the grim necessity to get more heads, even at the risk of losing their own. . . .

Instances of head-hunting have been reported from many other parts of the world than those already mentioned. Assam was once famous for its head-hunters, the Naga tribesfolk long indulged in it, and so did some of the tribes on the North-west frontier of India. Hill tribes in Formosa and tribes in the interior of the Philippines once practised it, and in New Guinea and indeed through the lands and islands of the South Seas it was practically universal.

Nor has Europe been without its examples. As late as 1912, in the course of the ferocious struggle of the Balkan Wars, the semi-barbarous Montenegrins were reported to have made a practice of cutting off the heads of their Turkish enemies and carrying them around by a forelock of hair or the moustache as ghastly trophies of victory.

Chapter 6

Widows for the Burning

"SUTTEE" is the English word for the rite of widow-burning, i.e., burning the widow alive on her husband's funeral pyre, that was once widely practised among certain Hindu castes in India, more especially among the Rajputs. The word is properly *Sati*, which is Sanskrit for "good woman" or "true wife", and the Sanskrit term for the act itself is *sahagamana*, meaning "keeping company" or "dying together".

One of the first European writers to give an account of the rite was the Greek historian Diodorus Siculus, who lived in the times of Julius Caesar and Augustus. It occurs in that part of his "universal history" in which he describes the invasion of India by Alexander the Great and his immediate successors, and the date is about 317 B.C. An Indian general serving under Eumenes, the Greek commander, had just died, and his two widows disputed the honour of burning themselves on the corpse of their lord. One of the wives could not be burnt since she was with child, but the other marched up to the funeral pile adorned as for a wedding, crowned with myrtle, and preceded by a number of her relatives singing hymns in praise of her intention. She distributed her jewels among her friends and domestics, and then, "having taken leave of those of her household, she was set upon the pyre by her own brother, and was regarded with wonder by the crowd that had run together to the spectacle, and heroically ended her life". Before the pyre was kindled, the army marched three times round it. The sight of the woman, "laying herself beside her husband, and even in the violence of the flames giving utterance to no unbecoming cry," stirred pity in the minds of some of the beholders and in others "excess of eulogy", while some of the Greeks reprobated the rite as barbarous and cruel.

Of course it was, but it was one backed by the authority of centuries and that had acquired the sanctity of religion. For a thousand years at least it had been practised in India by the Aryan aristocracy, and wherever the Brahminical religion had obtained predominance. Very likely the Aryans had brought it with them from their homeland somewhere in central Asia. In those parts of the sub-continent where the aboriginal inhabitants had not been driven out or exterminated the custom never took firm root, and was even sternly prohibited.

Ancient though the practice was, it was not prescribed in the Vedas, the oldest and most authoritative of the Hindu scriptures, nor is it included in the Code of Manu, the most primitive collection of Indian laws. It was only by the skilful manipulation of the sacred texts by the Brahman theologians that they were deemed to accord it the sanction of religion.

But while it was not, to begin with, a legal or a religious obligation, it very soon became very definitely a social one. It was not forced upon the woman, but she was made to feel that not only would her own happiness and that of her husband in the next life or incarnation depend upon her offering herself as a *sati*, but that the alternative would be to live on only in misery and degradation. For that was, and still is, the widow's customary lot in India.

One of the first Europeans to witness suttee was the celebrated French traveller Jean Baptiste Tavernier, who between 1640 and 1667 made a number of voyages to India and travelled extensively in the interior. His *Six Voyages* was published in 1677, and in this there is a chapter entitled,

"How the women burn themselves with the bodies of their deceased husbands in India", which is a remarkable piece of descriptive reporting.

"It is an ancient custom among the Idolaters of India," he begins, "that on a man dying his widow can never remarry; as soon, therefore, as he is dead she withdraws to weep for her husband, and some days afterwards her hair is shaved off, and she despoils herself of all the ornaments with which her person was adorned, she removes from her arms and legs the bracelets which her husband had given her, when espousing her, as a sign that she was to be submissive and bound to him, and she remains for the rest of her life without being of any consideration, and worse than a slave, in the place where previously she was mistress. This miserable condition causes her to detest life, and prefer to ascend a funeral pile to be consumed alive with the body of her defunct husband, rather than be regarded for the remainder of her days with opprobrium and infamy by all the world. Joined to which the Brahmins induce the women to hope that by dying in this way, with their husbands, they will live again with them in some other part of the world with more glory and more comfort than they have previously enjoyed. These are the two reasons which make these unhappy women resolve to burn themselves with the bodies of their husbands; to which it should be added that the priests buoy them up with the hope that at the moment when they are in the fire, before they yield up their souls, *Ram* [God] will reveal wonderful things to them, and that after the soul has passed through several bodies it will attain to an exalted degree of glory for all eternity."

But (Tavernier goes on to explain) before a woman could burn herself with the body of her husband she had to obtain permission from the Governor of the place where she was living, and those Governors who were Mohammedans—as most of them were, for he was writing of northern India, which was then under the rule of the powerful Mogul emperors of Delhi—"hold this dreadful custom of self-destruction in horror, and do not readily give permission". Widows with young children were not permitted under any circumstances to commit suttee, but were obliged to live to continue to watch over the education of their offspring. But those women who were peremptorily refused permission to immolate themselves were not much better off, since they were required to "pass the remainder of their lives in severe penances and in doing charitable deeds. There are some who frequent the great highways either to boil water with vegetables, in order to give it as a drink to passers-by, or to keep fire always ready to light the pipes of those who desire to smoke tobacco. There are others among them who make a vow to eat nothing but what they find undigested in the droppings of oxen, cows, and buffaloes, and who do still more absurd things".

In many cases, however, and probably in most, the Governor's permission was granted, perhaps in return for a bribe slipped into the hand of the great man's secretary, and "at length he allows them to do what they wish, and in a rage tells all the idolaters who accompany them that they may 'go to the devil'."

Immediately the permission had been obtained, "all the relatives and friends of the widow congratulate her on the good fortune which she is to acquire in the other world, and on the glory which all the members of the caste derive from her noble resolution. She dresses herself as for her wedding-day, and is conducted to the place where she is to be burnt. A great noise is made with the instruments of music and the voices of the women who follow, singing hymns to the glory of the unhappy one who is about to die. The Brahmins accompanying her exhort her to show resolution and courage, and many Europeans believe that in order to remove the fear of that death which man naturally abhors, she is given some kind of drink that takes away her senses and removes all apprehension which the preparations for her death might give rise to."

Tavernier had seen women burnt in three different ways. "In the kingdom of Gujarat, and as far as Agra and Delhi, this is how it takes place: On the margin of a river or tank, a kind of small hut, about twelve feet square, is built of reeds and all kinds of faggots, with which some pots of oil and other drugs are placed in order to make it burn quickly. The woman being seated in a half-reclining position in the middle of the hut, her head reposing on a kind of pillow of wood, and resting her back against a post, to which she is tied by her waist by one of the Brahmins, for fear lest she should escape on feeling the flame. In this position she holds the dead body of her husband on her knees, chewing *betel* all the time; and after having been about half an hour in this condition, the Brahmin who has been by her side in the hut goes outside, and she calls out to the priests to apply the fire; this the Brahmins, and the relatives and friends of the woman who are present, immediately do, throwing into the fire some pots of oil, so that the woman may suffer less by being quickly consumed. After the bodies have been reduced to ashes, the Brahmins take whatever is found in the way of melted gold, silver, tin, or copper, derived from the bracelets, earrings, and rings which the woman had on; this belongs to them by right."

Next Tavernier describes the method adopted in the kingdom of Bengal. This was the land of the Ganges, holiest of India's rivers, and "a woman in that country must be very poor if she does not come with the body of her husband to the margin of the Ganges in order to wash it after he is dead, and to bathe herself before being burnt. I have seen them come to the Ganges more than twenty days' journey, the bodies being by that time altogether putrid, and emitting an unbearable odour. There was one of them who, coming from the north, near the frontiers of the Kingdom of Bhutan, with the body of her husband which she had conveyed in a carriage, travelled all the way on foot herself, without eating for fifteen or sixteen days, till she arrived at the Ganges, where after having washed the body of her husband, which stank horribly, and having bathed herself also, she had herself burnt with him with a determination which surprised those who saw it. I was there at the time."

Bengal, like the rest of the country along the Ganges, was very short of fuel (Tavernier goes on to explain), and the poor women who had resolved to burn themselves used to send out to beg for wood out of charity with which to prepare the pile. This was like a kind of bed, with its pillow of small wood and reeds, in which pots of oil and other drugs were placed in order to consume the body quickly. "The woman who intends to burn herself, preceded by some drums, flutes, and hautboys, and dressed in her most beautiful ornaments, comes dancing to the funeral pile, and having ascended it she places herself, half-lying, half-seated. Then the body of her husband is laid across her, and all the relatives and friends bring her, one a letter, another a piece of cloth, this one flowers, that one pieces of silver or copper, saying to her, give this from me to my mother, or to my brother, or to some relative or friend, whoever the dead person may be whom they have most loved while alive. When the woman sees that they bring her nothing more, she asks those present three times whether they have any more commissions for her, and if they do not reply she wraps all they have brought in a *taffeta*, which she places between her lap and the back of the body of her defunct husband, calling upon the priests to apply fire to the funeral pile. This the Brahmins and the relatives do simultaneously. As there is, as I have remarked, but little wood in the Kingdom of Bengal, as soon as these miserable women are dead and half burnt, their bodies are thrown into the Ganges with those of their husbands, where they are eaten by the crocodiles."

Now we come to the practice along the Coromandel coast. "A large hole of 9 or 10 feet deep, and 25 or 30 feet square, is dug, into which an abundance of wood is thrown, with many drugs to make it burn fast. When the hole is well heated, the body of the husband is placed on the edge, and then his wife comes dancing, and chewing *betel*, accompanied by all her relatives and friends. The woman then takes three turns round the hole, and at each time she kisses all her relatives and friends. When she completes the third turn, the Brahmins throw the body of the deceased into the fire, and the woman, having her back turned to the hole, is also pushed by the same Brahmins, and falls in backwards. Then all the relatives throw pots of oil and other drugs of that kind, as I have said is elsewhere done, so that the bodies may be the sooner consumed."

In the greater part of the Coromandel coast, however, it was the custom to *bury* the widow with her husband's body instead of burning her. A hole was dug in the ground by the Brahmins, about a foot deeper than a man's height, and preferably in a sandy soil. Then the woman and the corpse were placed in it together, and "each of those who have accompanied them, having filled a basket of sand, throw it on the bodies until the hole is full and heaped over, half a foot higher than the ground, after which they jump and dance till they conclude that the woman is smothered".

As a rule, the woman submitted to her fate, in fear and trembling, in sullen resentment, in hopeless resignation; and even when they might perhaps have made their escape their superstitious dread made them go through with the ordeal.

Tavernier mentions a case of a woman—not in India but in one of the districts in the East Indies where there were Dutch traders—who *did* escape, but not for long. An "Idolater" had died, and his wife, who had no children and had obtained the permission of the Governor, went to the pit with the priests and her relatives to be burnt according to their custom. The fire was already lit, and they were making the three circuits that were customary, when a sudden storm broke, and the priests, wishing to take shelter, threw the woman into the pit and made off. But the rain was so heavy and kept on so long that it put out the fire and she was not burnt. At midnight she struggled out of the pit and made her way to the house of some relatives and knocked at the door. They let her in, and she was seen there by some "Hollanders" and a Capuchin friar named Father Zenon. She was in a frightful state, hideous and disfigured, and so grim and ghastly looking that it was enough to scare them. "However, the pains she had suffered did not so far terrify her, but that three days later, accompanied by her relatives, she went and was burned according to her first intention."

A still more extraordinary tale is told by Alexander Hamilton, a young Scotsman who, as he tells us, "having a rambling mind and a fortune too narrow to travel like a gentleman", went out to the East Indies in 1688 and remained there till 1723, engaged in a series of commercial adventures. His *New Account of the East Indies* (1727) is so graphically written that he has been compared not unfavourably with Herodotus. The subject of the tale was a certain native lady who, so he had been told, "had received addresses from a Gentleman, who afterwards deserted her, and her Relations obliged her to marry another. Her husband died shortly after their marriage, and according to custom she was laid on the funeral pile. The fire was well kindled and she was going to act the Tragedy on herself when she espied her former Admirer, and beckoned to him to come to her. When he came, she took him in her arms, as if she had a mind to embrace him; but being stronger than he, she carried him into the flames in her arms, where they were both consumed, with the Corpse of her Husband."

Hamilton had first-hand knowledge of suttee as it was performed in the East Indies, to which the custom had spread from India. "It is reported," he writes, "that before the Brahmins invented this law, poison was so well known and practised, that the least quarrel that happened between a married couple cost the husband his life, and this law put a great stop to it; and now custom so far prevails that if any faint-hearted lady has not courage enough to accompany her spouse to the other world, she is forthwith shaved and degraded, and obliged to serve all her husband's family, in all kinds of drudgery."

Then we have the statement, "I have seen several burned several ways". In Canara "they dig a pit about 10 feet long and 6 feet broad, and fill it with logs of wood. One great piece is set at the brim of the pit, ready to fall down on pulling a bit of string. When all is ready, there is a good store of oil or butter thrown on the wood, and then the husband's corpse is placed about the middle of the pile, and fire set to it, which blazes in an instant. Then the spouse takes her leave of all friends and acquaintances, and drums, trumpets, and hautboys playing cheerfully—she walks three or four times round the fire, which by this time is all in a great blaze, and then she leaps in on the corpse. As soon as she has leaped in, a priest draws the string, and down falls the great log of wood, at least 500 pounds weight, over her body, and all are consumed together."

In other parts, he continues, "they do not use pits, but a pile is built, and the corpse laid on it, and fire put to it; and the victim dancing round it for a little time, to the noise of loud music, leaps in; and, if she hesitates, the priest thrusts her in with long poles, making such a hideous noise that she cannot be heard; and all the while she is burning, the priests dance round the fire. Others again take somnific medicine, and stand by the pile till they fall on it while asleep. . . ."

Tavernier is good, and so is Hamilton, but the Abbé Dubois is better. From 1792 till 1823 Dubois was a Roman Catholic missionary in India. From his own account, he was a far from successful missionary, but from the beginning he formed the resolve to gain the Indians' confidence by living as they did, and the result was his book *Hindu Manners, Customs, and Ceremonies* (first published in 1818 but not complete until 1897), which is still of immense value. As an explorer of Indian life in all its aspects he is in a class by himself. Many of his best pages are devoted to a description of suttee as he saw it.

Some Indian widows, he says, committed "this folly" of

dying on their husband's pyre readily enough, spurred on as they were by the thought of the wretchedness of widowhood, by vanity, by the hope of acquiring notoriety, and perhaps also in some cases by a genuine feeling of enthusiasm. It should be remembered that they were awarded boundless honours, and were even deified after death. Vows were made and prayers addressed to them, and their intercession was sought in times of sickness and adversity. Such remnants of their bodies as were not entirely consumed by the fire were most devoutly gathered together, and on the spot where they had sacrificed themselves small monumental pyramids were erected to transmit to posterity the memory of "these brave victims of conjugal affection"—a tribute all the more conspicuous because the erection of tombs is something almost unknown amongst Hindus. "In a word, women who have had the courage to deliver themselves so heroically to the flames are numbered among the divinities, and crowds of devotees may be seen coming in from all sides to offer them sacrifices and to invoke their protection."

To these "inducements of vain and empty glory—sufficient of themselves to make a deep impression on a feeble mind—must be added the entreaties of relatives, who, if they perceive the slightest inclination on the part of the widow to offer up her life, spare no means in order to convince her and force her to a final determination. At times they go so far as to administer drugs, which so far deprive her of her senses that under their influence she yields to their wishes. This inhuman and abominable method of wheedling a consent out of the unhappy woman is in their opinion justified, because her tragic end woud bring great honour and glory to the whole of their family."

When a woman, after mature deliberation, had once declared her desire to be burnt alive with her deceased husband, her decision was considered irrevocable. She could not afterwards retract; and should she refuse of her own free will to proceed to the funeral pyre she would be dragged there by force. The Brahmins who regulated all the proceedings of the tragedy, and also her relatives, came up by turns to congratulate her on her heroic decision and on the immortal glory which she was about to acquire by such a death. All possible means which fanaticism and superstition could suggest were brought to bear upon her in order to keep up her courage, exalt her enthusiasm, and excite her imagination. And when at last the fatal moment had drawn nigh, she was adorned with rare elegance, bedecked with her jewels, and thus led to the funeral pyre.

"It is impossible for me to describe the finishing scenes of this dreadful ceremony without feelings of distress," says Dubois. One of the suttees he describes took place in 1794, in a village of the Tanjore district. A man of some importance belonging to the Vaisya caste had died, and his widow, a woman of about thirty, forthwith announced her intention of accompanying her deceased husband to the funeral pyre. The news of her intention spread rapidly, and a large concourse of people flocked from all quarters to see the spectacle. When everything was ready for the ceremony, and the widow had been richly clothed and adorned, bearers placed her husband's corpse—which had been clothed in his richest attire, covered with jewels, and the mouth filled with betel—in a sort of shrine, which was ornamented with costly stuffs, garlands of flowers, green foliage, etc. The corpse was seated, with crossed legs. Immediately after the funeral car in the procession followed the widow, borne in a richly decorated palanquin. An immense crowd of onlookers watched her go past, and lifted up their hands in admiration and rent the air with cries of joy. For already (as they viewed the matter) she was as good as translated to the paradise of the great god Indra, and what could they do but envy her happy lot.

Slowly the funeral procession moved along, and the spectators, especially the women, tried to get as near her as possible in order to congratulate her on her good fortune, and at the same time hoping that she would be pleased to predict the happy things that might befall them here below. She obliged them. With gracious and amiable mien she declared that one would enjoy the favours of fortune, another would be the mother of numerous children, a third would live long and happily with her husband who would never cease to love and cherish her. Then she distributed among them leaves of betel, and the way in which they fell over themselves to receive them was evidence of their reputed value as relics. Beaming with joy, the women then withdrew, each in the full hope that the promised blessings of wealth and happiness would be showered upon her and hers.

During the whole procession, which was a very large one,

the widow preserved a calm demeanour. Her looks were serene, even smiling. But when she reached the fatal place where she was to yield up her life, it was observed that her firmness suddenly gave way. "Plunged, as it were, in gloomy thought, she seemed to pay no attention to what was passing around her. Her looks became wildly fixed upon the pile. Her face grew deadly pale. Her very limbs were in a convulsive tremor. Her drawn features and haggard face betrayed the fright that had seized her, while a sudden weakening of her senses betokened that she was ready to faint away."

The Brahmins who were conducting the ceremony, and also her near relatives, saw her plight and ran quickly to her side. They urged her to keep up her courage and did everything in their power to revive her sinking spirits. All to no avail, however; the woman was bewildered and distracted, and turned a deaf ear to all their exhortations, and preserved a deep silence.

Now she was made to leave the palanquin. She was scarcely able to walk of her own, and her people helped her to drag herself to a pond near the pyre. Here she plunged into the water just as she was, with all her clothes and ornaments on, and immediately afterwards she was led, dripping, to the pyre on which the body of her husband had been already laid. It was surrounded by Brahmin priests, each with a lighted torch in one hand and a bowl of ghee (clarified buffalo butter) in the other. Also standing round in a double line were the woman's relatives and friends, several of them armed with muskets, swords, and other weapons. Dubois was told that this display of armed force was intended not only to intimidate the unhappy victim in case terror might lead her to make an attempt to run away, but also to overawe any persons who might be moved by a natural feeling of compassion and sympathy to attempt her rescue.

At length the *purohita* (chief officiating priest) gave the fatal signal. Instantly the poor widow was divested of all her jewels, and dragged, more dead than alive, to the pyre. There she was compelled, according to the established custom, to walk three times round it, two of her relatives supporting her by the arms. The first round she accomplished with tottering steps, but during the second her strength forsook her and she fainted away in the arms of her conductors, and in the third round they were obliged to complete the ceremony by dragging her along with them. Then she was cast, unconscious, upon the corpse of her husband on the summit of the pile. The air resounded with noisy acclamations. The Brahmins emptied the contents of their bowls on the dry wood and applied their torches. "In the twinkling of an eye the whole pile was a blaze. Three times was the unfortunate woman called by her name. But, alas! she made no answer."

The second suttee described by the Abbé Dubois occurred in 1801, when the king of Tanjore died. The king left behind him four lawful wives, and the Brahmins decided that two of these should be burnt with the body of their husband. They made the selection, and the two who were chosen, whatever their private feelings may have been, made a virtue of necessity and seemed perfectly ready to yield to the terrible lot which awaited them.

A single day was all that was required to make the preparations for the royal obsequies. At a distance of some miles from the palace a square pit was dug, not very deep and about 12 or 15 feet square, and within this was erected a pyramid of sandalwood resting on a kind of scaffolding. The posts which supported this were so arranged that they could easily be removed, when the whole structure would collapse.

Now the procession made its way to the funeral pyre. First came a large body of soldiers, followed by a crowd of trumpeters and other musicians; and then the dead king's body was carried along in a splendid open palanquin, while his guru, or spiritual adviser, his chief officers and nearest relatives walked alongside, wearing no turbans as a token of mourning. Now came the two queens, the destined victims. Each was borne in a richly decorated palanquin, and they were not so much decked as loaded with jewels; they were accompanied by some of their favourite women, with whom they conversed from time to time, and on either side strode a line of soldiers to keep back the excited crowds. A number of relatives of both sexes came next, and bringing up the rear was a great multitude of Brahmins and persons of all castes.

On reaching the fatal spot, the two queens performed the ablutions and other ceremonies required of them, and they went through the whole without hesitation or showing the least sign of fear. But when it came to walking round the pyre, on which the body of their deceased lord was now laid, their features underwent a sudden change, and notwithstanding their obvious efforts to suppress their natural feelings their strength seemed about to forsake them.

Still wearing their rich ornaments, the two queens were compelled to ascend the pyre, and to lie down beside the corpse, one on the left and the other on the right. Then they joined hands across it. Now the Brahmins recited several mantras, or prayers, after which they sprinkled the pile with holy water and emptied jars of ghee over the wood. Suddenly, the guru and several other Brahmins on one side, and the dead king's nearest relatives on the other, thrust lighted torches into the wood. The flames spread quickly, and the props having been removed, the whole pyramidal structure collapsed. Whereupon all the spectators shouted aloud for joy.

The two unhappy women must have been crushed to death when the pile collapsed, but some of the relatives called to them several times by name, and it was said that they heard, issuing from amid the flames, the word *"Yen?"* ("What?"), distinctly pronounced. But this, comments the Abbé, was a ridiculous illusion on their part, for by now the victims were in no state to hear or to speak.

Two days afterwards, when the fire had been completely extinguished, the remnants of bone that had not been entirely consumed were carefully collected and placed in copper urns, which were sealed with the new king's signet. Some time later, thirty specially selected Brahmins carried these relics to Benares, and tipped them into the Ganges. But a portion of the bones had been preserved for a special purpose: they were reduced to powder, mixed with boiled rice, and then eaten by twelve Brahmins. This "revolting and unnatural act", explains Dubois, had for its object the expiation of the sins of the deceased, it being generally believed that the sins were transmitted to the bodies of the persons who had swallowed the ashes. Any repugnance that these men might have felt for "such disgusting food" was overcome by the promise of a new house apiece.

Where the suttee had been performed was erected in due course a large domed mausoleum, and thither the reigning monarch came from time to time, prostrating himself humbly and offering sacrifices to the spirits of his predecessor and his two "worthy and saintly spouses". Henceforth these latter were regarded as divinities, and crowds of devotees came to implore their succour in the various troubles of life. "In the year 1802," says the Abbé in conclusion, "I have heard various accounts of a great number of so-called miracles performed through their intercession."

The whole business filled Dubois with loathing. He was well aware of the "eccentricities and inconsistencies of the human mind", but all the same he found it impossible to understand how "these Brahmins, who are so scrupulous and attach so much importance to the life of the most insignificant insect, and whose feelings are excited to pity and indignation at the very sight of a cow being slaughtered, can, with such savage cold-bloodedness and wicked satisfaction, look upon so many weak and innocent human beings, incited by hypocritical and barbarous inducements, being led with unaffected resignation to a punishment so cruel and undeserved".

Nor did he find at all easy to understand the British attitude to the practice. Nobody could have said nicer things about the British in India than this Frenchman who, "cast away, as it were, on the shores of this foreign land at a time when my own country was a prey to all the horrors of a disastrous revolution, never failed to receive from them the warmest hospitality, even when a desperate war might have given rise to bitter prejudice against everything French". He praised their justice and humanity and "perfect tolerance", but surely they were carrying their tolerance too far in continuing to permit the "infamous practice" of suttee.

If the Abbé had lived only a few more years in India he would have had cause to write very differently. He returned to France in 1823, in which year there were 575 widows burned in Bengal Presidency, of whom 109 were above 60 years of age, 226 from forty to sixty, 208 from twenty to forty, and 32 under twenty. Then in 1828 Lord William Bentinck became Governor-General of Bengal—the man who, according to the inscription written by Lord Macaulay for his statue in Calcutta, "abolished cruel rites, gave liberty to the expression of public opinion, whose constant study was to elevate the intellectual and moral character of the nations committed to his charge". Bentinck resolved to prohibit suttee absolutely, and, in the face of strenuous opposition, both from Europeans and natives, but with the support of some official and public opinion and of such enlightened Indian reformers as Rammohun Roy, he carried a regulation in Council, on

4 December, 1829, by which all who abetted suttee were declared guilty of "culpable homicide".

Thenceforth suttee, from being a quite common occurrence, became increasingly rare, until by the middle of the century it was supposed to be practically extinct. But it lingered on where devotion to ancient custom was most profoundly experienced, and even in our own time cases are occasionally reported in the newspapers. Thus in 1954 the widow of an officer of the Maharajah of Jodhpur's household died on her husband's pyre, and was acclaimed as a holy woman; and two years later a young widow in Rajasthan, with four children, died in the flames, pillowing her dead husband's head on her lap.

Chapter 7

The Daggers of Hara-Kiri

ONE of the peculiarly distinctive things about the Japanese is their way of committing suicide. Outside Japan this is generally known as *hara-kiri*, but the Japanese themselves generally prefer to use the synonym *seppuko*, which, being derived from the Chinese, has a rather more elegant sound. The literal meaning of hara-kiri is "belly-cutting", although it has sometimes been translated as "the happy dispatch". But this is an euphemism. What the operation consists of *is* "belly-cutting", neither more nor less.

When the Japanese first adopted this decidedly messy way of putting an end to their existence is not known. The ancient Japanese performed suicide by strangulation, as we may learn from an edict issued by the Emperor Kotoku in A.D. 646. "When a man dies," so this runs, "there have been cases of people sacrificing themselves by strangulation, or of strangling others by way of sacrifice, or of compelling the dead man's horse to be sacrificed, or of burying valuables in the grave in honour of the dead, or of cutting the hair and stabbing the thighs and then pronouncing a eulogy on the dead. Let all such customs be entirely discontinued."

Even so early, then, it had become the practice for human sacrifices to be made on the death of a great lord or *daimyo,* and Kotoku's edict does not seem to have had much permanent effect. With the rise of the military power in Japan it became quite the accepted thing for a man's retainers to follow their master into the grave, in order that they might continue to give him the service that was his due. This practice was known as *junshi,* and the method adopted was suicide by the sword, or what became known as hara-kiri; it is surmised that it was introduced from China, the source of so much else in the Japanese military code of behaviour. By the sixteenth century junshi had become an honoured custom among the Samurai, the class of military men—sometimes the term has been translated "gentry"—that included the retainers of the numerous daimyos or feudal lords. The practices continued into the time of Iyeyasu, who became ruler of the country in 1603, thus establishing the long line or dynasty of Tokugawa Shoguns which governed Japan until the restoration of the Mikado in 1868 that launched Japan into the modern age.

An able general and firm ruler, Iyeyasu was resolved on breaking the power of the daimyos, and one of the blows he directed against them was the formal abolition of junshi. "Although it is undoubtedly the ancient custom for a vassal to follow his lord in death," he declared, "there is not the slightest good reason for the practice. In future it will be strictly forbidden, more especially to retainers of the first rank but extending also to those of the lowest. A man who disobeys this prohibition is the very opposite of a faithful servant, and any property he leaves behind him will be confiscated as a warning to those who take upon themselves to disobey the laws."

This decree ended the practice among Iyeyasu's own vassals, but it continued, or was revived, after his death. Cases occurred right up to the reign of Mutsu-hito, the great modernizing emperor who ruled from 1867 to 1912, and even since then occasional cases of this traditional expression of loyalty to the death have been reported.

But hara-kiri was performed not only as junshi but as a self-inflicted penalty exacted by the traditions of the Samurai discipline. The military class established it as a custom and a privilege, something that they might claim as a right when they were confronted by the choice of death or dishonour. By about the close of the fifteenth century the military custom of permitting a Samurai to perform hara-kiri instead of subjecting himself to the shame of public execution was well established. Officers who had suffered defeat in battle and were about to fall into the enemy's hands would thus put an end to themselves rather than be executed by their captors. In course of time it became the recognized thing for a Samurai to commit hara-kiri when he received the order from his liege lord. Often a Samurai would not wait for the order. If he had fallen in some mission with which he had been entrusted; if he had committed some breach of trust, however innocently; if he had made a foolish mistake, or had shown himself to be incompetent or unworthy; or even if his lord had happened to frown upon him and show his displeasure—in all these and many other similar circumstances he might pass sentence upon himself and perish by a self-inflicted disembowelling. Hara-kiri might also be a form of protest. Thus a retainer who had been unable to convince his master that he was following the wrong course or was doing something unworthy of him, might commit hara-kiri as the only way left open to him of persuading his lord to correct the error of his ways.

Japanese literature contains many instances of hara-kiri committed for such motives as these. Perhaps the most famous is that of the "Forty-seven Ronins" which for two hundred and fifty years has been enshrined in the popular memory as a classic illustration of Japanese virtues.

The story begins in the spring of 1701, when a Japanese noble named Asana, Lord of Ako, was at Yedo (Tokyo) in attendance on the Shogun, who was the real ruler of the country although nominal supremacy was invested in the emperor, or Mikado. An envoy from the Mikado was announced, and Asana was called upon to receive him with traditional honours. Now Asana was better as a warrior than as a courtier, and he therefore took counsel with another nobleman, named Kira, whose vast knowledge of ceremonies and court etiquette was equalled only by the meanness of his disposition. Kira instructed Asana in all that was expected of him, but Asana did not pay him enough for his information and assistance. Whereupon Kira jeered at Asana for a country lout unworthy of the name of Daimyo. Asana suffered in silence for a while, but Kira so far presumed as to order Asana to bend down and fasten up his footgear. Asana felt so insulted that he drew his sword and gave Kira a great slash across the face, and would no doubt have killed him if he had not sought safety in flight. The palace was soon in an uproar. In brawling within its precincts Asana had committed a crime punishable with death and the confiscation of all his property. That same evening he was condemned to perform hara-kiri, while his castle was forfeited, his family declared extinct, and the members of his clan disbanded. To use the Japanese term, his retainers or followers became *ronins*, "wave-men", that is, wanderers who were without lord or country. The sentence was carried out in April, 1701.

Asana was dead, but he might be avenged. Oishi Kuranosuke, the senior of his retainers, took counsel with forty-six of the most trusty members of the clan, and they all vowed to avenge their lord, even though it would mean death for themselves. For although the action they contemplated was prescribed by social custom, it was just as imperatively forbidden by law. After a number of consultations in secret, the forty-seven decided to separate in order to throw their enemy off the scent, as well as to obtain essential information concerning his habits and movements. Several of the ronins obtained jobs as carpenters, smiths, and merchants, by which means they managed to obtain access to Kira's mansion and learnt their way about its corridors and gardens. Oishi himself went to Kyoto, where he plunged into drunkenness and debauchery; he even put away his wife and children and took up with a common harlot. All these things were reported to Kira by his spies in due course, and he was lulled into a feeling of complete security.

Then suddenly, on the night of 30 January, 1703, the Forty-seven Ronins, during a blinding snow-storm, attacked the Kira mansion. The outer gates were forced, and they stormed into the interior. Those retainers who put up any resistance were cut down, and Kira was dragged out from an outhouse in which he was hiding among the firewood and charcoal. He was taken before Oishi, who proceeded to address him with the respect which was felt proper in a mere gentleman addressing a great noble. Kira was requested to perform hara-kiri, as befitted one of his rank; but he was too cowardly to save his honour in this way, and there was nothing for it but to kill him like the scoundrel that he was. Then they cut off his head, and bore it with them as they marched, in military order, through the streets to the temple of Sengakuji. As they went along, the people flocked to cheer them on their way, and a great daimyo whose palace they passed sent out his servants with refreshments and messages of goodwill. Arrived at the temple, they were received by the abbot, who conducted them to the place in the grounds where their master had been buried. On his grave they laid the head of his enemy (which, according to the time-honoured custom, had been carefully washed). Then Oishi read from a manuscript they had brought with them. Addressing Asana as though he were still alive, they informed him that they had come that day to pay him homage, "forty-seven men in all, from Oishi Kuranosuke down to foot-soldier Terasaka Kichiyemon", who were all ready to lay down their lives on his behalf. They had done what they did because they simply could not do otherwise. Even though he might not have approved of their action, they felt that they who had eaten his bread could not leave him unavenged. So they had slain Kira Kotsuke-no-Suke with a dirk, or dagger, which Asana had valued, and now they placed the dirk on his grave beside the head of his enemy. The manuscript also was deposited on the grave, and then the forty-seven avengers turned away and marched off to meet whatever fate might be decreed.

It was what they had expected. The official sentence was soon pronounced: they were all to commit hara-kiri. And this they did, separately, in the mansions of the great daimyos into whose care they had been entrusted on their arrest. Then they were all buried together alongside their master. And from that day to this the grave of the Forty-seven Ronins in the grounds of the Sengakuji temple in Tokyo has been a place of popular pilgrimage.

Up to 1868 no foreigner had ever witnessed hara-kiri, but in that year, shortly after the Mikado had reassumed his full powers and dignities, the representatives of the foreign legations were invited to witness the hara-kiri of a Japanese officer who had brought discredit on his country by firing upon the foreign settlements at Hiogo. One of the witnesses was A. B. Mitford (later Lord Redesdale), who was second secretary to the British Legation in Japan, and he fully described the event in his book *Tales of Old Japan* (1871).

The condemned man was Taki Zenzaburo, an officer of the Prince of Bizen, and the ceremony, ordered by the Mikado himself, was arranged for 10:30 in the evening in the temple of Seifukuji, headquarters of the Satsuma troops at Hiogo. Seven witnesses from the foreign legations were present. They were conducted to the temple by officers of the Princes of Satsuma and Choshiu, and although the ceremony was to be conducted in the most private manner news of it had evidently leaked out, judging from the remarks they heard as they passed through the crowd assembled at the gate. The courtyard was crowded with soldiers standing in knots around large fires, which threw a flickering light over the heavy eaves and quaint gable-ends of the sacred buildings. The seven foreigners were ushered into a waiting-room, and after what seemed a long time the Governor of Hiogo came in and took down their names and informed them of the seven witnesses who were to attend on behalf of the Mikado. An opportunity was given to them to put questions to the condemned man, but this they declined.

After some further delay, they were invited to follow the Japanese witnesses into the *hondo* or main hall of the temple, where the ceremony was to be performed. "It was an imposing scene," wrote Mitford. "A large hall with a high roof supported by dark pillars of wood. From the ceiling hung a profusion of those huge gilt lamps and ornaments peculiar to Buddhist temples. In front of the high altar, where the floor, covered with beautiful white mats, is raised some three or four inches from the ground, was laid a rug of scarlet felt. Tall candles placed at regular intervals gave out a dim mysterious light, just sufficient to let all the proceedings be seen. The seven Japanese took their places on the left of the raised floor, the seven foreigners on the right. No other person was present.

"After an interval of a few minutes of anxious suspense, Taki Zenzaburo, a stalwart man, thirty-two years of age, with a noble air walked into the hall, attired in his dress of ceremony, with the peculiar hempen-cloth wings which are worn on great occasions. He was accompanied by a *kaishaku* and three officers, who wore the *jimbaori* or war surcoat with gold-tissue facings. (The word *kaishaku* is one to which our word 'executioner' is no equivalent term. The office is that of a gentleman; in many cases, it is performed by a kinsman or friend of the condemned, and the relation between them is rather that of principal and second than that of victim and executioner. In this instance the *kaishaku* was a pupil of Taki Zenzaburo, and was selected by the friends of the latter from among their own number, for his skill in swordsmanship.) With the *kaishaku* on his left hand, Taki Zenzaburo advanced slowly towards the Japanese witnesses, and the two bowed before them; then drawing near to the foreigners, they saluted us in the same way, perhaps even with more deference; in each case the salutation was ceremoniously returned.

"Slowly, and with great dignity, the condemned man mounted on to the raised floor, prostrated himself before the high altar twice, and seated himself—in Japanese fashion, his knees and toes touching the ground, and his body resting on his heels—a position in which he remained until his death, on the felt carpet with his back to the high altar, the *kaishaku* crouching on his left-hand side. One of the three attendant officers then came forward, bearing a stand of the kind used in temples for offerings, on which, wrapped in paper, lay the *wakizashi*, the short sword or dirk of the Japanese, 9½ inches in length, with a point and an edge as sharp as a razor's. This he handed, prostrating himself, to the condemned man, who received it reverently, raising it to his head with both hands, and placed it in front of himself.

"After another profound obeisance, Taki Zenzaburo, in a voice which betrayed just so much emotion and hesitation as might be expected from a man who is making a painful confession, but with no sign of either in his face or manner, spoke as follows: 'I, and I alone, unwarrantably gave the order to fire on the foreigners at Kobe, and again as they tried to escape. For this crime I disembowel myself, and I beg you who are present to do me the honour of witnessing the act.' Bowing once more, the speaker allowed his upper garments to slip down to his girdle, and remained naked to the waist. Carefully, according to custom, he turned his sleeves under his knees to prevent himself from falling backwards; for a noble Japanese gentleman should die falling forwards.

"Deliberately, with a steady hand, he took the dirk that lay before him; he looked at it wistfully, almost affectionately; for a moment he seemed to collect his thoughts for the last time; and then stabbing himself deeply below the waist on the left-hand side, he drew the dirk slowly across to the right side, and, turning it in the wound, gave a slight cut upwards. During this sickeningly painful operation he never moved a muscle of his face. When he drew out the dirk, he leaned forward and stretched out his neck; an expression of pain for the first time crossed his face, but he uttered no sound. At that moment the *kaishaku*, who, still crouching by his side, had been keenly watching his every movement, sprang to his feet, poised his sword for a second in the air; there was a flash, a heavy, ugly thud, a crashing fall; with one blow the head had been severed from the body.

"A dead silence followed, broken only by the hideous noise of the blood throbbing out of the inert heap before us, which but a moment before had been a brave and chivalrous man. It was horrible.

"The *kaishaku* made a low bow, wiped his sword with a piece of paper which he had ready for the purpose, and retired from the raised floor; and the stained dirk was solemnly borne away, a bloody proof of the execution. The two representatives of the Mikado then left their places, and, crossing over to where the foreign witnesses sat, called us to witness that the sentence of death passed on Taki Zenzaburo had been faithfully carried out."

Concluding his account, Mitford paid tribute to the extreme dignity and punctiliousness with which the terrible ceremony had been carried out. It was impossible not to be filled with admiration of the firm and manly bearing of the sufferer, and of the nerve with which the *kaishaku* performed his last duty to his master. "Nothing could more strongly show the force of education. The Samurai, or gentleman of the military class, from his earliest years learns to look upon the hara-kiri as a ceremony in which some day he may be called upon to play a part as principal or second. In old-fashioned families, which hold to the traditions of ancient chivalry, the child is instructed in the rite and familiarized with the idea as an honourable expiation of crime or blotting out of disgrace. If the hour comes, he is ready for it, and bravely faces an ordeal which early training has robbed of half its terrors. In what other country of the world does a man learn that the last tribute of affection which he may have to pay to his best friend may be to act as his executioner?"

Japanese women might (and sometimes did) commit suicide, but (since disembowelling was thought to be altogether too unfeminine) not by hara-kiri but by *jigai*—that is to say, by piercing the throat with a dagger so as to sever the arteries by a single thrust-and-cut movement. In time of war Japanese ladies might commit jigai to preserve their honour. Many cases are known of Japanese wives who have committed suicide out of loyalty to their deceased husbands. Samurai maidens who have been crossed in love have done likewise, as is told in many a tale that has come down from the days of feudal chivalry. The women members of a daimyo's household have also shown themselves not to be behindhand in demonstrating in this fashion their loyalty to their master, who would surely need their services in the world of the dead just as he had received them in life. And equally with men, Japanese women have committed suicide as a moral protest, when their lord and master (for that is what a Japanese husband has always been) has done some shameful thing, turning a deaf ear to the protests of his wife and his relations and friends. We read of a case that occurred in 1892, when a local magnate who had promised to support one candidate at an election gave his vote to his rival: the voter's wife was so disgusted at his behaviour that she performed jigai after the old Samurai manner. For long afterwards the brave woman's grave was decorated with flowers, and incense was burned in reverence.

Japanese war-widows have sometimes committed hara-kiri. A well-remembered instance was in 1895, the woman being the wife of one Lieutenant Asada, who had fallen in battle against the Chinese. On being told of her husband's death, the twenty-one-year-old girl at once, and having obtained her father's consent, resolved to follow him. First she thoroughly cleaned their house in Tokyo, and put all her affairs in good order. Then she arrayed herself in her best clothes, laid mattings on the floor opposite the alcove in the guest-room, placed her husband's picture in the alcove, and set offerings before it. When everything had been arranged in accordance with the ancient ritual, she seated herself on the floor before the portrait, took up a dagger which had been a wedding-present from her husband, and cut her throat with a single skilful thrust.

Although what may be described as mandatory hara-kiri was prohibited by law in 1868, the unofficial practice of this form of committing suicide continued in isolated instances. On the occasion of the funeral of the Emperor Mutsuhito in 1912, his most distinguished general, Count Nogi, together with his wife, committed hara-kiri in the solemn fashion of the Samurai to which the Count belonged. Numerous instances of hara-kiri were reported in the course of the Second World War, and the spirit that inspired it was evinced by the Japanese suicide-pilots who dive-bombed the warships of the British and American fleets.

Chapter 8

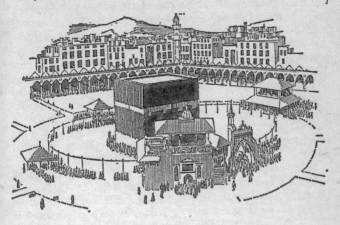

With the Pilgrims to Mecca

IN all the world there is no more famous place of pilgrimage than Mecca; indeed, so famous is this ancient Arabian city that, to quote the dictionary, "any outstanding place reverenced or resorted to" is referred to as a Mecca.

Mecca attracts its immense crowds of pilgrims primarily because it was the birthplace (in A.D. 570) of the Prophet Mohammed. It is the holiest city of the world—religion of Mohammedanism, or Islam, as it is more properly styled; and at the times of daily prayer every Moslem, wherever he may be and whatever he may be doing, turns himself in the direction of Mecca. In every Moslem mosque there is a semicircular recess or niche in the wall, facing the entrance, which indicates to the worshipper the right way to turn when making his devotions. Moslem dead are buried with their feet towards the holy city, so that they may be ready to spring up facing the Prophet, when as the trump of doom sounds he will lead the faithful to the Judgment-seat of God—or Allah, to use the Moslem word.

To visit Mecca as a pilgrim at least once in a lifetime is a sacred obligation imposed on every Moslem, although in practice the great majority of the pilgrims have always been men, owing to the reluctance of women in Arabia and other eastern lands to being seen in public. It is expressly commanded in the Koran, the holy book of Islam, and Mohammed is reported to have declared that a man who dies without having made the pilgrimage to Mecca might just as well die a Jew or a Christian. There is, however, the saving clause, that the would-be pilgrim is "able", e.g., he must be possessed of sufficient means to cover the expenses of the *hadj* and to maintain those dependent upon him at home while he is away. But for this proviso, the pilgrims would number millions annually, but even as it is the figure may reach 200,000 in a year.

If it were not for its religious importance—it has been well styled the Metropolis of Islam—Mecca is hardly the sort of place that would attract the tourist. It lies in a narrow, barren valley, 45 miles to the east of Jedda, its seaport on the Red Sea, with which it is now connected by a tarmac road. It is ringed with gaunt hills, and beyond stretch the empty wastes of the desert. There are no industries worth speaking of, and from time immemorial the townsfolk have depended on the tourist traffic, providing the pilgrim hosts with food and accommodation, acting as guides to the holy places, and furnishing them with whatever else they may require. Travellers have described them as lively, polished, and frivolous, and very definitely "on the make". Of late years, the town has been considerably improved, as the royalties from the American companies operating the Arabian oil-wells have flowed into the national exchequer; but most of the streets are dirty and unpaved, and sanitation still leaves a good deal to be desired. Pilgrims are found lodgings in the houses, built of stone and of several storeys for the most part, that climb the hills on either side, and there are charitable institutions in which the poorest pilgrims may find accommodation. Public baths and hospitals are among the modern amenities. Then of course there are innumerable shops and bazaars, in which the tourist may purchase provisions and souvenirs of his stay.

Nothing is known of the early history of the town, but it was a place of religious pilgrimage long before Mohammed's time, for within its walls stood a temple which all the pagan tribes of the Arabian peninsula held to be most holy. This structure was called the Kaaba, from the Arabic word for "cube", and it was in fact a cube-shaped, unpretentious, squat, and rather ugly building, in which were housed some hundreds of idols of the Arabian gods and goddesses. Embedded in a corner of its outer wall was a stone which, so the townsfolk believed, had fallen from heaven; originally this had been white, but in the course of ages it had been blackened by the kisses bestowed upon it by the lips of sinful men. And close by was a well called Zem-Zem, perhaps from the noise that the water made as it bubbled up out of the ground.

These were the things that the ancient Meccans revered, the things the pagan tribesfolk flocked to the city to see. And they are still there. There is reason to believe that the Prophet would have abolished the pilgrimage to Mecca if he could, since it was so closely associated with the pagan cults. But circumstances were too strong for him, and he had to content himself with the abolition of its idolatrous accompaniments. The idols were tipped off their pedestals and smashed, but the "Holy House" of the Kaaba was preserved and made into the holiest shrine of the new faith. A fresh history was invented for it. It was revealed that Adam, after his expulsion from Paradise, had begged of God that he might erect a building like one that he had seen there, whereupon a representation of the house in question was lowered from Heaven and set up at Mecca. After Adam's death, his son Seth built a house in the same form of stones and clay; this was destroyed by the Deluge, but was rebuilt by Abraham and his son Ishmael, at God's command, after the original model. If any were inclined to doubt this story, he might be shown a stone, enclosed in an iron chest, which was the one that Abraham had stood upon when he built the Kaaba. . . .

Then the well Zem-Zem—this was now identified as the very spring which gushed out of the sand when Ishmael (who is held to have been the progenitor of the Arab peoples) was dying of thirst as he wandered in the desert with Hagar his mother.

These are some of the stories that were now told to explain the Kaaba and its surroundings—stories which reflect the conversations that the Prophet had had as a young man with Jews whom he had met in the course of his caravan trips into Syria. The Meccans had small hesitation in accepting them as true, since they provided a new justification for the pilgrimage to their city. Whereas before, in the times of paganism, the pilgrims came to worship the idols in the Kaaba, now they flocked thither to worship this new god of Mohammed's preaching, this Allah. What did it matter, so long as the pilgrims still came? Their profits were as great as before, even better. . . .

Although there is a constant stream of pilgrims to Mecca throughout the year, tradition decrees that the best month, the one most pleasing to Allah and therefore of greatest religious benefit, is the twelfth month of the Moslem year. Since the Moslem calendar is based on the phases of the moon and not like ours on the movements of the sun, this most favourable month may fall at all seasons of the year. Most of the pilgrims come from hot climates; but even so, when the month falls in the summer, conditions are almost unbearable, when the heat is staggering, the ground scorches one's feet, and one seems to be moving, or trying to move, through a fiery furnace.

No allowance is made, however, for the changes of temperature. The pilgrim's dress is always the same, and comes as nearly as possible to what is believed to have been the Prophet's own wish, that those who go to Mecca should wear no clothing at all. As it is, male pilgrims when they enter the sacred territory that surrounds the city lay aside all their clothes and don a special garment called the *ihram*. This consists of two pieces of cotton cloth about the size of bath-towels, one of which is fastened round the waist and the other draped over the shoulders. The head must be completely shaved, and is left bare, thus adding to the risk of heat-stroke; the beard is left on, however. The nails must be carefully pared. The feet are shod with a peculiar kind of sandal or slipper, which "covers neither the heel nor the instep". Female pilgrims wear a less-revealing costume, comprising five garments, viz., trousers or drawers, over-dress, green frock, black robe, and veil which hides the face completely save for two slits for the eyes.

While wearing this habit, says George Sale—whose "preliminary discourse" attached to his translation of the Koran, made in 1734, is still most valuable—the pilgrims "must neither hunt nor fowl (though they are allowed to fish), which precept is so punctually observed, that they will not kill even a louse or a flea, if they find them on their bodies; there are some noxious animals, however, which they have permission to kill during the pilgrimage, as kites, ravens, scorpions, mice and dogs given to bite. During the pilgrimage it behoves a man to have a constant guard over his words and actions, and to avoid all quarrelling or ill language, and all converse with women and obscene discourse, and to apply his whole intention to the good work he is engaged in."

Until not so long ago the pilgrim hosts converged on Mecca on foot or in camel caravans, taking weeks and months and even years to complete the journey. It was considered a remarkable instance of modern enterprise when in 1886 the Government of India appointed the already world-famous firm of Thomas Cook and Son "pilgrim agents" for the whole of India. Today travel agents offer cheap trips to Mecca, and the pilgrimage is very big business indeed. Most of the pilgrims land at Jedda and make the journey down the road by bus or car or truck, but increasing numbers arrive by air at Jedda airport which has connections with all the continents. However he gets there, the pilgrim cannot but feel the sudden revelation of the holy city as the most dramatic moment in his life.

Mecca is situated near the eastern end of the sacred area already referred to, the Haram as it is styled, which forms a rough diamond about 25 miles long by about 12 miles across. The boundaries of the Haram are marked by pillars, beyond which no non-Moslem is permitted to penetrate. In the past a handful of Europeans have ventured to make the pilgrimage in disguise, while knowing full well that detection must bring with it a speedy end to their adventure and life itself. Within the Haram no killing of any living creature is allowed, except domestic animals required for food and criminals condemned to death by the courts. The wearing of the pilgrim dress is, of course, obligatory.

The ceremonies which are prescribed for the Faithful in Mecca during the month of pilgrimage are many and elaborate. The first thing to be done is to visit the Kaaba, the "ancient house" which was once a heathen temple but was adapted by Mohammed thirteen hundred years ago, to the worship of Allah, the One True God. This stands in the courtyard of the Great Mosque, and although it has been several times rebuilt (most recently in 1627) it retains the form of the temple that Mohammed knew. It is about 40 feet long, 33 feet wide, and 50 feet high, built of stone, with a flat roof.

There are no windows, and there is only one door. Usually it is covered with a black veil or carpet—the *kisweh*—that is adorned with a broad band embroidered with texts from the Koran in the flowing Arabic script.

In the Kaaba the chief object of veneration is something that was almost certainly a fetish of the ancient Arab paganism, something that is the last survivor of the idols that stood all round the sanctuary up to the time of Mohammed. This is the Black Stone, which is fixed in the building's south-east corner, about five feet above the ground. It has been often described, but never better than by the daring Swiss traveller John Lewis Burckhardt, who in 1814 made the pilgrimage to Mecca. (Burckhardt, it may be mentioned, was one of the very first Christians to do so; he spent years in preparation, disguised himself under the name of Sheikh Ibrahim Ibn Abdallah, and so mastered the language and ideas of his fellow pilgrims that after a critical examination the most learned Moslems entertained no doubt of his being what he professed to be, a learned doctor of the Islamic law.) The Black Stone, he wrote in his account of his travels (published some years after he had died a victim to dysentery at Cairo in 1817 and had been buried there as a holy pilgrim in the Moslem burial-ground), "is an irregular oval, about seven inches in diameter, with an undulated surface, composed of about a dozen smaller stones of different sizes and shapes, well joined together with a small quantity of cement, and perfectly smoothed: it looks as if the whole had been broken into many pieces by a violent blow, and then united again. It is very difficult to determine accurately the quality of this stone, which has been worn to its present surface by the millions of touches and kisses it has received. It appeared to me like a lava, containing several small extraneous particles, of a whitish and of a yellowish substance. Its colour is now a deep reddish brown, approximating to black: it is surrounded on all sides by a border, composed of a substance which I took to be a close cement of pitch and gravel, of a similar, but not quite the same brownish colour. This border serves to support its detached pieces; it is two or three inches in breadth, and rises a little above the surface of the stone. Both the border and the stone itself are encircled by a silver band, and the lower part of the border is studded with silver nails."

Modern geologists have expressed the opinion that the Black Stone is very likely a meteorite, and in this case the Moslems are not so very far wrong when they assert that it "fell from heaven".

The Kaaba is opened to the public on a few days in the year, when there is a scramble for admission and a great clamour for baksheesh from its custodians and from the beggars who crowd round the door. There is but one room, the roof of which is supported on two pillars. The upper part of the walls are hung with hangings of red silk, in which are interwoven flowers and inscriptions from the Koran. Walls and floor are of white marble, and from the ceiling hang numerous lamps—sometimes said to be of solid gold—which have been presented by worshippers in days gone by. In one corner is a stairway giving access to the roof, and in another is a chest containing the stone which, according to tradition, was pressed by Abraham's feet.

On a day when Burckhardt found the door being opened, he joined in the crush. He reports that sobbing and moaning filled the room, and he thought that much of it was genuine. "I could not stay longer than five minutes; the heat was so great that I almost fainted, and several persons were carried out with great difficulty, quite senseless." As he came down the steps into the courtyard, he was hailed by a "sherif" who held out to him the silver key of the Kaaba for him to kiss, in return for a fee of course; and gratuities had also to be given to a eunuch who sat by the sherif, and to other eunuchs and a collection of minor officers and servants of the shrine who were lying in wait.

Arrived at the Kaaba, the pilgrim is required to compass it seven times, beginning at the corner where the Black Stone is placed. But here we cannot do better than to revert to the classic account of another great traveller, the Englishman Sir Richard Burton, who made the pilgrimage to Mecca almost exactly forty years after Burckhardt. Hardly in disguise, however, for Burton had transformed himself into a Moslem, and had no difficulty in finding acceptance as such. Here, to begin with, is Burton's description of the Kaaba as he saw it for the first time.

"There at last it lay, the bourn of my long and weary pilgrimage, realizing the plans and hopes of many and many a year. The mirage medium of Fancy invested the huge catafalque and its gloomy pall with peculiar charms. There were no giant fragments of hoar antiquity as in Egypt, no remains of graceful and harmonious beauty as in Greece and Italy, no barbaric gorgeousness as in the buildings of India; yet the view was strange, unique, and how few have looked upon the celebrated shrine! I may truly say that, of all the worshippers who clung weeping to the curtain, or who pressed their beating hearts to the stone, none felt for the moment a deeper emotion than did the Haji [pilgrim] from the far north. It was as if the poetical legends of the Arab spoke truth, and that the waving wings of angels, and not the sweet breeze of morning, were agitating and swelling the black covering of the shrine. . . ."

Few Moslems (he goes on) contemplate for the first time the Kaaba without fear and awe. He had with him a young Arab boy, Mohammed by name, who knew the customary procedure. After leaving him to his devotions for a few minutes, the boy approached Burton and told him that it was time to begin. They entered the courtyard of the Mosque through the "Gate of the Sons of the Old Woman", so named because, according to the popular legend, when Abraham and his son Ishmael had been ordered by God to build the Kaaba they found the site already occupied by an old woman, who only consented to remove her dwelling on the condition that the key of the new temple should be entrusted to her descendants for ever and ever. There, after uttering certain prescribed prayers and supplications, they moved across the pavement to the well Zem-Zem, where they performed the usual two prostrations in honour of the mosque. "This was followed by a cup of holy water, and a present to the Sakkas, or carrier, who for the consideration distributed a large earthen vaseful in my name to poor pilgrims. The produce of Zem-Zem is held in high esteem. It is apt to cause dysentery and boils, and I never saw a stranger drink it without a wry face. The flavour is salt-bitter, much resembling an infusion of a teaspoonful of Epsom salts in a large tumbler of tepid water. Moreover, it is exceedingly 'heavy' to the taste."

Next the pair advanced to the corner in which is the Black Stone, "and standing about ten yards from it, we repeated with upraised hands, 'There is no god but Allah alone, whose covenant is truth, and whose servant is victorious. There is no god but Allah, without sharer, his is the kingdom; to him be praise, and he over all things is potent.' After which we approached as close as we could to the stone. A crowd of pilgrims preventing our touching it at that time, we raised our hands to our ears in the first position of prayer, and then lowering them, exclaimed, 'O Allah, (I do this), in thy belief, and in verification of thy book, and in pursuance of thy Prophet's example—may Allah bless him and preserve! O Allah, I extend my hand to thee, and great is my desire to thee! O accept thou my supplication, and diminish my obstacles, and pity my humiliation, and graciously grant me thy pardon.' After which, as we were still unable to reach the stone, we raised our hands to our ears, the palms facing the stone, as if touching it, recited the Takbir, the Tahlil, and the Hamdilah [prayers], blessed the Prophet, and kissed the finger-tips of the right hand."

Then commenced the ceremony of the *Tawaf* or circumambulation of the Kaaba over the low oval of polished granite that surrounds it. "I repeated after my Mutawwif (guide), or cicerone, 'In the name of Allah, and Allah is omnipotent! I purpose to circuit seven circuits unto almighty Allah, glorified and exalted!'" So they passed round the building, saying at each corner the prescribed prayers and invocations; and at one, the Yemen or southern corner, finding the crowd less dense, "we touched the wall with the right hand, after the example of the Prophet, and kissed the finger-tips." Two more circuits had then to be made at the same pace, what Burton describes as being "very similar to the French *pas gymnastique*, that is to say, 'moving the shoulders as if walking in sand'." After this they had to make four circuits at a much slower and more leisurely pace.

This concluded the Tawaf, and now Burton decided to make a further effort to kiss the stone. "For a time I stood looking in despair at the swarming crowd of Bedouin and other pilgrims that besieged it. But the boy Mohammed was equal to the occasion. After vainly addressing the pilgrims, of whom nothing could be seen but a mosaic of occiputs and shoulder-blades, the boy collected about half a dozen stalwart Meccans, with whose assistance, by sheer strength, we wedged our way into the thin and light-legged crowd. The Bedouins turned round upon us like wild cats, but they had no daggers. The season being autumn, they had not swelled themselves

with milk for six months; and they had become such living
mummies that I could have managed single-handed half a
dozen of them. After thus reaching the stone, despite popular
indignation, testified by impatient shouts, we monopolized the
use of it for at least ten minutes. Whilst kissing it and rubbing hands and foreheads upon it I narrowly observed it, and
came away with the impression that it is a big aerolite."

Gratified by their success, Burton and the boy pushed their
way thorugh the crowd and, after several more prostrations at
various points, arrived again at the door of the building in
which was the well Zem-Zem. Here Burton was "condemned
to another nauseous draught, and was deluged with two or
three skinfuls of water dashed over my head *en douche*", an
ablution which, he remarks with considerable satisfaction,
"causes sins to fall from the spirit like dust". Then they returned to the Black Stone corner, and recited some more
prayers, but they were unable to get near enough to touch it
again. By this time Burton confesses that he was thoroughly
worn out, with scorched feet and a burning head—under-
standable enough when, as he reminds us, these had to be
kept bare throughout the ritual.

That same evening, however, accompanied by the boy
Mohammed, and by a man carrying a lantern and a prayer-
rug, he again repaired to the "Navel of the World", as the
Moslems sometimes call it. The scene was now very different.
The moon, approaching the full, tipped the brow of the
surrounding hills, and lit up the spectacle with a solemn light.
"In the midst stood the huge bier-like erection,

> 'Black as the wings
> 'Which some spirit of ill o'er a sepulchre flings'—

except where the moonbeams streaked it like jets of silver
falling upon the darkest marble. It formed a point of rest for
the eye; the little pagoda-like buildings and domes around it,
with all their gilding and fretwork, vanished. One object,
unique in appearance, stood in view—the temple of the one
Allah, the God of Abraham, of Ishmael, and of his posterity.
Sublime it was, and expressing by all the eloquence of fancy
the grandeur of the One Idea which vitalized El Islam, and
the sternness and steadfastness of its votaries. The oval pave-

ment round the Kaaba was crowded with men, women, and children, mostly divided into parties, which followed a mutawwif; some walking staidly, and others running, whilst many stood in groups to pray.

"What a scene of contrast! Here stalked a Bedouin woman, in her long black robe like a nun's serge, and poppy-coloured face-veil, pierced to show two fiercely flashing orbs. There an Indian woman, with her semi-Tartar features, nakedly hideous, and her thin parenthetical legs, encased in wrinkled tights, hurried round the fane. Every now and then a corpse, borne upon its wooden shell, circuited the shrine by means of four bearers, whom other Moslems, as is the custom, occasionally relieved. A few fair-skinned Turks lounged about, looking cold and repulsive, as their wont is. In one place a fast Calcutta 'khitmuger' stood with turban awry and arms akimbo, contemplating the view jauntily, as those gentlemen's gentlemen will do. In another, some poor wretch, with arms thrown on high, so that every part of his person might touch the Kaaba, was clinging to the curtain and sobbing as though his heart would break. Late in the evening I saw a negro in the state of religious phrenzy. He was a fine and powerful man, as the numbers required to hold him testified. He threw his arms wildly about him, uttering shrill cries, which sounded like le! le! le! le!, and when held, he swayed his body, and waved his head from side to side, like a chained and furious elephant, straining out the deepest groans.

"That night I stayed in the Haram till 2 a.m. Numerous parties of pilgrims sat upon their rugs, with lanterns in front of them, conversing, praying, and contemplating the Kaaba. The cloisters were full of merchants, who resorted there to 'talk shop', and vend such holy goods as combs, tooth-sticks, and rosaries. Presently, my two companions, exhausted with fatigue, fell asleep; I went up to the Kaaba, with the intention of 'obtaining' a bit of the torn, old kiswat or curtain, but too many eyes were looking on. The opportunity was favourable, however, for a survey, and with a piece of tape, and the simple processes of stepping and spanning, I managed to measure out the objects concerning which I was curious. At last sleep began to weigh heavily upon my eyelids. I woke my companions, and in the dizziness of slumber they walked with me through the tall, narrow street to our home in the Shamiyah. The town appeared safe; there were no watchmen, and yet people slept everywhere upon cots placed opposite their open doors. . . ."

The ceremony of the Tawaf should be repeated every day during the first seven days of the pilgrimage. The next ceremony is partly to run and partly to walk seven times between two hills or mounts—they are called that, although they are in fact low platforms arched over—that bear the names of Safa and Marwah. In pagan times the Arabs used to worship idols at these spots, where now the pilgrims utter prayers to Allah and recite verses from the Koran. The rest of the day is spent in visiting other holy places in the vicinity, feeding the pigeons that congregate on the mosque roofs, drinking the waters at Zem-Zem, and in public worship.

If it is Friday, the Moslem sabbath, the Great Mosque's central area will be filled with perhaps thirty thousand worshippers, all wearing the simple and ghostly-looking pilgrim garb and going through the ritual with the most devout precision. In other mosques, wherever they may be, the worshippers are arranged in straight lines with their faces turned towards Mecca, but here they are formed in circles round the Kaaba and the white marble pulpit that stands a few yards away. Up the steps of the pulpit moves the imam or leader—he should not be called "priest" since there are no priests in Islam—and from his place beneath the gilded spire of the little edifice he leads the vast congregation in their devotions. As he bends and sways, lowers himself to the ground and then stands erect with arms upraised, all the company do as he does, all perfectly attuned in the time-honoured ritual of praise and prayer. The moment the service is over, there is a rush to perform once more the circumambulation of the Holy House.

The eighth, ninth, and tenth days of the pilgrimage should be devoted to visiting Mt. Arafat, a small hill lying just outside the sacred precincts. This is the most important item in the programme. Neglect of other parts of the ceremonial may be compensated for by offerings, but to miss the "stand on Arafat" is to deprive oneself of all the virtues accruing from the pilgrimage, and only one who has performed it is entitled to receive the honourable title of *Hadj*. The arrangements are believed to follow closely the movements of Mohammed when he performed his "farewell pilgrimage" in A.D. 632, not long before his death. The pilgrim leaves Mecca between sunrise and ten a.m. with a vast host of others, bare-headed, bare-footed, some mounted on camels, some in motor transport, but the greater number plodding along on foot. As the column plunges on there is a roar of hurrying feet and the dust spreads for miles around. That night should be spent in devotion, but the coffee-booths do a lively trade and songs and tales are perhaps as common as prayers in the groups huddled round the camp fires.

Next forenoon the pilgrim may move about the hill, and at midday answers the summons to hear a sermon, which may last for several hours. Perhaps he will be moved to tears by the discourse, join vehemently in the accompanying prayers; perhaps, on the other hand, his attention will be distracted as Burton's was. . . .

"I had prepared a *cachette,* a slip of paper, and had hid in my ihram a pencil destined to put down the heads of this rarely heard discourse," he writes. But "close to us sat a party of fair Meccans, apparently belonging to the higher classes, and one of these I had already several times remarked. She was a tall girl, about eighteen years old, with regular features, a skin somewhat citrine-coloured, but soft and clear, symmetrical eyebrows, the most beautiful eyes, and a figure all grace. There was no head thrown back, no straightened neck, no flat shoulders, nor toes turned out—in fact, no elegant barbarisms, but the shape was what the Arabs love, —soft, bending, and relaxed, as a woman's figure ought to be. Unhappily she wore, instead of the usual veil, a 'yashmak' of transparent muslin, bound round the face; and the chaperone, mother, or duenna, by whose side she stood, was apparently a very unsuspicious or compliant old person. Flirtilla fixed a glance of admiration upon my cashmere [the shawl he was wearing about his shoulders]. I directed a reply with interest at her eyes. She then, by the usual coquettish gesture, threw back an inch or two of head-veil, disclosing broad bands of jetty hair, covering a lovely oval. My palpable admiration of the new charms was rewarded by the partial removal of the yashmak, when a dimpled mouth and a rounded chin stood out from the envious muslin. Seeing that my companions were safely employed, I ventured upon the dangerous ground of raising hand to forehead. She smiled almost imperceptibly, and turned away. The pilgrim was in ecstasy. . . ."

But now the sermon came to an end, and the assemblage

broke up and engaged in what is very rightly called the "hurry from Arafat", a mad stampede down the hill in the direction of the half-way station at Muna. "Every man urged his beast with might and main; it was sunset, the plain bristled with tent-pegs, litters were crushed, pedestrians trampled, and camels overthrown; single combats with sticks or other weapons took place; here a woman, there a child, and there an animal were lost; in brief, it was a state of chaotic confusion." Burton mounted his camel and tried to push his way through the mob in pursuit of the pretty Meccan, who was being borne away in her litter. But alas, "the charming face that smiled at me from the litter grew dimmer and dimmer—I lost sight of the beauty. . . ."

Before sunrise the next morning a second "stand" is prescribed on Arafat, but before the sun is fully up the pilgrims should be gathered at Muna, where they are required to throw stones at "the Devils". These are represented by three pillars which are said to mark the position of idols that were destroyed by the Prophet; and the ceremony is, therefore, a way of showing Moslem contempt for the heathen gods. But according to another legend, the procedure is in imitation of Abraham who was at his devotions in this place when he was disturbed by the devil, and threw stones at him to drive him away.

After the "throwing" the pilgrim should sacrifice a goat or a sheep to Allah, and then he returns as speedily as possible to Mecca, where he for the last time runs round the Kaaba and kisses the Black Stone. This completes the pilgrimage, and he is now at liberty to attend to his toilette and resume his ordinary dress. The Hadj, so far as he is concerned, is at an end, and as a full-qualified *haji* he may take the road for home.

Chapter 9

Bushman Artists

BETWEEN ten and fifteen thousand years ago the first true men are supposed to have moved from the grasslands of the Sahara into Europe by way of the land bridges that then existed at Gibraltar and Sicily. The last Ice Age was drawing to its close; and as the ice slowly receded towards the pole, so these ancestors of ours followed up its retreat, gaining a bountiful livelihood from the herds and hordes of wild beasts that they hunted with spear and arrow and caught in carefully prepared traps.

Yes, they were skilful hunters, these men in the springtime of human history. But they were something more. They were artists; and still in the caves that were their homes we may see painted on the walls the figures of the beasts they pursued up above in the light of day. We cannot be sure what was their motive, if there was anything beyond the sheer joy of artistic creation; but it has been very plausibly surmised that their art was a species of sympathetic magic.

These hunter-artists not only drew and painted, but they displayed their craft in carving little figures out of soapstone, including in particular figures of women of extraordinary anatomical development—women who are grossly fat, with breasts as big as pumpkins and immense haunches and buttocks, and their hair arranged in tufted spirals. An outstanding example of this kind of female representation—or may it be styled, portraiture?—is the so-called Venus of Willendorf, a small statuette of an exceedingly fat woman that was found in the Austrian village of that name. In most or all of these figures the sexual characters are emphasized almost to the point of exaggeration, and it has been suggested that they were fertility charms.

For a long period—how long is a matter of guesswork, but it must have extended over many centuries—the hunter-artists of what is called the Aurignacian culture (after a grotto near Aurignac, in the south of France, where evidences of their culture were first discovered) continued to practise their art Then their genius seems to have deserted them. Steadily their technique declined, until we find men producing nothing better than painted pebbles. The great age of Palaeolithic, or Old Stone Age, art was over.

However much we puzzle our heads with the "why and wherefore" we shall never be much the wiser. But there is another question that may be put, which is of greater practical interest. We may put it in the words of Professor W. J. Sollas: "What has become of this gifted Aurignacian race? Has it wholly vanished out of ken, either by extinction, or by transformation into some conquering race, like say the Egyptians, or does it possibly still survive, retaining, more or less, its primitive characters?"

This is the question that Professor Sollas put in his book *Ancient Hunters;* and the rest of the book's title, *And Their Modern Representatives,* suggests the answer at which he arrived. In attempting to answer this question (he wrote) we may begin by confining our attention to the mural paintings and endeavour to discover whether there is any race existing at present which practises the same art. Yes, there is such a race, a people still in the same stage of culture as the Aurignacians, a people who live in caves and decorate the walls with paintings, both in monochrome and polychrome, which recall in the closest manner some of the most successful, as well as some of the least successful, efforts of the Aurignacian artists. This race is the Bushmen of southern Africa.

Perhaps it is only to be expected that the "modern representatives" should be a people that among the races of mankind is accorded a very low place indeed, perhaps the lowest of all, way down below even the Australian aborigines. The Bushmen are nomadic hunters, whose social organization is based on family groups. In days gone by they were wont to roam over much of Africa south of the Zambezi, but they have been steadily compressed into the most remote and ill-favoured regions, the Kalahari desert in particular. They hunt game with the bow and poisoned arrows, throwing-sticks and sometimes spears, and when game is scarce they live on locusts, frogs, snakes, lizards, and ants' eggs. Their dress is mainly skins, and they live in caves or holes in the ground roofed over with matting.

But there are things about them that are strikingly reminiscent of the Aurignacians of so long ago. First, there is their appearance. They are thin and wiry and short in stature, but their backs are hollowed, the stomach protuberant, and the lower spine curved in such a way as to give a most prominent appearance to the posterior. Furthermore, there is a fatty accumulation about the buttocks which makes the Bushman—and still more, the Bushwoman—the most steatopygous of the human kind. In most of these things they would seem to resemble very closely the hunter-artists of the Old Stone Age.

Even more significant is what they evince of something that may be fairly described as an artistic instinct. Among them both sexes love to adorn themselves after their fashion. The men paint their bodies (dirty and grease-encrusted as they generally are) with red, yellow, or black stripes in various patterns, and wear necklaces made from fragments of ostrich-shells which show up well against the warm brown skin. The women, for their part, go in for quite an elaborate toilette, sprinkling their heads and necks with a green powder obtained from copper ore, and dusting their hair with flakes of mica after dressing it with a pomade of red ochre. Clearly they have a sense of colour and of design, and this is even more in evidence in their habitations, for any flat surface that happens to be available is pretty sure to be covered with some form of ornamental drawing, or at least it may be painted in broad stripes with red ochre.

These drawings were among the first things about the Bushmen to catch the attention of European travellers who ventured into their territory in the early part of the last century. One of the most sympathetic and understanding was John Barrow (later Sir John), who in 1803 published an account (*Travels in the Interior of Southern Africa*) of the extensive excursions he had made, on horseback and on foot and very occasionally in a covered waggon, that occupied many months and extended over a thousand miles in the then hardly known and mostly unexplored regions of southern Africa.

First impressions were not too favourable. "Whether they are considered as to their persons, their turn of mind, or way of life, the Bosjesmans"—as Barrow calls them, explaining the term as meaning "men of the bushes, from the concealed manner in which they make their approaches to kill and to plunder"—"are certainly a most extraordinary race of people." After studying them closely, and having taken their measurements, he concluded that "the Bosjesmans are amongst the ugliest of all human beings". He remarks on the "apeish character" of their visage, which "their keen eye, always in motion, tends not to diminish", and their uncommonly protuberant bellies and hollow backs.

In one of his chapters Barrow describes "A Journey into the Country of the Bosjesmans", this being in the neighbourhood of the township of Graaf-Reinet, on the edge of the Karroo desert. He visited a "horde or kraal" that consisted of five-and-twenty huts, or holes in the ground rather, which had been hollowed out like the nest of an ostrich. It was customary, he was told, for each man to have two wives, one of them old and past child-bearing and the other young. The men he met were entirely naked, and most of the women were very nearly so. "Their only covering was a belt of springbok's skin, with the part which was intended to hang before cut into long threads, but the filaments were so small and thin that they answered no sort of use as covering; nor indeed did the females, either old or young, seem to feel any sense of shame in appearing before us wholly naked. Whether, in the confusion and the hurry, they had scrambled among the rocks before they had time to adjust their only dress, or whether they were indifferent about concealing any particular part of their bodies, I do not pretend to say, but their aprons appeared to have been put on very carelessly. The fringed part of some of them was hanging behind; of others, on the exterior side of the thigh; and some had fallen down as low as the knee. Yet they were not entirely without notions of finery. A few had caps made of the skins of asses, and bits of copper, or shells, or beads, were hanging in the neck, suspended from their little curling tufts of hair. All the men had the cartilage of the nose bored, through which they wore a piece of wood or a porcupine's quill."

There is much more in Barrow's account that is of deep interest, as when he tells us that, while the "Bosjesmans" are generally confined to their hovels in the daytime, for fear of being surprised and taken by the Boer settlers who were their deadly enemies, "they sometimes dance on moonlight nights from the setting to the rising of the sun. They are said to be particularly joyful at the approach of the first thunderstorm after the winter, which they consider so infallible a token of the summer having commenced, that they tear to pieces their skin-coverings, throw them in the air, and dance for several successive nights". But there is one more piece of information that is very much to our present purpose.

In one of the caverns which served the little people as homes, Barrow noticed on the smooth rock faces drawings of animals that "these savages" had made from time to time. Some were nothing more than caricatures, but others were so well executed that there was no difficulty in recognizing the animals represented. One of a zebra was remarkably good; and among the rest were elands, springboks, qua-chas (quaggas, the wild ass), baboons, and ostriches. One had only to go outside the cave and see these creatures roaming the veldt. The force and spirit shown in the drawings was truly remarkable, as also the attempts to indicate the effects of light and shade. Well might Barrow say that this was not the sort of thing one would expect from savages, whose materials were only charcoal, pipe-clay, and the different ochres.

Since Barrow's day many more caves and rock faces have been discovered in various parts of southern Africa, bearing drawings and paintings in which are depicted, often with remarkable accuracy and true-to-life effect, the scenes in which Bushmen have played a part, and the animals with which they were familiar and upon which they depended for their existence. Some of the scenes would seem to be historical events, although in the absence of written records we shall never be sure; others represent beyond a doubt martial forays,

yet others what may be supposed to be religious or magical
ceremonies in which the dance is prominent. But most are of
hunting scenes, and very possibly these had a magical significance, such as the somewhat similar scenes in the prehistoric
art-galleries are supposed to possess. Probably the most famous of these is the one in a cave in the Herschel district of
Cape Province, in which a Bushman is shown disguised in
the skin of an ostrich and stalking these birds from inside
the flock.

Nothing is known, of course, of the individual artists, but
it is presumed that they were men who showed a gift for
artistic expression and were encouraged by the tribe to concentrate on their craft. They were men who knew where to
find their natural pigments, and having found them, how to
grind them to powder with heavy stones and mix them with
fat or marrow-oil, and then how to apply them with brushes
made of feathers or specially prepared animal tendons. When
completed, the paintings must have been regarded with superstitious reverence or dread, and yet instances have been found
of one painting having been made over another: sometimes
four or five such superimposed pictures have been found, as
in a rock-shelter on the banks of the Imvani, in the Queens-
town district of the Cape.

Perhaps we should be grateful for this, since the practice
has provided us with a key to their age. An old Bushman told
G. W. Stow (as he reports in his book, *The Native Races of
South Africa*) that the pictures of an artist were always
respected as long as any recollection of him was preserved in
his tribe; during this period, no one, however daring, would
attempt to deface his paintings by placing others over them.
But when his memory was forgotten, some aspirant after
artistic fame might appropriate the limited rock-face of
the shelter for his own performances, and unceremoniously
painted over the efforts of those who preceded him. If we
calculate that the memory of any artist would be preserved
among his people for at least three generations, this would
give a probable antiquity of five hundred years to the oldest
pictures in the Imvani rock-shelter. But elsewhere there are
many which, there is reason to believe, are much older than
this.

Paintings are not the only instances of Bushman art. There
are also numerous engravings, in which the outlines of the

design have been incised on the rock face, and then the design has been filled in by "pecking" the surface all over within the outline. The difficulties involved in this process, when the only tools available were pointed stones, will need no emphasis. On the whole, the engravings have not the quality and value of the paintings, but they have one advantage, in that they are much more durable. It is hardly too much to say that they will last indefinitely, while the paintings are exposed to the ravages of the weather, obliteration through cattle rubbing themselves against them, the smoke of fire lit by herdsmen, and the vandalism of visitors. Nor is this all. Some fine examples have been ruined by attempts made to remove them to places of presumed greater safety or where they might be more conveniently studied.

While some of the drawings and paintings have been irretrievably lost, a large number have been recognized for what they are, an altogether exceptional expression of the artistic impulse among the most primitive of mankind, and steps have been taken to preserve them. Furthermore, first-rate copies have been made of many of them, and these are available for study and comparison in the great museums of the world.

Such comparison has led to a realization of some close resemblances between Bushman art and that of the prehistoric Aurignacian cave artists. Of course, there are differences, as Professor Sollas himself pointed out; thus we may note that in the Bushman paintings the various figures are not thrown on to the wall in a disorderly crowd as in the prehistoric paintings, but are grouped into a picture, which tells a tale of its own. At the same time, the differences are outweighed by the similarities. The technique is very much the same. There is the same striving after realistic truth, the same quality of movement in the animal forms represented. All in all, it may be claimed that "of all existing hunting tribes the Bushmen make the closest approach in their art to the Aurignacian age".

Of course it does not follow that "we can argue from identity of cult to identity of race", but if we attentively examine the Bushmen as they are represented in their paintings we shall perceive a peculiarity in their outline, namely, that excessive development which is known as steatopygia.

Direct observation of existing Bushmen shows them to be just as "fat-buttocked" as their ancestors depicted on the cave walls. Barrow certainly noticed it. "The great curvature of the spine inwards and the remarkably extended posterior, are characteristics of the whole Hottentot race, but in some of the small Bosjesmans they are carried to such an extravagant degree as to excite laughter. If the letter S be considered as one expression of the line of beauty to which degrees of approximation are admissible, some of the women of this nation are entitled to the first rank in point of form. A section of the body, from the breast to the knee, forms really the shape of the above letter." So interested was Barrow in the phenomenon, he invited some of the Bosjesman ladies to submit themselves for measurement. "The projection of the posterior part, in one subject, measured five inches and a half from the line touching the spine. This protuberance consisted entirely of fat, and, when the woman walked, it exhibited the most ridiculous appearance imaginable, every step being accompanied with a quivering and tremulous motion, as if two masses of jelly had been attached behind her."

There was something more about the female form among the "Bosjesmans" that drew Barrow's attention, "an extraordinary character that distinguished them from the women of most nations". He had often heard it said that Hottentot women possessed "an unusual appendage in those parts that are seldom exposed to view"; and now he discovered that, "ridiculous as it may appear, it is perfectly true with regard to the Bosjesmans. The horde we met with possessed it in every subject, whether young or old; and, without the least offence to modesty, there was no difficulty in satisfying our curiosity in this point". Now while this peculiar anatomical feature is sometimes found to a slight degree among European women, it is most unusual to find women who are "longinymph" and also steatopygous; in fact, the association of these two characteristics is almost confined to women of the Hottentot and Bushman tribes. The greater the development of these features, the nearer is the approach to their ideal of beauty. But (and this is indeed a strange thing) they would seem to have been present together in the females of the Aurignacian race.

This would not be apparent if all we had to go upon was the paintings with which the ancient artists decorated the walls of their caves, since, as Sollas expresses it, "for some inscrutable reason the Aurignacian usually refrained from depicting the human form". But "he had no scruple about sculpturing it in the round", and "he seems to have taken a special pleasure in carving figurines, which almost invariably represent woman in the nude", for example, those in the cave of Brassempouy and in caves in France and Belgium, and of course the "Venus of Willendorf" referred to earlier. Some of these show women possessing just those characters which have been remarked upon as being peculiar to the Bushmen. Professor Sollas would seem to be on sure ground, then, in asserting that the artists who carved the figurines in the Aurignacian caves have shown in the clearest manner that they were intimately acquainted with women who presented a close anatomical resemblance to the existing Bushwomen, and the presumption is that these were women of their own race. This presumption is supported by such evidence as is available from the remains of the Aurignacians themselves.

Are we then entitled to argue that the Bushmen of today are the physical descendants of the Aurignacians of ten or fifteen thousand years ago? On the available evidence, that would be going too far; certainly it cannot be demonstrated. But at least there remains a supposition, a possibility, of the most suggestive value.

Many questions about the Bushmen may be asked, and most of them must remain unanswered. We know nothing of Bushman history, even of the last hundred years or so. They are such out-of-the-way folk, so insignificant in the family of races and nations, so backward in all that makes for culture. And yet, we have their art. In their paintings and engravings we have abundant evidence that they, or their ancestors, were endowed with a measure of artistic sensibility and power of execution that is unique among the primitive races of mankind.

This is the strangest thing about them, and it is all the more to be regretted that their fate has been such a hard one. A terrible war of extermination was waged against them by the Boers in the last century. Incidents in the struggle have been reported that are shocking to our humanity, and it is impossible to refuse a tribute of admiration to the brave little people who in almost every instance preferred death to surrender. Among the few exceptions was a chief who kept up the fight until he had no more arrows left; he then at length accepted the offer of quarter that had been made to him and gave himself up. And what happened to him? He had his brains blown out.

The last to be killed in this terrible war was one of the painters. When his body was picked up, there was found a leather belt upon it, from which were strung twelve little horns, each containing a different pigment.

Professor Sollas is unstinted in his praise. "The more we know of these wonderful little people," he writes, "the more we learn to admire and like them." They had many solid virtues—untiring energy, boundless patience, fertile invention, steadfast courage, devoted loyalty and family affection—and to these they added a native refinement of manners and a rare aesthetic sense. "In their golden age, before the coming of civilized man, they enjoyed their life to the full, glad with the gladness of primeval creatures. The story of their later days, their extermination, and the cruel manner of it, is a tale of horror on which we do not care to dwell. They haunt no more the sunlit veldt, their hunting is over, their nation is destroyed; but they leave behind an imperishable memory, they have immortalized themselves in their art."

Chapter 10

Killing the Sacred Bear

REMOTELY placed in the most northern parts of the Japanese islands live the Ainus. There are only a few thousand of them, but in days gone by they were much more numerous and widely spread. They seem to have come from the north, not long before the Japanese started to arrive from the southwest, and were gradually pressed back towards the east and north. It was only in the eighteenth century that they were completely subjugated. Most of them live on the northern island of Hokkaido, but there are a few hundred in the southern half of Sakhalin and the Kurile islands, which since the Japanese defeat in 1945 have been included in the Russian dominion.

Racially, they are an enigma. They are quite distinct from the Japanese: they constitute a white-skinned drop in a vast yellow ocean. The word Ainu means in their language "man". They are reputed to be the hairiest race in the world, their luxuriantly thick black beards (which they never cut or trim) and the abundance of hair on their bodies giving them an appearance which is in marked contrast with the smoothness of the Japanese. As though not to appear too different, Ainu women have tattooed moustaches on their upper lip, besides geometrical patterns tattooed on their hands.

Both men and women are strongly built, toughened by the hard conditions of their life. They are hunters of deer and bears, fishers who have trained their dogs to aid them in catching salmon, foragers for roots and berries, nuts and fungi. Their dwellings are huts made of reeds and thatch, without furniture of any kind, mats spread on the earth floor serving as seats and beds. In the middle of the one room is the hearth, which is revered as the abode of the Fire Goddess; the smoke escapes through a hole in the roof. There is only one window, and that faces east and is considered to be sacred. Lighting is from an oyster-shell lamp burning fish-oil, or from a torch of birch bark. At night the inmates huddle together to keep warm beneath a heavy load of animal skins, and there is not much regard for the decencies. Both sexes wear garments of cloth woven from birch bark fibre, and these are generally embroidered with colourful patterns.

In days gone by the Ainus had a reputation for a fiercely martial spirit, and their women joined with the men in resisting the advance of the Japanese invaders. Today, however, they display a mild and amiable disposition, and the visitor is assured of a friendly welcome. But they are often filthily dirty, the practice of bathing being altogether unknown, and they wash their hands and faces only on ceremonial occasions. They are also strongly addicted to getting drunk on saké or rice beer. Before putting their lips to the cup the men make use of a "moustache-lifter", a wooden contrivance about nine inches long by an inch wide which is often shaped to represent some animal and has a ritual significance. Women are as great boozers as the men, at least when they get the chance. But (so the Rev. John Batchelor reported, in his account of the Ainus published towards the end of the last century) they "get what their husbands choose to give them, which is some-times very little indeed".

No one has described the Ainus with more intimate understanding than Isabella Bird (later Mrs. Bishop). Here is a passage from that intrepid Englishwoman's *Unbeaten Tracks in Japan*, published in 1878 after she had spent some months wandering about the country, on foot or on horseback, and alone save for a Japanese youth as an attendant. She describes the scene as she sits in an Ainu hut after dark.

"The birch-bark chips beam with fitful glare, the evening saké [rice beer] bowls are filled, the fire-god and the garlanded god receive their libations, the ancient woman splits bark, and the younger women knot it, and the log-fire lights up as magnificent a set of venerable heads as painter or sculptor would desire to see—heads, full of—what? They have no history, their traditions are scarcely worth the name, they claim descent from a dog, their houses and persons swarm with vermin, they are sunk in the grossest ignorance, they have no letters or any numbers above a thousand, they are clothed in the bark of trees and the untanned skins of beasts, they worship the bear, the sun, moon, fire, water, and I know not what, they are uncivilizable and altogether irreclaimable savages, yet they are attractive, and in some ways fascinating, and I hope I shall never forget the music of their low, sweet voices, the soft light of their mild, brown eyes, and the wonderful sweetness of their smile. . . ."

From time immemorial the Ainus have taken delight in bear-hunting, and they are justly commended for the daring and resource with which they track down the bears in their mountain haunts and follow them deep into their caves and dens. It is a dangerous sport indeed, in which a man armed only with a knife strives to overcome a powerful mountain bear in a fight to the death. Fully-grown bears are killed for food, but a young cub may be taken alive to play its part in a ritual which is the most original and distinctive feature of Ainu religious ceremonial.

Usually a bear cub is caught in the late winter. It is brought into the village and found a place in one of the huts where it is tended with the greatest care and consideration. The story has often been told that an Ainu woman has been known to take the little cub and give it her breast as though it were a child. Mr. Batchelor, who spent so many years among the Ainus as a missionary, at first strenuously denied this; but in the later editions of his book he told how he had at length actually seen it being done. The cub may be fed by hand or by mouth, usually on a dish of millet and fish boiled into a soft pap. It will play with the children, and becomes quite one of the family. This goes on for two or three years, by which time it has become big enough to hurt with its huggings and scratchings, and it is then placed in a stout cage with wooden bars.

But at length the time arrives when it becomes the victim of a cruel and barbarous rite. This is ordinarily in September or October, and the occasion is known as the "Feast of sending away", by which is meant that the cub is about to be despatched as an envoy to that world where the spirits of departed bears are supposed to live.

A man who decides on giving a bear-feast sends invitations to his friends and neighbours in the village, and also to many who live in distant villages. The invitation may run somewhat as follows: "I am about to sacrifice the dear little divine thing who resides among the mountains. My friends and masters, come to the feast; we will then join in the great pleasure of sending the god away. Come!" Allured by the prospect of getting drunk for nothing the invitees need no second bidding, and on the appointed day they crowd into the hut, where they sit round the fire, the men in front and the women behind, partaking of millet cakes and rice beer, especially beer.

When all the guests have arrived, a number of *inao* are prepared: these are sticks of willow that are whittled near the top to form a sort of bush. After a prayer to the goddess of the hearth to convey these to the other divinities, the *inao* are taken outside and fixed to posts stuck in the ground beyond the sacred window in what is called a *nusa*. At their base are laid two stout poles.

When these preparations have been completed, one of the Ainu men goes to the bear and, sitting down before its cage, informs it that it is about to be sent to its forefathers. He craves pardon for what they are about to do, expresses the hope that it won't be angry, and tries to comfort it with the consolation that ever so many *inao* and plenty of cakes and drink will be sent along with it on its long journey. One of these speeches that he had heard is given by Batchelor in his account. "O thou divine one," it runs, "thou wast sent into the world for us to hunt. O thou precious little divinity, we worship thee; pray hear our prayer. We have nourished thee and brought thee up with a deal of pains and trouble, all because we love thee so. Now, as thou hast grown big, we are about to send thee to thy father and mother. When thou comest to them, please speak well of us, and tell them how kind we have been; please come to us again, and we will sacrifice thee."

Next another Ainu goes to the bear's cage, and catches the victim's head in a rope with a noose in it. The noose is made to pass round the neck and under a foreleg, so as not to choke the animal when it struggles. Another noose is then made in a second rope, and this is passed over the bear's head in the same way, excepting that the end of this rope comes out on the opposite side; thus, when the bear leaves the cage, it is led along by two men, one on each side.

Now (to quote Mr. Batchelor's account) "the ancients of the people form a ring and sit down, while the younger people stand, and try to work the bear up into a passion. The two men lead the poor animal round and round the ring, whilst the people shoot at it with blunt arrows. The shouting of the people is quite deafening, and the rage of the bear furious. When the animal shows signs of exhaustion, a stake is driven into the ground in the centre of the ring, and it is tied to it. Now blunt arrows are shot at it with double vigour, and the poor animal tears and rages till thoroughly tired out.

"Then comes the test of valour and bravery. All at once some brave young Ainu will rush forward and seize the poor brute by the ears and fur of the face, whilst another suddenly rushes out and seizes it by the hindquarters. These two men both pull at the animal with all their might. This causes the animal to open its mouth. Then another man rushes forward with a round piece of wood about two feet long; this he thrusts into the beast's mouth. The poor beast, in its rage, bites hard at this, and holds it tight between its teeth.

"Next, two men come forward, one on each side of the bear, and seize its forelegs and pull them out as far as they can. Then two others will, in like manner, catch hold of the two hind-legs. When all this has been done quite satisfactorily, the two long poles which were laid by the *nusa* are brought forward. One is placed under the bear's throat, and the other upon the nape of its neck. Now all the people rush forward, each eager to help squeeze the poor animal till it dies. And so the poor beast is choked to death. It is indeed a brutal scene. . . ."

As soon as the animal is dead, it is skinned and cut up, and sometimes the men will drink its warm blood and besmear their bodies and clothing with it in the most ghastly fashion. The head is cut off and set in the east window of the house. A piece of its own flesh is placed under its snout, together with a cup containing some of its meat that has been boiled, with some millet dumplings and dried fish. A moustache-lifter may also be laid within easy reach. Then prayers are uttered to the dead animal, inviting it to return to earth after it has visited its parents in the afterworld, when it may once again be granted the honour of being sacrificed. When the bear is supposed to have finished dining off its own flesh, the master of ceremonies takes the cup containing the boiled meat, salutes it, and proceeds to divide the meat between all present, young and old, men, women, and little children. Everyone must have a taste, all must share in what is a kind of sacramental meal. Then the rest of the flesh is cooked and similarly divided and partaken of by all the participants in the grim ceremony. After this, the bear's head is set up on a long pole behind the *inao* behind the hut, where it remains until nothing is left but the bare white skull. Batchelor was assured by his Ainu informants that they believed the spirits of the slain animals to reside in the skulls preserved in this way, and this was why they were wont to address them as "divine preservers" and "precious divinities".

Similar accounts of "killing the sacred bear" have been given by travellers who have visited the other principal centres of Ainu life. So impressed have some of these been, that they have called the bear the chief divinity of the Ainus, and have regarded the ritual as a piece of "idolatrous veneration", a form of "worship after their fashion". Certainly there are some features of the procedure which can be so described, as, for instance, the prayers that are offered to the victim both when alive and dead; the offerings of food, including portions of its own flesh; and the solemn participation of the whole company in a meal that has some resemblance to a sacrament. The Ainus also refer to the bear that is killed as one of their *kamui,* or gods.

But it can hardly be maintained that the victim of the bear-festival is in the same category as the principal divinities of Ainu worship, in particular the Fire Goddess, or Goddess of the Hearth, who is known by a term which means "Grandmother" or "Old Woman", and her mate, the "Ancestral Governor of the House", both of whom are held in high veneration and are addressed most devoutly on all important occasions. Those observers are nearer the mark who stress the part played by the "sacred bear" as a messenger from the Ainu to their spiritual overlords. This aspect of the celebration is well brought out in what we are told of the practice among the Ainu tribes of Sakhalin.

About the middle of the night before the bear is to be killed, or very early the same morning, an Ainu man with a glib tongue takes up his stand before the cage in which the bear is confined and makes a long speech, in which he reminds the bear how well they have taken care of him while he has been with them, what good meals they have provided him with, how they have taken him down to the river for a bathe, and have made him warm and comfortable. And now, he goes on, the time has come when they will be holding a great festival in his honour. "Don't be frightened. We are not going to hurt you. All we are going to do is to kill you and send you to the god of the forest who loves you. We are about to give you a good dinner, the best dinner you have ever eaten among us, and we will all weep for you together. Then the Ainu who is the best shot among us is going to kill you. Look, there he is, over there; he is weeping, and he asks your forgiveness in advance. You will understand that we cannot feed you always. We have done enough for you; now it is your turn to sacrifice yourself for us. You will ask the gods to send us, for the winter, plenty of otters and sables, and for the summer, seals and fish in abundance. Don't forget our messages. We really love you very much, and our children will never forget you."

Then when the bear has been trotted round the village and tied up to a tree, the orator again addresses him at such a length that he finishes only at daybreak. "Remember," he cries, "remember! Think of all we have done for you. It is now up to you to do something in return. Do your duty. Don't forget to tell the gods to give us riches, that our hunters may return from the forest laden with rare furs and animals good to eat, that our fishers may find lots of seals on the beach and in the sea, and that their nets may come near to breaking under the weight of the fish. You are our only hope. We have given you food and joy and health. The evil spirits laugh at us, and threaten us with famine and other horrible things. But now we are about to kill you in order that you in return may send riches to us and to our children." To this discourse the bear will listen without conviction, as he plods along, with many a lamentable howl, at the end of his rope. Then just as the first beams of the sun appear above the horizon, the marksman sends an arrow through the poor beast's heart. Whereupon the people sob in mourning, then hurry to skin the victim and banquet off its flesh. They will be feeling quite pleased with themselves, for they have the happy confidence that the messenger whom they have just sent on his way to the gods will not forget what he has been told, but will render a good report, with the result that all the good things they have asked for will erelong be forthcoming.

This is the festival of Killing the Sacred Bear among the Ainus—or we should say, this *was* the festival . . . since the efforts of the missionaries and of the Japanese government officials have made it a thing of the past. It is now a memory, and the people who practised it for so long—they, too, are in the way of becoming a memory, as they are caught and submerged in the relentless stream of civilization.

Chapter 11

The Tragedy of the Meriah

TUCKED away in a remote corner of Bengal lived a race of primitive barbarians known as the Khonds, or Kandhs. They were aborigines, descendants of people who were already living in India before the first Aryans trekked in their ox-carts from beyond the Himalayas; and for many hundreds of years they maintained behind their ramparts of rock and forest and marsh the ways and manners of their forefathers.

Government among their tribes was patriarchal. Marriage was by capture. Murder was punished by the blood-feud. Personal disputes were settled by duels, or by such ordeals as thrusting a bare hand and arm into a pan of boiling oil or taking up a bar of red-hot iron. Population was kept within bounds of infanticide, unwanted girl babies being turned out into the jungle to die from exposure or wild beasts.

Husbandry and war were the only pursuits considered worthy of a Khond. All the hard and dirty work of the community was performed by an order of serfs, whom the Khonds believed were descended from folk who were living in the land when their own ancestors came and dispossessed them. One thing more should be said about these primitives: they were a highly religious people, and in the end it was their religion which brought them to the notice of the outside world and led to the break up of their time-honoured pattern of living.

Many were the divinities they worshipped, but there were two in particular. One was Boora Pennu, the "god of light", who was looked upon as the supreme being, the creator of all that was; and the other was his female consort, whose name was Tari Pennu, and she was the parent of all evil. But she was also the Earth-goddess, on whom depended the reproductive capacity of plants and animals and of men and women. As such she had to be fed, and the Khonds were in no doubt that there was nothing she liked so much as blood—human blood.

Among the Khonds, then, human sacrifice was a regular institution. There was nothing secret about it, nothing of which they felt the slightest reason to be ashamed. It was performed in public by tribes and villages, both at social festivals held at regular intervals and also when special reasons demanded something out of the ordinary.

For a long time the bloody rites were known to the surrounding peoples only by rumour, since the Khonds believed very firmly in keeping themselves to themselves. But in 1835 their territory came under British control, and although it was the policy of the East India Company, through whom that control was exercised, not to interfere more than was absolutely necessary with the religious practices of the native people, a line had to be drawn somewhere, and human sacrifice was very definitely outside it. The first thing to be done was to discover the facts, and in 1837 a young officer in the Company's Madras Army, Lieutenant S. C. Macpherson, was sent on a mission of inquiry and survey into the unexplored parts of Gumsur, one of the principal Khond districts in Orissa. Macpherson did his job well, and on his return submitted a report in which the Khond human sacrifices were described in the fullest detail.

The sacrifices (he reported) were of several kinds. The most important were those celebrated at the time of sowing or planting the principal crop, since it was held to be essential that every villager should be enabled to procure a shred of human flesh with which to fertilize his fields, otherwise they

would not bear. But there were also special celebrations, as
when there had been an extraordinary number of deaths from
sickness or tigers, or when a number of women had died in
childbed, or when the crops showed signs of failure. Any particularly untoward happening in the family of the local rajah
might also be taken as an indication that the Earth-goddess
was athirst and must be appeased in the only way that she
approved. For Tari was very particular in her tastes. . . .

Persons selected for the sacrifice were known as *Meriahs*.
They might be of either sex, and of almost any age and race;
but to be acceptable to Tari they must have been acquired by
purchase, or have been destined to the sacrifice from birth,
i.e., they were the children of meriahs or had been devoted by
their parents or guardians in infancy. As a rule, they were
made available through the efforts of a race of men known as
Panwas, a small number of whom were to be found in most
villages. The Panwas acted as middle-men. They made business trips into the plains and bought unwanted children from
the poorer classes of Hindus, but if the supply ran short they
had no hesitation in resorting to kidnapping. When they were
completely out of stock, they had been known to repair the
deficiency from their own children.

"An intelligent witness informed me," wrote Macpherson,
"that he once chanced to see a Panwa load another with
execrations and finally spit in his face because he had sold for
a victim his own child, whom the former wished to have
married. A party of Khonds who saw the proceeding immediately pressed forward to console the seller of the child,
saying, 'Your child has died that all the world may live, and
the Earth-goddess herself will wipe the spittle from your
face'."

When a child had been bought, or otherwise procured, he
was handed over to the village headman, who lodged him in
his own house. He might be fettered if there seemed any like-
lihood of his trying to get away, but usually he was left free
to roam about as he willed. In any event he was treated with
kindness and deep respect as a consecrated being. He would
be made welcome in every household, and when he had
arrived at puberty he might be eagerly sought out by Khond
wives and daughters and enticed into sexual relations, after
which they would express their profound thanks to the goddess for having been allowed such distinction. A wife was

generally given to a meriah when he had reached maturity, the bride being herself among the destined victims, and the couple were granted a piece of land and a supply of farm stock in order that they might fend for themselves. Any children born of such a union were so many additions to the sacrificial "stock". So they might go on, living happily for years, and they might well come to think that the reprieve would continue indefinitely. But there they were mistaken. However long and often the sacrifice was postponed, the day would come at last when the meriah, and perhaps his wife and family as well, would be immolated.

Ten or twelve days before the day appointed for a sacrifice, the victim was "devoted" by cutting off his hair, which till then had been left unshorn. The villagers also made themselves ready, washing their clothes and joining in prayers for the successful completion of the rite. As the day drew near, crowds assembled, for since the sacrifice was "for all mankind" none might be excluded.

The celebration was spread over three days. On the first of these days, and the following night, the crowd engaged in drunken feasting and frantic dancing, under the excitement which (so they believed) the goddess had inspired and which it would be impious to resist. Then on the second morning the victim, who had been kept fasting since the previous evening, was carefully washed, dressed in new garments, and then led forth to join the merry-making throng. A procession was formed, and the meriah, surrounded by a crowd of singing and dancing villagers, was taken to a grove in the forest which had always been kept sacred from the axe. Here in the course of the day a post was set up, and the meriah was seated at its foot and tied to it. In this position he was anointed with oil, ghee (clarified buffalo butter) and turmeric (a reddish paste made from the plant of that name), and garlanded with flowers.

Throughout this day the meriah was treated with a reverence not far short of adoration, and the worshippers strove to procure the smallest personal relic—a particle of the turmeric paste with which he had been smeared, perhaps, or a drop of his spittle, this latter being most highly esteemed by the women, who considered it to be charged with sovereign virtue. From time to time the crowd danced round the post with its bound figure, and as they danced they cried out, "O god, we offer this sacrifice to you; do you give us good crops, seasons, and health." Then, turning to the victim, they explained, "We bought you with a price, and did not seize you; now we are going to sacrifice you according to our custom, and no sin rests with us."

All through that night the orgy of drunkenness and debauchery continued. Then in the morning the victim, still tied to the post, was refreshed with a little milk and palm sago. For hours more the jubilations went on, but at noon they abruptly terminated. The hour of sacrifice was at hand, and with stunning shouts and pealing music the crowd heralded its consummation.

Once more the meriah was anointed with oil, and as many of the people as could get near enough touched the anointed parts and strove to transfer some of the oil to their own heads. Then the victim's bonds were undone, for he must not suffer bound, and he might be given a stupefying draught of opium. Sometimes the bones of his arms were broken, and perhaps those of his legs as well. This was done to make it impossible for him to attempt to escape, since there had been instances of meriahs managing to get away at the last moment. Macpherson mentions one such case, of a young man who, after he had been untied, induced the officiating priest—the *Janni,* as he was called—to lend him his axe and bow so that he might join in the dance as a free man for the last time. The priest agreed, and just as the dance was ending the meriah clove in his skull with the axe and dashed away down the gorge and across a foaming torrent. The infuriated crowd hotly pursued him, but he took refuge with a local chieftain, who refused to surrender him.

Now followed a kind of dramatic dialogue, in which the part of the victim, and also sometimes the parts of the priest and the village chief, were sustained by the best impersonators that might be found. The victim was made to entreat that another might be substituted for him—some useless child perhaps, some skulking coward; but he was told that the goddess would not be at all pleased if this were done. It was pointed out to him that if he wanted to blame anybody, it was his parents who had sold him for the sacrifice. "But did I share the price," he was made to say; "did the love and respect you have all showed me up to now lead me to expect any such end?" In reply he was told to think of the glorious future that awaited him after death, and the immense boon that his sacrifice would confer on mankind. Then the entreaties turned to imprecations, and after warning the Janni of how he would punish him when he should have become a god, the victim was made to abandon the struggle and bid them "now do your will on me".

At some place in the dialogue the priest called upon the Earth-goddess by name, and recited an invocation of which Macpherson gives a lengthy version. "O Tari Pennu! When we omitted to gratify you with your desired food, you forgot kindness to us. We possess but little and uncertain wealth. Increase it, and we shall often be able to repeat this rite. We do not excuse our fault. Forgive it, and prevent it in future by giving us increased wealth. We here present to you your food. Let our houses be so filled with the noise of children that our voices cannot be heard by those within. Let our cattle be so numerous that neither fish, frog, nor worm may live in the drinking-ponds beneath their trampling feet. Let our cattle so crowd our pastures that no vacant spot shall be visible to those who look on them from afar. Let our folds be so filled with the soil of our sheep that we may dig in them as deep as a man's height without meeting a stone. Let our swine so abound that our home fields shall need no ploughers but their rooting snouts. Let our poultry be so numerous as to hide the thatch of our houses. Let the stones at our fountains be worn hollow by the multitude of our brass vessels. Let our children have it but for a tradition, that in the days of their forefathers there were tigers and snakes. Let us have but one care, the yearly enlargement of our houses to store our increasing wealth. Then we shall multiply your rites. We know that this is your desire. Give us increase of wealth, and we will give you increase of worship."

When the dialogue had come to a conclusion at last, the meriah was dragged to the place chosen the night before as the one most acceptable to the goddess for the sacrifice. The priest, assisted by one or two of the village elders, took a branch that had been split down the middle in readiness; and into the cleft, several feet deep, they thrust the meriah's body, so that his chest or his throat was firmly gripped. Cords were then twisted round the open end of the branch and pulled tight. Then the priest gave a slight wound to the victim with his axe. This was the signal the crowd had been waiting for.

They flung themselves on the unhappy meriah, and tore the flesh from his bones with their fingers, or sliced it off with their knives. The head and intestines were left untouched.

As soon as a man had been able to snatch a piece of the bleeding flesh he dashed away with it through the forest to his own village, where the people had been fasting and staying indoors until it should arrive. When he had got well away from the scene of the sacrifice, he reverently wrapped the gobbet (which he may have been carrying in his mouth) in a covering of leaves, and on drawing near to his village he laid it on a cushion of grass. On arrival he deposited the parcel in the place of general assembly, and soon all the people ran to the place. Unwrapping the piece of flesh from its coverings, the priest carefully divided it into two portions, one for the Earth-goddess and the other for the worshippers. This done, he addressed the goddess. "O Tari Pennu, our village has offered such and such a person as a sacrifice, and the flesh has been divided among the people in honour of the gods, and here is a piece for you. Be not displeased with the amount; we could only give them as much. If you will give us wealth, we will repeat the rite." Having thus spoken, he then scraped a hole in the ground with his fingers and, with his back turned and not looking, deposited the piece of flesh in it, after which each man came up and helped to cover it with a little earth. The priest then sprinkled water on it from a gourd.

The piece reserved for the worshippers was divided into as many shreds as there were men involved. Each man as he received his piece rolled it in a covering of leaves and proceeded to bury it in his favourite field, just as the priest had shown him how to. When all the pieces had been buried, the villagers met together again and for three days feasted and rejoiced.

Meanwhile, what had been happening in the sacred grove? On the night after the sacrifice the remains of the meriah— his head and bones and intestines—were watched over by a strong guard of villagers. The next morning the priest and his assistants burned them on a funeral pile, together with a sheep slaughtered as a final sacrifice. The ashes were carefully collected and either scattered over the fields or pasted on the houses and granaries. Two things more remained to be done. First, the father of the meriah was presented with a bullock in full and final settlement of any claims he might have on the village. Secondly, a bullock was killed for a feast in which everybody joined, and this was made the occasion for yet another address to the goddess. "O Tari Pennu," said the priest, "you have afflicted us greatly, you have brought death to our children and to our bullocks, and failure to our corn. But we do not complain of this. It is your desire only to compel us to perform your due rites, and then to raise up and enrich us. We were anciently enriched by this rite; do you now enrich us. . . . We are ignorant of what is good to ask for. You know what is good for us. Give it to us!"

Such was the Meriah Sacrifice of the Khonds. Macpherson's report was not completed when in 1839 he fell sick with fever and was sent to the Cape to recuperate. Other reports had been coming in, however, and the authorities in Madras were already fully resolved on the suppression of the horrid rite. Some had urged strong measures: let sepoys be sent into the Khond country, prepared to use their bayonets if the besotted villagers would refuse to come to heel. Others had counselled caution, however, and they had prevailed. It had been decided to send some picked officers of the Company's service into the area to see what they could do by persuasion, and among these was Captain John Campbell (later Major-General Sir John Campbell, C.B.). Campbell spent altogether thirteen years among "the wild tribes of Khondistan, for the suppression of human sacrifices," to quote from the title of the book in which he described his experiences, and he was completely successful.

What he called his "first crusade" opened in December, 1837, when he summoned all the chiefs of the Khond villages to meet him at the little hill fort of Bodiagherry. On the appointed day they nearly all put in an appearance, bringing with them a number of their followers, so that Campbell had an audience of three thousand when he addressed them. He took his place in the shade of a tree, and the Khonds squatted on the ground in a semicircle or stood at the back, smoking vigorously. What he had to say was conveyed to them through interpreters. He told them how painfully the British Government had been affected by the discovery of the horrible sacrifices that were offered annually with a view to averting the wrath of the Earth-goddess. The time had arrived when this savage and impious ceremony must terminate for ever. He assured them that a new order had dawned for them. They were no longer subjects of an ignorant Rajah, who took no interest in their welfare or happiness, but by the fortune of war they had become subjects of the British Government, in whose dominions such a revolting ceremony as he had come to denounce could not be tolerated for a moment.

"I thought it best to confess," he says in his "personal narrative", "that we, like them, had once sacrificed human beings; like them, we had indulged in similar cruel offerings; like them, we had believed that the judgment of the gods could be averted only by a bloody expiation and the slaughter of our fellow-men. But this was in the days of gross ignorance, when we were both fools and savages, knowing nothing, and living in a debased and brutal life; but we emerged from this darkness, gradually obtained light, and at last gave up for ever our barbarous and unholy practice. And what has been the consequence? All kinds of prosperity have come upon us since we abolished those sinful rites; we now possess learning and wisdom, and see clearly the great folly we had committed. . . ."

Then he entreated them to bear in mind that he had not come to interfere with their religion or subvert their faith, but simply and solely to prohibit a custom unsanctioned by the laws of God or man—his only wish being that they might abandon such wicked and cruel acts and, under the protection of the Government whose subjects they now were, enjoy the fullest measure of prosperity, and live at peace among themselves and with their neighbours.

After some discussion among themselves, the Khonds expressed their considered opinion through a spokesman. "We have always sacrificed human beings," this man pointed out, "our fathers handed down the custom to us. They thought no wrong; neither did we. On the contrary, we felt we were doing what was right. We were then the subjects of the Rajah of Goomsur, now we are the subjects of the British Government, whose orders we must obey. If the earth refuses to produce, or disease destroys us, it will not be our fault; we will abandon the sacrifice, and will, if permitted, sacrifice animals like the inhabitants of the plains."

Captain Campbell had good reason to be pleased, and he promptly invited the people to meet him again on a certain day, when they should bring with them all the meriahs in their possession. The day came, and nearly a hundred per-

sons, male and female, were handed over to his charge. The
the assembled chiefs took an oath. Seated on tiger skins, an
holding in their hands a little earth, rice, and water, they eac
spoke as follows: "May the earth refuse its produce, ric
choke me, water drown me, and tiger devour me and my chi
dren, if I break the oath which I now take for myself and m
people, to abstain for ever from the sacrifice of huma
beings."

But there were some isolated cases of resistance. One suc
incident occurred when Campbell was on leave at the Cape
and Captain Frye was in charge of his agency. News reache
Frye that a sacrifice was on the eve of being consummated
He hastened at once to the place mentioned, with a sma
body of troops, and arrived just in time to rescue the victim
a handsome girl of fifteen or sixteen. The assembled Khond
were half-mad with religious excitement, but when they sav
Frye meant business they yielded up the girl. He would hav
liked to lecture them on the iniquity of their proceeding, bu
since they were in such a "wild and irritated state" he ver
prudently judged that the moment was not opportune, an
marched off with his prize back to camp. Scarcely was he ou
of sight (so he learnt afterwards) when the infuriated moun
taineers said among themselves, "Why should we be debarre
from our sacrifice? See, here is our aged priest, seventy sum
mers have passed over his head—what further use is he? Le
us sacrifice *him*". No sooner said than done; the old ma
"was barbarously slaughtered, to satisfy their superstitiou
cravings."

Notwithstanding occasional setbacks, the work of rescu
went on, and Campbell was greatly encouraged by what h
calls a "romantic incident" in which the chief character wa
a woman who had been brought up as a meriah but ha
been rescued and, with her three children, placed in the asy
lum that had been established at Sooradah. Only when sh
had been there some little time did she reveal that she ha
another child, a boy, who was a destined meriah. The mothe
had until quite recently gloried in the fact, but now she ha
had a complete change of heart, and she implored Campbe
to send out a party to rescue the boy. This he was unable t
do at the time, but he promised to despatch one the nex
season, and hoped that it would be in time to save the boy
life. But this promise failed to satisfy the mother.

"Immediately afterwards," wrote Campbell in his report, although the rains were at their height, for it was the monsoon period, it was reported to me that she had escaped from the asylum, but without taking her children. A month passed away, and there was no news of the fugitive, and I began to despair of ever seeing the woman again; but about the fortieth day after her flight from Sooradah she appeared before me, bringing her little boy with her, much to my gratification. I learnt from her lips the history of her perilous adventure."

So great and complete had been the change in her feelings about the practice since she had been at the asylum, that she had not been able to rest or sleep while she knew that her boy was in danger of being sacrificed. Her distress became so overpowering that she resolved to save him at all costs. So she fled from Sooradah, and at length reached the hills, although not without utmost difficulty and danger, since tigers and snakes abounded in the jungle through which she had to pass. She dared not let herself be seen by friendly tribes, for fear that she would be sent back to the asylum as a runaway; while if any of the wilder or unpledged tribesfolk had caught sight of her she would have been delivered over at once to her former owners. So her danger was equally great from friend and foe.

"The poor creature, therefore, travelled only under cover of the night; and what nights they were at such a season! A perfect deluge of water was pouring from the heavens; the mountain torrents were roaring, and bursting from their banks; and the wild beasts howling in concert with the elements. But this brave woman, the instincts of whose better nature had now for the first time been awakened, was not disheartened. She crouched in the forests by day, lest she should be seen, and pursued her journey only when the people of the villages were asleep—subsisting on what wild roots she could find, when the small stock of parched rice she had carried away from the asylum was exhausted. At last she reached the village, and hovered about it for three days, not daring to enter when the inhabitants were there, but waiting her opportunity when, as is generally the case in the rainy season, all the villagers should be absent in their fields. The fortunate moment arrived; she saw her son, and, no one being present, carried him off, and fled with all the strength which desperate resolution lends to courage."

In a few nights she reached the territory of the friendly tribes, and had nothing more to fear. She could tell them what she had done, and pray them to help her back by easy stages to the first military station. This of course they very readily did, and, wrote Campbell, "I do not know that I ever felt more satisfaction than when I welcomed this heroic woman and the little son she had so nobly rescued. I found her worn to a skeleton by suffering and exposure, sufficient to have made the strongest man succumb. It should be remembered that not four months previously she would have gloried in her son's sacrifice." To add to the story's happy ending, Campbell disclosed that "she and all her children were well cared for, and with the usual liberality of the Indian Government, comfortably provided for the remainder of their lives."

How many meriahs were sacrificed? It is impossible to say. Captain Campbell was of the opinion that, since each cluster of villages would most probably celebrate a sacrifice annually, and extra victims might be required when special causes made it necessary, the annual figure was in the neighbourhood of a hundred and fifty. The total number of meriahs rescued in the course of the operations among the Khonds with which he was concerned, between the years 1837 and 1854, was 717 males and 789 females, or 1,506 altogether. Of this number 342 were restored to relatives and friends or given for adoption to persons of character living in the plains; 267 were given in marriage to Khonds, etc.; 306 were settled as cultivators in villages; 200 were placed in missionary schools at Cuttack, Berhampore, and Balasor; 75 were in a position to support themselves; 82 were placed in the asylum at Sooradah (referred to in Captain Campbell's story), which was established for the reception of unmarried females and young girls; 15 died; and 77 deserted and nothing was known of their fate.

Chapter 12

Poor Little Chinese Girls!

BEFORE the Revolution in 1911 it was a most common practice in China for parents to bind their daughters' feet. This was something that had been done for a very long time. Generations of women had been crippled and disabled, and even among the women themselves there were few to question it. Not until the arrival of the Christian missionaries was there any considerable opposition, and very often this was denounced as foreign "interference".

On the face of it, the custom was shockingly unnatural. It was also exceedingly cruel. The required size and shape of the feet could be attained only by a dislocation which caused great pain to begin with, prolonged suffering, and permanent crippling.

This is how it was done. At an early age, usually when the girl was four or five years old, the process began with the feet being tightly bound round in the intended shape by a strong bandage of cotton cloth, two yards long and about three inches wide. The four smaller toes were bent under the foot, the big toe was sometimes brought backwards on the top of the foot, and the instep was forced up and back. In this way the foot was clubbed, and forced into a shoe that was only three or four inches in length.

Every night and morning the bandage was drawn tighter, and if the bones were refractory and tended to spring back, the foot was given a hammering by a heavy wooden mallet such as was used in beating clothes after being washed. Immediately after each binding, the little girl was made to walk up and down, for fear that mortification might otherwise set in. Then she was put to sleep in a bed beside her mother's, and if she kept her parents awake with her crying she might be thrust into an outhouse where the noise she made would no longer be heard.

The first year was the worst. Unquestionably the little victims suffered great pain, but as a rule the skin, which at first was dreadfully abrased, became generally hardened and less sensitive. For at least two years more the process was carried on with, until the feet had become permanently misshaped. As the girl grew into womanhood, she began to walk as on pegs, and the calf of the leg gradually shrivelled up for want of exercise. There was a Chinese proverb which had only too much truth in it: "For each pair of bound feet there has been shed a whole *kang* (bath) of tears."

Not all Chinese girls were subjected to this torture. The degree of severity with which the feet were bound differed widely in the various classes of society. The women in the humbler classes were generally left in a position to walk about with ease—otherwise how would they have been able to engage in their household tasks and manual labour in the fields? The women of the boat-population, who spent their lives on the trading junks, and in particular the Hakka people of Canton, never had their feet bound. At the other end of the social scale, the ladies of the Manchu court circles and aristocracy were also exempted, although (such is the force of fashion) some of them attempted to evade the prohibition.

But the little girl who was expected to grow up into a lady had to submit to the operation as a matter of course. Perhaps in her case her feet would still answer all that would be required of them—which is not saying much, since a Chinese lady hardly walked at all. If she went out, she was conveyed either in a sedan-chair or, in the northern parts of the country, in a carriage; while within doors she hobbled about as best she could, leaning on a stick or the shoulder of a waiting-maid, or was carried on the back of a servant.

What was the reason for this practice, which was all the more objectionable since Chinese women (and men too, for that matter) are said to be generally gifted with finely shaped extremities?

An explanation commonly given is that it was an attempt to copy the peculiarly shaped feet of a certain beautiful empress or lady of the court, but there was no agreement as to her identity. One candidate for the distinction was P'an-fei, a favourite of the Emperor Ho-Ti, whose capital city was Nanking; she was so lovely that golden lilies were supposed to spring out of the ground wherever she stepped. According to another tradition, it was T'an-ki, wife of the last emperor of the Shang dynasty, about 1100 B.C.: she seems to have been a semi-mythical character, a changeling of fairy parentage, who had "hind's feet" covered with fine hair, which she disguised by binding them round and wearing dainty little fairy shoes. Coming to much later times, a ruler of the Sung dynasty (about A.D. 970) had a favourite wife whom he delighted to see posing or dancing upon golden lotus-flowers; she had the most beautiful little feet, and to make them appear even more beautiful than they were he used to wind strips of coloured satin round them till they came to resemble a crescent moon or a bent bow.

Leaving the realm of fantasy, one explanation that has been put forward is that foot-binding was a class distinction: as already indicated the poor and servants never had their feet bound. Another view is that the practice served to distinguish the Manchu conquerors from the mass of Chinese, but it may be noted that the Manchu emperors never enforced it upon their subjects. Then it has been suggested that foot-binding was a symbol of the seclusion and subjection of women, more especially of the upper and leisured classes. A Chinese gentleman wanted to keep his womenfolk at home, where they would always be under his eye and control. On this view, foot-binding was a means of restraining the gadding-about propensities of Chinese ladies!

Perhaps there is more to be said for the opinion that foot-binding had a sexual significance. It is generally recognized that sexual interest may become concentrated in non-sexual parts of the body, such as the hair, the neck, the hands and the feet. On this view, a tightly bound foot may constitute a love-fetish, something capable of arousing intense erotic feeling, especially under conditions when the normal incitements to sexual gratification have begun to lose their power. In this connexion it may be observed that the custom of foot-binding most probably had its rise amid the licentious and luxurious surroundings of the imperial court. Beyond any doubt, to the Chinese male, the spectacle of a woman or girl mincing along, with protruding chest and hips pushed out behind, was charged with the most erotic meaning. Chinese poets seem never to have tired of describing not only the leaf-shaped eyebrows and the willow waists of their lady-loves, but those swaying movements which they likened to boughs gently waving in answer to the caresses of the wind.

For many years only the Christian missionaries inveighed against foot-binding, but in the years between the Boxer Rebellion of 1900 and the outbreak of the Revolution in 1911 there were some enlightened Chinese who strove to abolish the practice along with others that hindered the modernization of their country. However, it was not until the triumph of Sun Yat-sen's revolutionary movement that it really went out of fashion. In the Communist China of the present, foot-binding has become a thing of the past.

Chapter 13

Fakirs and Fanatics

WITH what morbid relish Gibbon must have written those pages in his *Decline and Fall* in which he describes the rise and spread of the ascetic movement in the early Christian centuries! We may imagine him, sitting in his pleasant retreat beside the lake at Lausanne, looking out over the blue water to the white-capped peaks lining the further shore; and then, in his mind's eye, transporting himself to the burning sands of Egypt, where creatures hardly recognizable as human passed their days and nights in self-inflicted horrors.

"Such dreadful fellows", he must have mused, these ascetics who "seriously renounced the business, and the pleasures, of the age; who abjured the use of wine, of flesh, and of marriage; chastised their body, mortified their affections, and embraced a life of misery, as the price of eternal happiness."

"Unhappy exiles from social life," is what he calls them, men and women who were "impelled by the dark and implacable genius of superstition". A few pages later on he brings into our view the hermits "who sunk under the painful weight of crosses and chains", and whose "emaciated limbs were confined by collars, bracelets, gauntlets and greaves of massy and rigid iron. All superfluous incumbrance of dress they contemptuously cast away; and some savage saints of both sexes have been admired, whose naked bodies were only covered by their long hair". Then after a reference to those who "aspired to reduce themselves to the rude and miserable state in which the human brute is scarcely distinguished above his kindred animals", he goes on to mention those who "often usurped the den of some wild beast whom they affected to resemble", and "buried themselves in some gloomy cavern, which art or nature had scooped out of the rock". The most perfect hermits were supposed to have passed many days without food, many nights without sleep, and many years without speaking, "and glorious was the *man* (I abuse that name) who contrived any cell, or seat, of a peculiar construction, which might expose him, in the most inconvenient posture, to the inclemency of the seasons".

One most abominable fellow there had been, who had achieved immortality by "the singular invention of an aerial penance". His name was Simeon, he was a Syrian by birth, and at the age of thirteen he deserted his profession of a shepherd and became a novice in a monastery. But the austerities of the place were not harsh enough for him, and eventually he established himself on the top of a column, sixty feet above the ground. In this lofty station, Simeon the Stylite (Greek, *stylos,* a column) "resisted the heat of thirty summers, and the cold of as many winters. Habit and exercise instructed him to maintain his dangerous situation without fear or giddiness, and successively to assume the different postures of devotion. He sometimes prayed in an erect attitude, with his outstretched arms in the figure of a cross; but his most familiar practice was that of bending his meagre skeleton from the forehead to the feet; and a curious spectator, after numbering twelve hundred and forty-four repetitions, at length desisted from the endless account. The progress of an ulcer in his thigh might shorten, but it could not disturb, this *celestial* life; and the patient Hermit expired, without descending from his column."

Yes, truly a disgusting creature; and the urbane little historian (we may suppose) reached for his snuff-box and took another pinch. But of course this sort of behaviour was a thing of the past, at least among all those peoples who might be accounted civilized. In this enlightened age, towards the end of the eighteenth century, when society seemed so polished, so secure, so essentially humane, such senseless austerities, such cruel and useless penances, might be found only among the most barbarous and backward of the human family. If Gibbon really thought along these lines, he was very far out in his reckoning. For in India, where, as he knew well enough, men had been leading a civilized existence for centuries without number, Simeon Stylites would have been made to feel quite at home.

Gibbon finished his *History* in 1787, and he died in 1794. But he was still living when the young Abbé Dubois left Paris and went out to India as a missionary, where he remained until 1823. In another chapter we have quoted Dubois's account of the Suttees that came to his notice, or he may have actually witnessed, and now we turn to his pages for an account of the religious devotees whom he had encountered along the roads and in the villages and towns of the Indian peninsula.

"Silly fanatics," is what he calls them, "who make it their task to torture themselves and to mutilate their bodies in a hundred different ways." First in his picture-gallery of human horrors is the devotee who is "often seen stretched at full length on the ground and rolling in that posture all round the temples, or, during solemn processions, before the cars which carry the idols. It is a remarkable sight to see a crowd of fanatics rolling in this manner, quite regardless of stones, thorns, and other obstacles." Then there are those who, "inspired by extreme fanaticism, voluntarily throw themselves down to be crushed under the wheels of the car on which the idol is borne. And the crowds that witness these acts of madness, far from preventing them, applaud them heartily and regard them as the very acme of devotion."

Some of the most horrible tortures were inflicted on themselves by the devotees of the goddess Mari-amma (one of the many names given to the consort of the Great God Siva), whom he denounces as the most evil-minded and bloodthirsty of all the deities of India. "At many of the temples consecrated to this cruel goddess," he writes, "there is a sort of gibbet erected opposite the door. At the extremity of the crosspiece, or arm, a pulley is suspended, through which a cord passes with a hook at the end. The man who has made a vow to undergo this cruel penance places himself under the gibbet, and a priest then beats the fleshy part of his back until it is quite benumbed. After that the hook is fixed into the flesh thus prepared, and in this way the unhappy wretch is raised in the air. While suspended he is careful not to show any sign of pain; indeed, he continues to laugh, jest, and gesticulate like a buffoon in order to amuse the spectators, who applaud and shout with laughter. After swinging in the air for the prescribed time the victim is let down again, and, as soon as his wounds are dressed, he returns home in triumph!"

Then there are some votaries who make a vow to walk with bare feet along a heap of burning coals. "For this purpose they kindle a large pile of wood, and when the flames are extinguished and all the wood consumed, they place the glowing embers in a space about twenty feet in length. The victim stands at one extremity with his feet in a puddle expressly prepared for the purpose, takes a spring, and runs quickly over the burning embers till he reaches another puddle on the other side. In spite of these precautions very few, as one can imagine, escape from the ordeal with their feet uninjured."

Another kind of torture that Dubois had observed "consists in piercing both cheeks and passing a wire of silver or some other metal through the two jaws between the teeth. Thus bridled, the mouth cannot be opened without acute pain. Many fanatics have been known to travel a distance of twenty miles with their jaws thus maimed, and remain several days in this state, taking only liquid nourishment, or some clear broth poured into the mouth. I have seen whole companies of them, condemned by their self-inflicted torture to enforced silence, going on a pilgrimage to some temple where this form of penance is especially recommended."

One man in particular the Abbé recalled seeing, standing at the gate of a temple dedicated to the cruel goddess. What an imbecile he was! His lips were pierced by two long nails, which crossed the face so that one point reached to the right eye and the other to the left. "The blood was still trickling down his chin; yet the pain he must have been enduring did not prevent him from dancing and performing every kind of buffoonery before a crowd of spectators, who showed their admiration by giving him abundant alms."

Not content with the great number of ordinary forms of penance that were open to them, "devout Hindus try unceasingly to invent new methods of self-torture". There was one fanatic, for instance, who, having made a vow to cut half his tongue off, proceeded to do so, put the amputated portion in an open coconut shell, and offered it on his knees to the divinity. Others had bound themselves to go on pilgrimage to some distant shrine, but not in the ordinary way: beginning at their very doors, they stretched themselves on the ground, rose to their feet, advanced two steps, lay down again, rose again . . . and so on until they arrived at their destination. Persons had been seen attempting to measure their length in this way along the entire road running from the sacred city of Benares to the temple of Jagannath at Puri. This was a distance of more than two hundred leagues, but "I should not like to swear that they really accomplished such a feat".

Some of the penitents went about quite naked, "the object of this indecent practice being to convince the admiring public that they are no longer susceptible to the temptations of lust". There were also religious mendicants who showed themselves in public in "a state of nature". This was, of course, no new thing in India. When Alexander the Great reached the city of Taxila in the Punjab in 326 B.C. he was amazed to be met by naked ascetics whom the Greek writers denominated "Gymnosophists", i.e., "naked wise men". Strabo, three hundred years later, mentions them in his *Geographica*, and they have caught the attention of almost every traveller since. Thus the French physician François Bernier, who lived for twelve years in India as personal physician to the Mogul emperor Aurungzebe and wrote on his return to France a vivid account of his travels that was published in 1670, relates how the great Moslem ruler was so tolerant of his Hindu subjects' practices that religious devotees might often be seen walking through the towns stark naked, "men, women, and girls looking at them without any more emotion than may be created when a hermit passes through our streets".

James Forbes, who served in India as an officer of the East India Company from 1766 to 1783, says in his *Oriental Memoirs* (1813) that in Warren Hastings's time these Gymnosophists, "robust handsome men, generally entirely naked", used to roam about the country in such swarms that battalions of sepoys had to be sent out to disperse them. Forbes also tells us that among the devotees he had encountered was

one of these Gymnosophists, who seemed more like a wild
beast than a man; he had made a vow, it appeared, to hold
up his arms straight above his head, and now they had become withered and dried up, while his outstretched fingers
with long nails of twenty years' growth, had the appearance
of extraordinary horns. "His hair, full of dust, and never
combed, hung over him in a savage manner, and except in
his erect position, there appeared nothing human about him."
Since he was quite unable to feed himself, Hindu women of
distinction contended for the honour of putting food in his
mouth.

Perhaps as often as not, a Hindu devotee is called a *fakir*
but in the strict use of the term this word should be applied
only to the ascetics and holy men of the Moslem faith. The
Hindu religious mendicant is properly styled a *sannyasi*,
particularly if, as most of them are, he is a worshipper of the
great god Siva.

Among sannyasis, caste rules are abrogated; anyone may
join their ranks, even Sudras and outcastes, and they may eat
together and share the same roof. They are supposed not to
partake of flesh meat or spirits; they rub ashes over their
bodies and wear salmon-coloured robes and a tiger-skin when
they can get hold of one; and as a distinguishing badge they
hang round their necks a string of rudraksha berries, or fail-
ing that, at least one berry. Their equipment includes a conch-
shell used as a trumpet, and a pair of iron tongs.

The daily life of the sannyasi is regulated by six prohibi-
tions and as many commandments. The "don'ts" are: never
to sleep on a couch, under any circumstances; never wear
white clothes; never speak to a woman, or even think of one;
never sleep in the daytime; never ride on a horse or other
animal, or in any vehicle whatsoever; and never to allow one's
mind to be agitated in any way. Then the "musts" are: leave
his habitation only for the sake of begging such food as is
necessary, once a day; say his prayers every day; bathe once
a day; contemplate daily the image and likeness of Siva; practise purity and cleanliness; and perform the worship of the
gods.

A number of sects of these holy men are recognized. One
is the Dandis, so-called after the staff *(danda)* which they invariably carry. Another is the Lingaits, or Lingavats, who
always wear hanging round their necks on a thread a repre-

sentation of the lingam (the phallus, or male organ), which is
the special symbol of Siva. Then there are the Aghoris, or
Aghora-pathins, whose endeavour it is to propitiate Siva with
the most revolting austerities and practices. Among the latter
is their preference for human carrion, obtained by digging up
corpses from the graveyards. "And why not?" they argue,
when reproached for this disgusting habit; "according to the
philosophy we hold, everything is a manifestation of the
Universal Soul, and *nothing* can be unclean!" It is said that
women—Aghorinis—are often associated with these human
ghouls, and they are even more filthy and shameless in their
habits than their male companions. Mention should also be
made of the Yogis, who combine intense mental concentra-
tion with such physical behaviour as the adoption of special
postures, often forced and painful, and the deliberate suppression of breathing for as long as possible, all in the hope
and with the intention of bringing the body under control and
liberating the indwelling spirit.

"Fakir" is derived from the Arabic word *fakhar*, which
means "poor". Like their Hindu counterparts, the Moslem or
Mohammedan religious mendicants and ascetics take upon
themselves vows of poverty which cut them off from the
cares of the world and enable them to give themselves up entirely (so at least is their plea) to contemplation of the Deity.
Mohammed, the first preacher of Islam, as this world religion
is properly styled, was no ascetic, and he taught that the followers of Allah might enjoy all the good things of life in a
reasonable moderation. All the same, among the early Moslems there were some who reacted against the easy living of
Damascus and Baghdad, and devoted their lives to austerity
and prayer and other religious exercises. When the Arabs
conquered almost all India in the centuries following upon
Mahmud of Ghazni's invasion in A.D. 1001, they were brought
into close contact with Hindu ideas and practices, and there
arose in Islam a strong movement of *fakirism* in which a
good deal of the Hindu element was incorporated. Likewise
in Persia the fakir became a frequent and well-recognized
figure, while in Turkey and Egypt and adjacent countries there
sprang up orders of religious fanatics known as Dervishes.
Thirty-two of these have been listed, the most celebrated being those known popularly as the Howling and the Dancing

Dervishes, on account of the outstanding features of their extraordinary performances.

India, however, has been, and remains, the principal centre of religious asceticism, both Moslem and Hindu, and in both the great states into which the sub-continent has been divided the Mohammedan fakir and the Hindu sannyasi (or *sadhu*, to employ another term for the Hindu holy man) continue to flourish. When Tavernier was in India in the seventeenth century he estimated the number of religious devotees at over a million; modern estimates range from two or three millions to even four millions. Wherever you go, from the Himalayas to Cape Comorin, you will not be able to go far without your encountering the half-naked or naked figure, often bearing on his meagre body the marks of self-inflicted pain, slowly moving along the road with his begging-bowl held out in mute appeal, or sitting cross-legged in the dust by the wayside.

Chapter 14

Tattooed Skins

Of all the many strange things that Captain Cook noticed when voyaging among the islands of the South Pacific in 1769, perhaps the one that most attracted his attention was the practice of tattooing, and it was through the account that he gave in his *Journal* that the term was first introduced into Europe.

The word is derived from the Tahitian *tatau,* which in turn comes from *ta,* meaning "to strike". This is a clear indication of the proper meaning of the term. There have been many peoples, in ancient times and modern, who have painted their bodies—did not our own ancestors "dress themselves in woad"?—but tattooing in its strict sense refers to skin marks produced on the bare flesh by a pointed instrument, followed by the introduction of a pigment that gives visibility and prominence to the designs. This is a very widespread practice, so widespread that Charles Darwin asserted that "not one great country can be named, from the Polar regions in the north to New Zealand in the south, in which the aborigines do not tattoo themselves", but it is in Polynesia and the adjacent New Zealand and Australia that the practice has reached its highest development.

Among the accounts of tattooing given by men who encountered it in all its original freshness, a high place must be accorded to that of William Ellis, who for nearly ten years, until his recall to England in 1825, laboured under the auspices of the London Missionary Society in the South Sea Islands, for much of the time on Oahu, in the Hawaiian group, but including a visit to Tahiti. It was here that he came across *tatauing,* as he most correctly calls it.

"The fondness of the Tahitians for these ornaments," he writes, "as they considered the marks so impressed, is truly remarkable. It is not confined to them, but pervades the principal groups, and is extensively practised by the Marquesans and New Zealanders. Although practised by all classes, I have not been able to trace its origin. It is by some adopted as a badge of mourning, or memorial of a departed friend; and from the figures we have sometimes seen upon the persons of the natives, and the conversations we have had, we should be induced to think it was designed as a kind of historical record of the principal actions of their lives. But it was, we believe, in modern times, adopted by the greater number of the people purely as a personal adornment.

"It must have been a painful operation," he goes on to say, "and was seldom applied to any extent at the same time. There were *Tahua,* professors of the art of tatauing, who were regularly employed to perform it, and received a liberal remuneration. The colouring matter was the kernel of the candle-nut, called by the natives *tiairi.* This was first baked, and then reduced to charcoal, and afterwards pulverized, and mixed with oil. The instruments were crude, though ingenious, and consisted of the bones of birds or fishes, fastened with fine thread to a small stick. Another stick, somewhat heavier, was also used, to strike the above when the skin was perforated. The figure or pattern to be tataued was portrayed upon the skin with a piece of charcoal, though at times the operator was guided only by his eye."

A number of what the missionary describes as idolatrous ceremonies preceded the operation; and then, when these were finished, "the operator, immersing the points of the sharp bone instrument in the colouring matter, which was a beautiful jet black, applied it to the surface of the skin, and, striking it smartly with the elastic stick which he held in his right hand, punctured the skin and injected the dye at the same time, with as much facility as an adder would bite and deposit his poison. So long as the person could endure the pain, the operator continued his work, but it was seldom that the whole figure was completed at once. Hence it proved a tedious process, especially with those who had a variety of patterns, or stained the greater part of their bodies".

Generally the natives began to impress "these unfading marks" upon their persons at an early age, frequently before they were seven or eight years old. Both sexes were "tataued", but the men more often than the women.

Of all the forms of tattooing that he had come across, the Tahitian displayed the greatest taste and elegance. Though some of the figures were arbitrary, such as stars, circles, lozenges, etc., the patterns were usually taken from nature, and were often most graceful. "A cocoa-nut tree is a favourite object; I have often admired the markings of a chief's legs, when I have seen a cocoa-nut tree correctly and distinctly drawn, its roots spreading at the heel, its elastic stalk pencilled as it were along the tendons, and its waving plume gracefully spread out on the broad part of the calf. Sometimes a couple of stems would be twined up from the heel, and divided on the calf, each bearing a plume of leaves. The ornaments round the ankle, and upon the instep, make them often appear as though they wore the elegant Eastern sandal. The sides of the legs are sometimes tataued from the ankle upward, which gives the appearance of wearing pantaloons with ornamented seams. In the lower part of the back, a number of straight, waved, or zigzag lines, rise in the direction of the spine, and branch off regularly towards the shoulders. But, of the upper part of the body, the chest is the most tataued. Every variety of figure is to be seen here. Cocoa-nut and bread-fruit trees, with convolvulus wreaths hanging round them, boys gathering fruit, men engaged in battle, in the manual exercise, triumphing over a fallen foe; or, as I have frequently seen it, they are represented as carrying a human sacrifice to the temple. Every kind of animal—goats, dogs, fowls, and fish—may at times be seen on this part of the body; muskets, swords, pistols, clubs, spears, and other weapons of war, are also stamped upon their arms and chests.

"They are not all crowded upon the same person, but each one makes a selection according to his fancy; and I have frequently thought that the tatauing on a man's person might serve as an index to his disposition and his character.

"The neck and throat were sometimes singularly marked. The head and the ears were also tataued, though among the Tahitians this ornament was seldom applied to the face. The females used to tatau more sparingly than the men, and with greater taste. It was always the custom for the natives to go barefooted, and the feet, to an inch above the ankles, were often neatly tataued; appearing as if they wore a loose kind of sandal, or elegant open-worked boot. The arms were frequently marked with circles, their fingers with rings, and their wrists with bracelets. The thin transparent skin over the black dye often gave to the tatau a tinge of blue.

"The females seldom, if ever, marked their faces; the figures on their feet and hands were all the ornament they exhibited. Many suffered with the pain occasioned by the operation, and from the swelling and inflammation that followed, which often continued for a long time, and ultimately proved fatal. This, however, seldom deterred others from attempting to secure this badge of distinction or embellishment of person."

When Charles Darwin visited Tahiti some ten years after Ellis had left, he, too, remarked on the tattooed figures of the men he came across. He thought they were very handsome fellows, and was not in the least put off by their dark colour. A white man bathing by the side of a Tahitian was, he commented, like a plant bleached by the gardener's art compared with a fine dark green one growing vigorously in the open fields. As regards the tattooing, he was similarly impressed by the tree-like patterns. "The simile may be a fanciful one," he remarked, "but I thought the body of a man thus ornamented was like the trunk of a noble tree embraced by a delicate creeper."

Among the Fijians (so we learn from Thomas Williams, who was a Wesleyan missionary in the islands for a number of years) it was common for the men to cut unsightly scars in their skins, and burn rows of wart-like spots along the arms and hands of their women, which they and their admirers thought most ornamental. Tattooing proper was also widely practised, but only the women were subjected to it, and it was performed only by female operators. Young women were ornamented with barbed lines on their hands and fingers, and the middle-aged with patches of blue markings at the corners of the mouth. Tattooing was also applied on other parts of the body, and oddly enough, especially on those parts which were covered by the *liku,* the kind of fringed band, made of the bark of the hibiscus and fastened round the waist, that was the women's only garment. In some of the islands tattooing was an indication that the women had borne children, but it was also resorted to to conceal the wrinkles of age. The custom was said to have been ordered by Ndengei, the chief of the Fijian gods, and it was believed that any woman who neglected to have it performed on her person could not possibly hope for happiness in the life beyond the grave.

The natives called it *qia,* and it was performed with an instrument made of four or five bone teeth fixed in a wooden frame. The required pattern was first outlined, and then the comb, having been dipped in a pigment composed of charcoal and candle-nut oil, was driven into the skin with sharp taps. Sometimes months were occupied in the process, which was very painful and was submitted to only from the motives of fear and pride.

According to the Fijians, the Tongans first observed the practice among them, and then introduced it into their own island. But with them the custom is confined to the *men,* instead of to women, and the Fijians had a humorous story to account for this difference. They said that the Tongan who first reported the custom to his countrymen, being anxious to state it correctly, repeated to himself in a sing-song voice as he went along, "Tattoo the women, but not the men; tattoo the women, but not the men". Then as ill-luck would have it, he struck his foot violently against a stump in the path, and in his confusion he reversed the order of his message, singing for the rest of his journey, "Tattoo the men, but not the women". And thus the Tongan chiefs heard the message, and thus it came about that the smart of the *qia* tooth was inflicted on the men instead of on their wives!

Whatever the Tongan practice, the general rule in the South Seas was for the women to be tattooed. One of the reasons for this was the religious one mentioned above, that a woman who had not been tattooed was ineligible for the native heaven. Another was to make the women more attractive to men. A third was ornamentation, but this can hardly have been altogether important since the markings were often so finely done as to be hardly visible, and moreover they were applied to portions of the body that were hidden by the *liku*. This suggests a sexual significance.

Among primitive peoples we often find the magico-religious concept that the sexual regions are exposed to very special dangers from evil spirits, and must therefore be specially protected. Tattooing is believed to constitute the most effective protection, and it is for this reason that, for example, in the tattooing of the girls of the Caroline Islands and in New Guinea, the most complicated part of the design is on the pubes. It is interesting to learn that the girls, who cannot be charged with immodesty, do not object to having the designs inspected and copied by inquisitive European investigators. Exposing the genital region in these circumstances does not matter, since the tattooing is regarded not as an erotic device but as a protection of this highly vulnerable part of the body against the machinations of wicked spirits.

The tattooing of the Tahitians was supposed to be of the first rank, but it was nearly approached by that of the native New Zealanders, the Maori tribesfolk. The word "tattoo" was not to be found in their vocabulary: they called it *"moko"*. When the Maoris first began to practise it is unknown, but it was probably subsequent to the discovery of New Zealand by the Dutch voyager Tasman in 1642, since he makes no mention of the practice, which he would surely have done if he had encountered instances of it.

The next European voyager to reach New Zealand was Captain Cook in 1769, and in his Journal he records that one day they shot a native whose face was marked down the sides with spiral lines of a regular pattern. Later on many other natives similarly marked were encountered. "The bodies and faces are marked with black stains they call *amoco*," wrote Cook; "broad spirals on each buttock—the thighs of many were almost entirely black, the faces of the old men almost covered." And again: "The marks in general are spirals drawn with great nicety and even elegance. One side corresponds with the other. The marks in the body resemble the foliage in old chased ornaments, convolutions of filigree work, but in these they have such luxury of forms that of a hundred which at first appear exactly the same no two were formed alike on close examination." Some of the Maori men were stained all over, with the exception of only a few narrow lines, so that at first sight they appeared to be wearing striped breeches.

Included in the company of Cook's ship the *Endeavour* was a clever draughtsman named Sydney Parkinson, who was employed by the expedition's naturalist, the famous Joseph Banks. On his return to England Parkinson published his own account of the voyage, in which he mentioned the tattooed New Zealanders and included some of his own drawings (now in the British Museum collections). At close quarters, the skins of some of the men looked like carving, but at a distance it would seem that they had been only smeared with black paint. Parkinson also had a special word for the women. "Their lips were in general stained of a blue colour, and several of them were scratched all over their faces as if it had been done with needles or pins."

The Maori ladies would not have been too pleased with his comment. In their society, red lips were looked upon as a reproach: they must be blue to be in the fashion. When Charles Darwin inquired into the matter, he was told that the missionaries had tried to persuade the girls not to be tattooed about the lips, but a famous operator had arrived from the south, and they declared: "We really must have just a few lines on our lips; else when we grow old, our lips will shrivel, and we shall be so very ugly."

Was the "famous operator" the man named Aranghie, the most celebrated of all the artists in Moko? Born a *kooky*, or slave, by his skill and industry he raised himself to a position of equality with the greatest men of his country; and as every chief who employed him made him some handsome present, he soon became a man of wealth. Augustus Earle knew him well, and in his *Narrative of a Nine Months' Residence in New Zealand in 1827*, from which we have already drawn passages on his contacts with the New Zealand cannibals, he gives a most interesting account of the man and his work.

By way of introduction, Earle says that "tattooing has been brought to such perfection here, that whenever we have seen a New Zealander whose skin is thus ornamented, we have admired him. It is looked upon as answering the same purposes as clothes. When a chief throws off his mats, he seems as proud of displaying the beautiful ornaments figured on his skin, as a first-rate exquisite is in exhibiting himself in his last fashionable attire." It is an essential part of warlike celebrations, he continues, and since the whole of the district of Ko-ro-ra-di-ka was now preparing for an imminent war Aranghie had been sent for to apply his "operating hands" to the persons of the mighty men who were gathering there.

"As this 'professor' was a near neighbour of mine, I frequently paid him a visit in his 'studio', and he returned the compliment whenever he had time to spare. He was considered by his countrymen a perfect master in the art of tattooing, and men of the highest rank and importance were in the habit of travelling long journeys in order to put their skin under his skilful hands. Indeed, so highly were his works esteemed, that I have seen many of his drawings exhibited after death. A neighbour of mine very lately killed a chief who had been tattooed by Aranghie; and, appreciating the artist's work so highly, he skinned the chieftain's thighs, and covered his cartouche-box with it."

Then Earle goes on: "I was astonished to see with what boldness and precision Aranghie drew his designs upon the skin, and what beautiful ornaments he produced; no rule and compasses could be more exact than the lines and circles he formed. So unrivalled is he in his profession, that a highly-finished face of a chief from the hands of this artist is as greatly prized in New Zealand as a head from the hands of Sir Thomas Lawrence is amongst us." Really, it was most gratifying to see the respect that these savages paid to the fine arts. Aranghie was constantly surrounded by the most important personages in the community, such as Pungho Pungho, Ricky Ricky, Kivy Kivy, etc.; and Earle's friend "King George" sent him every day the choicest things from his own table.

As a rule, Maori women were tattooed only on their faces and perhaps fingers. Captain Cook noted that it was only in New Zealand and the Sandwich Islands that they tattooed the face: "They have a singular custom amongst them, the meaning of which we could never learn—that of tattooing the tip of the tongues of the females." But women in New Zealand were sometimes tattooed much more extensively. This is rather amusingly evidenced by the account given by one Bidwell, in his *Rambles in New Zealand* (1839).

While crossing a creek one day, a native informed him that one of their party was tattooed behind just like the men. "I asked her if it was the case, and she said yes, and if I would wait and let her go on a bit ahead she would show me, which she accordingly did, to my great edification." Only very rarely had he come across a woman who was tattooed anywhere but on the lips and chin, so this was "quite a curiosity". But he could not imagine why the woman did it, since they were always covered.

If he had put the question to the revealing lady on the woodland path, or to any other of the tattooed dames, he would probably have had it explained to him, that it was what their husbands or lovers admired. Clearly they must have thought it well worth while, or they would not have submitted themselves to such a lengthy and painful operation. And so thinking, they could even manage a smile.

One day the French explorer Dumont d'Urville, who sailed the South Pacific about the same time that Darwin did in the *Beagle,* visited a native village in New Zealand where the chief's wife was having her back tattooed. "Half of her back was already incised with deeply cut designs, and a female slave was engaged in decorating the other half. The unfortunate woman was lying on her chest, and seemed to be suffering greatly, while the blood gushed forth abundantly from her shoulders. Still she did not utter even a sigh, and looked at me merrily with the greatest composure." The chief himself was standing by, and seemed to be taking pride in the new honour that his wife was receiving from the decorations on her skin.

The instruments used by the Moko practitioners were small, narrow chisels made from seabirds' wing-bones, sharks' teeth, stones, or hard wood, worked down to a fine point or edge. These were placed against the flesh along the pattern that had been already drawn, and hit with a wooden mallet, causing deep cuts or gashes. The pain was always considerable, but it became excruciating when the incisions were made on the most tender parts—the lips, the corners of the eyes and eyelids, the tip of the tongue, and the parting of the nostrils. Dreadful swellings often arose, and for weeks the unhappy subject might have to take nourishment through a feeding-tube. The blue-black tint of the designs was produced by a pigment or dye made from the burnt and powdered resin of the Kauri pine, mixed with oil or with dog's fat.

Heads that had been "mokoed" were held in high esteem. The Maoris used to cut off the heads of their enemies fallen in battle, stick them on poles about their homesteads, and carefully preserve them as trophies—"all of which," stated Major-General Robley in his classic study, *Moko: or Maori Tattooing* (1896), "was highly gratifying to the survivors, and the spirits of their late possessors". In the ordinary way, slaves were not permitted to be tattooed, so that tattooing was a recognized mark of distinction between the free man and the slave. But cases were reported of slaves' heads being tattooed for the special purpose of selling them; if the owners of the heads were too long in dying, their masters might expedite their demise. The tribal wars in New Zealand were brought to an end in the middle of the last century, just at about the time when the demand for tattooed heads by foreign museums was making itself felt, so that there may have been all too much truth in the saying that the increase in the number of Maori heads in European and American museums coincided with a reduction in the live population of New Zealand.

Another people that has gone in for tattooing on an extensive scale is the Ainus of Japan. Isabella Bird, in her book, *Unbeaten Tracks in Japan*, indignantly repudiates the charge that Ainu women and girls are ugly, although she admits that they are *very* dirty. They have also big mouths, but these look bigger than they really are, because of the broad band which is tattooed above and below them. A few unite the eyebrows by a streak of tattooing, and most of them have a band tattooed across the knuckles of each hand, and a series of tattooed bracelets extending to the elbow.

The process of disfigurement, as Miss Bird calls it, "begins at the age of five, when some of the sufferers are yet unweaned. I saw the operation performed on a dear little bright girl this morning. A woman took a large knife with a sharp edge, and rapidly cut several horizontal lines on the upper lip, following closely the curve of the very pretty mouth, and before the slight bleeding had ceased carefully rubbed in some of the shiny soot which collects on the mat above the fire. In two or three days the scarred lip will be washed with the decoction of the bark of a tree to fix the pattern, and give it that blue look which makes many people mistake it for a daub of paint." The little victim "held her hands clasped tightly together while the cuts were inflicted, but never cried. The pattern on the lips is deepened and widened every year up to the time of marriage, and the circles on the arms are extended in a similar way."

Why did the women do it? Miss Bird inquired, but the men could not give any reason for the universality of the custom, beyond that it was an old custom and part of their religion, and no woman could marry without it.

Nearly two thousand years ago a Chinese traveller reported that Japanese men "all tattoo their faces and ornament their bodies with designs, differences of rank being indicated by the position and size of the patterns". But from the dawn of authenticated history down to the middle ages tattooing in Japan seems to have been confined to criminals, who were dealt with in this way very much as they were branded in Europe. The swashbucklers of feudal times then took to it, apparently because some blood-and-thunder scene of adventure tattooed on their chest and limbs helped to give them a terrific air when for any reason they were stripped. Other classes whose avocations led to them baring their bodies in public followed suit, such as carpenters and running grooms; and we are told that when an artisan could not find the fee all at once, he was operated on by stages through a term of years, as money was forthcoming. Because of these lowly associations, the practice came to be considered ungentlemanly; and since foreigners might be expected to regard it as a barbaric survival, the Japanese reforming government of 1868 made tattooing a penal offence. But in 1881 (so it is said) the two young sons of the Prince of Wales, who were on a visit to Japan, took a fancy to it and were surreptitiously tattooed, and this made tattooing "respectable".

So far at least as the younger of the two princes is concerned, this statement would seem to be incorrect, however. Prince George (the future King George V) *was* tattooed, but not apparently until a year or so later, when he was on a tour of the Holy Land. "We have been Tatoed," he wrote to his mother (later Queen Alexandria), "by the same old man that tatoed Papa & the same thing too the 5 crosses. You ask Papa to show his arm."

Chapter 15

When Father "Lies In"

ON the face of it, the custom of "couvade" must appear too far-fetched altogether, as nothing better than an old wives' tale. Surely it cannot be true that, among any people anywhere at any time, a man should "lie in" instead of his wife when she is about to have a baby! And yet there is no doubt about it. Many travellers in various parts of the world, in ancient times and in modern, have reported its existence, and there is evidence that it has not completely died out. But, as we shall see, if not unbelievable it is unexplainable, at least to the satisfaction of the modern intelligence.

The word "couvade" was first used by E. B. Tylor about the middle of the last century. He derived it from the French word *couver,* meaning "to hatch" or "to brood", and he devised it as a technical term to describe the custom just alluded to. Briefly outlined, and in what may be termed its perfect form, it requires that the father of a child should, some time before the birth and even sometimes before the wife's pregnancy, take certain precautions and act in a certain way that, to those who are unacquainted with the custom, must appear more than strange.

To begin with, he is required to submit to a strict diet and avoid hard work or the handling of tools and weapons, and abstain from hunting, smoking, and other amusements and pursuits. When the time of the birth draws near, the husband takes to his bed and pretends to be lying in, sometimes simulating the groans and cries and contortions of a woman in the pains of labour. Whilst he is in bed he is fed on dainties, cossetted and made much of, and when the child is born he nurses it in his arms and receives the felicitations of his relatives and friends on his happy delivery. Sometimes he even puts on his wife's clothes to make the performance more exact.

More than two thousand years ago the couvade attracted the surprised attention of Greek and Roman writers. Strabo, who was writing his *Geographica* (which survived as a school-book well into the Middle Ages) at the beginning of our era, relates that the women of Iberia (Spain), after the example of the women of the Celts, Thracians, and Scythians, as soon as they were delivered used to quit their beds to give place to their husbands, whom they tended assiduously. Diodorus Siculus, a little earlier, says that in Corsica when a woman had given birth to a child her husband went to bed and remained there a certain number of days just as though he were lying in. Two hundred years before that, Apollonius of Rhodes described a people on the north-west coast of Asia, among whom, "as soon as married women are delivered, their husbands groan, lie on beds, and cover their heads. All this time their wives give them nourishing food, and prepare for them baths such as are suitable for women who are lying in". Marco Polo, the great Venetian traveller who seven hundred years ago crossed Asia to Peking, reported that in Chinese Turkestan the father of a newborn child had to retire to bed for forty days and was subjected to a number of restrictions, among them a prohibition of chewing betel-nut and washing himself. Very probably it was this report that suggested the lines in Samuel Butler's *Hudibras* (1663) about "Chineses" who "go to bed and lie in, in their ladies' stead", although the Chinese did not in fact practise couvade. Nor did the Japanese, although the aboriginal Ainus are reported to have done so.

About the same time the French voyager Du Tertre observed couvade among the Caribs of the West Indies, and wrote an interesting account. When a child is born (he says), the mother goes presently to her work, but the father begins to complain and takes to his hammock, and there he is visited as though he were sick and undergoes a course of dieting. "How they can fast so much and not die of it, is amazing to me, for they sometimes pass the first five days without eating or drinking anything; then up to the tenth day they drink *ouycou*, which has about as much nourishment in it as beer. These ten days passed, they begin to eat cassava only, drinking ouycou, and abstaining from everything else for the space of a whole month. During this time, however, they only eat the inside of the cassava, so that what is left is like the rim of a hat when the block has been taken out, and all these cassava rims they keep for the feast at the end of forty days, hanging them up in the house with a cord. When the forty days are up they invite their relations and best friends, who being arrived, before they set to eating, hack the skin of this poor wretch with agouti-teeth, and draw blood from all parts of his body, in such sort that from being sick by pure imagination they often make a real patient of him."

But this, the narrator goes on, "is so to speak only the fish, for now comes the sauce they prepare for him. They take sixty or eighty large grains of pimento or Indian pepper, the strongest they can get, and after well mashing it in water, they wash with this peppery infusion the wounds and scars of the poor fellow, who I believe suffers no less than if he was burnt alive; however, he must not utter a single word if he will not pass for a coward and a wretch. This ceremony finished, they bring him back to his bed, where he remains some days more; and the rest go to make good cheer in the house at his expense. Nor is this all, for through the space of six whole months he eats neither birds nor fish, firmly believing that this would injure the child's stomach, and that it would participate in the natural faults of the animals on which its father had fed; for example, if the father ate turtle, the child would be deaf and have no brains like this animal, while if he ate manati the child would have little round eyes like this creature, and so on with the rest."

No less interesting is the account of the practice given by the Jesuit missionary Martin Dobrizhoffer, who worked for a number of years from the middle of the eighteenth century among the Abipone tribesfolk of Paraguay, in the Gran Chaco region of South America. In his *History of the Abipones*, published in 1784, he writes: "No sooner do you hear that the wife has borne a child, than you will see the Abipone husband lying in bed, huddled up with mats and skins lest some ruder breath of air should touch him, fasting, and kept in private, and for a number of days abstaining religiously from certain viands; you would swear that it was he who had had the child. . . . I had read about this in old times, and laughed at it, never thinking I could believe such madness, and I used to suspect that this barbarian custom was related more in jest than in earnest, but at last I saw it with my own eyes among the Abipones. And in truth they observe this ancestral custom, troublesome as it is, the more willingly and diligently from being altogether persuaded that the sobriety and quiet of the father is affected for the well-being of the newborn offspring, and is even necessary."

By way of elaboration of his account, Dobrizhoffer proceeds to relate that one day he was walking with Francesco Barreda, the deputy of the royal governor of Tucuman in the neighbouring province of Argentina, when a native *cacique* or chief named Malakin approached to pay his respects. He had just left his bed, he informed them, to which he had been confined in consequence of his wife's delivery of a child. "As I stood by, Barreda offered the cacique a pinch of Spanish snuff; but seeing the savage refuse it, he thought he must be out of his mind, for he knew him at other times to be greedy of this nasal delicacy. So he asked me aside to inquire the cause of this abstinence. I asked Malakin in the Bipone tongue (for this Barreda was ignorant of, as the cacique was of Spanish) why he refused his snuff today? 'Don't you know?' he answered, 'that my wife has just been confined? Must I not therefore abstain from stimulating my nostrils? What a danger my sneezing would bring upon the child!' No more, but he went back to his hut to lie down again directly, lest the tender little infant should take some harm if he stayed any longer with us in the open air. For they believe that the father's carelessness influences the newborn offspring, from a natural bond and sympathy of both."

Towards the end of the last century Sir Everard im Thurn observed the couvade among the Indian tribes of the Guianas, and other travellers have reported it among some of the Red-skins of North America. Among many other instances in various parts of the world may be noted the practice of certain primitive tribes in southern India, when the woman, as soon as she feels the birth-pangs, informs her husband, who forthwith puts on some of her clothes, places on his forehead the mark which the women usually put on theirs, retires into a dark room, and lies down on the bed, covering himself with a long cloth. When the child is born, it is washed and placed on the cot beside the father, and asafoetida (an ill-smelling gum resin), jaggery (coarse dark sugar) and other articles are administered not to the mother but to the husband. Then during the days of ceremonial uncleanness prescribed by ancient custom, the man is treated just as other Hindus treat their women on such occasions, not being allowed to leave his bed but having everything brought to him.

All these instances are taken from more or less primitive peoples, but some suggestions of the couvade have been found in Britain. Here and there one may come across the belief that the pregnancy and confinement of a wife affects in some way her husband, and that if the husband undergoes some measure of pain his wife will be correspondingly relieved. In remote parts of Scotland the belief is said still to linger, that if the husband is the first to get up on the morning after the wedding, he will take upon himself all the pains of childbirth when the time arrives. There is also a belief, found in Ireland as well as in Scotland, that the nurse or midwife may be able to transfer some of the birth-pangs to the father, perhaps by taking some of his clothes and laying them on the wife. This belief was encountered by Thomas Pennant, who rambled over a good part of the British Isles in the second half of the eighteenth century. When at Langholm, in Dumfriesshire, in 1772 he was told that the midwives of the district had it in their power to transfer part of "the primeval curse bestowed upon our first great mother from the good-wife to the husband. I saw the reputed offspring of such a labour, who kindly came into the world without giving her mother the least uneasiness, whilst the poor husband was roaring with agony and in uncouth and unnatural pains."

Clearly there is a substantial element of "sympathetic magic" in some of the customs forming the couvade, but this is not a sufficient explanation. Many other "explanations" have been put forward from time to time. The most amusing, but hardly the most convincing, is that fathers are so pushed around and bossed about at the time of their wife's confinement, especially by their mother-in-law, that they have been made really ill and have taken to their beds in self-defence. A Norwegian writer once expressed the opinion that a woman about to bear a child likes to have her husband handy in case of emergencies, and an obvious way of making sure of this is to put him to bed. Interesting also is the suggestion that the couvade is a relic of the times when our ancestors were androgynous or hermaphrodites, and both sexes yielded milk and nourished their young and were treated in childbirth therefore very much alike.

An explanation which has received considerable support is based on the belief that birth is a specially dangerous period, since there are numerous evil spirits lying in wait to wreak evil on the newborn and its mother if they possibly can. Now a man is the natural protector of his wife and children, and he therefore takes upon himself as a matter of course to defend them against the powers of evil. In order to do this most effectively, he pretends to be the mother, by going to bed in her place when her time comes, receiving special care and attention, etc., while she remains modestly and unobtrusively in the background, going about her maternal and domestic duties without calling any special attention to herself or to her baby. Perhaps (so it is argued) in this way the evil spirits may be deluded into thinking that it is indeed the man who has given birth, and concentrate on him all their wrath and guile. And how disagreeably will they be surprised when they find that they have to deal not with a poor weak woman but with a man who is well capable of taking care of himself! Meanwhile the mother and child will be making progress and will soon be out of danger. From this it would seem that the primitive has not a very high opinion of the intelligence of the malicious spirits who are supposed to infest the world.

There is still another explanation, which has obtained a considerable measure of support. This is that the couvade arose in a matriarchal state of society, one in which the descent was recognized only through the mother, whether because the part played by the father in procreation had not become recognized or because there was a good deal of promiscuity and the paternity of a child was not easy to determine. But at length the male members of the society resolved to assert themselves and obtain their rights, and the couvade (so it is suggested) represents an attempt to convert the matriarchal state of society into a paternal one. By this gross mimicry of childbirth, the father asserted his own share in the creation of the child, openly affirmed his paternity, and doubtless laid claim to certain rights over his offspring. It showed that a man was no longer content with a share of the women of the tribe, but insisted on possessing a woman who was acknowledged as his, and that any children she bore were his likewise. "It is, in short," wrote Dr. Letourneau in his book on the evolution of marriage, "a revolt of individualism against primitive communism. The mimicry is gross and strange, but in a social condition where there exists neither lawyer, nor mayor, nor register of civil acts, testimonial proof is the great resource, and in order to make it sure and durable, men have willingly had recourse to striking and complicated practices which are calculated to engrave the remembrance of a fact on the memory of those present." But to this "plausible exhibition which gives to the couvade the value of our registry of birth" many objections have been raised, including the awkward fact that it has been found amongst peoples still in the stage where descent through the mother is generally recognized. But another objection is that the explanation implies that the people who practised, or practise, couvade take a lawyer's view of social arrangements; as A. E. Crawley puts it in his book *The Mystic Rose*, "the custom would be too much of a legal fiction if it meant all this originally".

Primitive man is not legal-minded, nor is he particularly rational; it is only we people who live in a matter-of-fact or scientific environment who worry our heads about "explanations". And it may well be that the custom of couvade never will be explained—to *our* satisfaction.

Chapter 16

Odd Doings Among the Todas

THERE are fewer than a thousand of them, and there can never have been very many more, since they have tried to keep their numbers under control. But numbers are not everything, and the Todas have many peculiar features that make them one of the most interesting of the smaller races that have managed to survive.

Their homeland is high up in the Nilgiri hills in southern India, and they have lived there from time immemorial. Their villages (or hamlets rather, since they consist of no more than half-a-dozen huts occupied by members of the same family) are spread out over the plateau, which they share with a number of Kota tribesfolk and a larger number of Badagas. All three are interdependent, for while the Badagas are agriculturists, producing far more than their own subsistence from the fertile soil, and the Kotas are artisans—weavers, blacksmiths, carpenters, etc.—the Todas are pastoralists.

In appearance they are very different from the other peoples of southern India, and in fact they are descended from the aborigines who were there before the Aryan invasions.

Tall and well-proportioned, with a deep brown skin colour, they let their hair grow to luxuriant lengths. Both sexes wear cloaks, patterned in bright colours. Their dwellings are like nothing so much as barrels half buried in the ground; they are made of rattan and brushwood, and since they have no windows they are often stuffy and evil-smelling. The beds are made of earth, covered over with a thick layer of cow dung, and there is no other furniture.

The Todas do not cultivate the soil, they do not fish or hunt. But they keep buffaloes. To them life without buffaloes would be hardly conceivable. The buffalo is the foundation of their society, and it is most closely bound up with their religion. Their food consists very largely of buffalo products—milk, ghee or clarified butter, buttermilk—supplemented with small quantities of grain or rice boiled in milk. The routine of daily life is regulated by the time-table of dairying operations.

Although the Toda buffaloes are a variety of the Indian water-buffalo, they are much finer beasts in appearance and far wilder in their ways. They are of two sorts, "sacred" and "ordinary", but you can hardly tell which is which by looking at them. The division would seem to be mainly a matter of personal selection, even though in the Toda mythology the sacred buffaloes were created in the beginning by On, one of the chief Toda divinities, while the ordinary buffaloes were made by his wife. But the two sorts are treated very differently. The sacred ones are cared for by men specially chosen and trained—a kind of holy milkmen—and their milking, etc., is done in special dairies and surrounded by an air of sanctity. The ordinary buffaloes, on the other hand, are looked after by "ordinary" men, and there is nothing special about it.

Taking the ordinary buffaloes first, the daily routine is simple. The buffaloes are kept at night in pens which are walled like the Toda villages. On rising in the morning, the men emerge from their huts and greet the sun with a gesture made with the bared right arm raised to the face. They open the gate of the pen, and the great beasts lumber out to the accustomed milking-place. The milking is done by a man or a boy—never by a woman—and at the same time other men will be churning the milk drawn on the previous evening. This is done inside the hut, and the milk is poured into an earthenware vessel and stirred vigorously by a bamboo stick. Milking over, the buffaloes are driven to their grazing-ground, where they stay till evening, when they make their way back of their own to be milked again. By the time this is done it will be getting dark. The buffaloes are taken back to their pen and shut up safely for the night. In each hut the lamp is lighted and is saluted by the men with the same gesture as when saluting the sun in the morning. The people take their meal, after which the door is made fast, the lamp is put out, and they all go to their rest.

When we come to the sacred buffaloes, we are confronted with a variety of procedures, an elaborate terminology, and a complicated classification of occupations. For there are different classes of sacred buffaloes, and each gives its name to a particular kind of dairy with its own specialized ritual. As already stated, milking takes place in a special dairy, one for each village. Typically, this consists of two rooms, and only the dairyman may enter the inner one and perform his dairying operations there. He is the nearest approach to a priest that the Todas have, and his life is regulated by custom. In the lowest grade of dairy—the least sacred, that is—he may be a villager who has been given the job because no one else was available, and he will be paid a small wage and given a couple of cloaks a year and the loan of a buffalo for the use of his family. Usually he sleeps in the dairy, but he may spend a night as often as he likes with his wife in the village, or with another woman. The ritual part of his duties may be nothing more than the ceremonial greeting in the morning, and a prayer in the evening for the welfare of the dairy and of its buffaloes.

Considerably higher in the social scale is the *wursol*, who is in charge of a dairy to which buffaloes of a greater degree of sanctity are attached. The Todas, it should be explained, are divided into two quite distinct groups known as the Tartharol and the Teivaliol, and a wursol in a Tartharol dairy must be a Teivali, and vice versa. He may be married, but if his wife belongs to the same group as himself he must forgo all intercourse with her as long as he holds his position in the dairy. He is given rather more clothing than the lower-grade dairyman. No ordinary person is allowed to touch him. He must wash his hands before starting work in the morning, bow in reverence before he crosses the threshold of his dairy, touch the dairy vessels with ceremonial gestures, recite a prayer when lighting his lamp and shutting up the buffaloes for the night, and "feed the bells", that is, give a smear of buttermilk to the bells which hang in the dairy.

At the top of the scale is the *palol,* who has charge of a number of dairies belonging to a clan. When he rises, he must wash not only his hands but his face, rinse out his mouth, and tie up his hair. He has more salutations to make, more prayers, more ritual touchings. He must not be touched by an ordinary Toda, and is approached with great reverence. He must not be married, but he is not expected to remain without women in his life, provided they keep out of the dairy.

After he has held office for a certain number of years he is required to perform a ceremony of a very peculiar kind. He names a woman from the clan to which his dairy belongs, and on a day that is appointed she is bathed, dressed in her best clothes, and adorned with all her ornaments, and sent to meet him in a glade in the forest. Sexual intercourse takes place, and the woman returns to her home in the village. But the *palol* remains, completely naked, in the wood until sunset, when he bathes in a stream, dresses, and goes back to his dairy. A remarkable feature of this performance is that it takes place in the daytime, which would normally be regarded as most immoral. But in all matters of sexual behaviour the Todas are very out of the ordinary.

As a rule, they marry very young, and usually to a cousin. The boy is taken to see his intended bride at her village, and makes her a wedding-gift of a small article of clothing. This gift is repeated year after year until the time comes for the couple to set up house together in the boy's village, which is generally when the girl is fifteen or sixteen. But some years before this she will have been deprived of her virginity by a man specially hired for the purpose and chosen for his strong physique and who belongs to any clan but the girl's. "This must take place before puberty," wrote W. H. R. Rivers in his classic account of the Todas, "and it seemed that there were few things regarded as more disgraceful than that this ceremony should be delayed until after this period. It might be a subject of reproach and abuse for the remainder of the woman's life, and it was even said that men might refuse to marry her if this ceremony had not been performed at the proper time."

Another extraordinary feature of Toda marriage is that when a girl marries she marries not one man only but all the brothers the man may have. From all accounts, the arrangement works very well. The brothers live together with their wife in the same house, and share her favours according to an agreed time-table. There are no feelings of jealousy, and disputes are almost unknown. When the woman becomes pregnant, the eldest brother among the co-husbands performs a queer little ceremony, in which he presents her with a small imitation bow and arrow, which is taken as a formal acknowledgment of parenthood. But the other brothers are all equally regarded as fathers of the coming child, and the responsibilities of parenthood are shared between them on equal terms.

From time to time observers have suggested that polyandry among the Todas is on the decline, since they have come across instances in which the brothers in a joint establishment had more than one wife between them. But on closer examination it has generally been found that even in these cases none of the husbands has a wife to himself, but they all hold the women in common.

In most of these polyandrous unions the husbands are "own" brothers, i.e., sons of the same mother, but in a few cases they are "clan brothers", i.e., they only belong to the same clan and are of the same generation. Sometimes the clan-brothers dwell in different villages, in which case the wife spends a month with each in turn.

Wherever polyandry has been practised, there, too, will generally be found the practice of female infanticide. The Todas afford no exception. They are said to have got rid of unwanted girl babies from time immemorial until quite recently, although they indignantly deny that it is still done. Not that they see anything particularly wrong in the custom, especially when they have been hard pressed to make a living. It has been suggested, however, that they have sometimes practised it in order to keep down the number of women, since under polyandry it is no longer necessary or even desirable that the number of the sexes should roughly balance.

One way of keeping their numbers under control was to place the baby girl just in front of the buffalo-pen, so that when the gates were opened in the morning she would be trampled to death. Another has been to drown the child in a jar of buffalo-milk; and a third, to get some old women to stifle her for a small consideration.

Not only are the Todas polyandrous, but their morals are said to be decidedly lax. Marriage as an institution is not taken very seriously among the dairy-folk. Wives have been often transferred from their husbands or group of husbands in return for a number of buffaloes. A man will take his wife to her new husband, accept delivery of the agreed number of buffaloes, take some slight refreshment that may be offered, and then return home, leaving his wife behind. A woman is not expected to be content with the man or men who are her husbands; to take a lover in addition is looked upon as the most natural thing in the world. If a man should grudge the use of his wife to a neighbour, he would be condemned by society as an unreasonable boor.

Furthermore, extra-marital unions are very common. Thus a woman may live with a man as though she were his wife, but any children born to them will be legally the children of the woman's husband, or of some other male member of her clan. More usually, the man visits the woman at her husband's house by arrangement, and with his permission, which may have been granted out of good-neighbourliness or something more tangible.

From this it will be seen that a Toda woman may have several recognized lovers as well as several husbands, and she may also indulge in intercourse with any male who happens to attract her wandering fancy, or who may make it worth her while. Among these promiscuous contacts are to be numbered the dairyman-priests of certain grades.

As against this sexual liberty, a wife may be put away by her husband with the greatest of ease: she may be divorced for being a fool, or for not doing what her husband bids her. But a man is not entitled to divorce his wife simply because she has proved barren. Not that this is likely to cause him much concern, since all he has to do is to take another wife—or if all the women are "booked", arrange to have a share in somebody else's.

Chapter 17

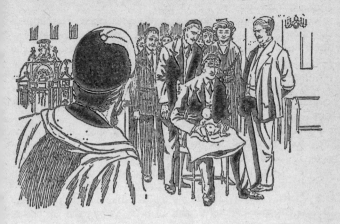

The Mark of a Jew

IN the first of the Bible books we are told that the Lord appeared unto Abraham and instructed him that "Every man child among you shall be circumcised", and that "in the self-same day as God had said unto him" Abraham "took Ishmael his son, and all that were born in his house, and all that were bought with his money, every male among the men of Abraham's house; and circumcised the flesh of their foreskin."

This was not the first appearance of circumcision in human history, however. It had already been practised by other peoples for a very long time indeed—for thousands of years if, as has been argued from surviving evidences of the Old Stone Age, some at least of the men of the Magdalenian culture were circumcised. It was practised by the ancient Egyptians as far back as the Fourth Dynasty, or 3000 B.C., and probably long before that. The ceremony is clearly portrayed on a temple at Thebes, and it is said that most of the male mummies which have been examined are found to have been circumcised. Herodotus states that: "Other men leave their private parts as they are formed by nature, except those who have learnt otherwise from them, but the Egyptians are circumcised." Some authorities have questioned Herodotus's assertion as being too sweeping, and have argued that only the sons of priests and others specially concerned with the sacred mysteries were so treated. But there is no reason to doubt Herodotus's further statement, that the Phoenicians and Syrians of Palestine learnt the practice from their intercourse with the Egyptians, and the Ethiopians might have done so also.

While it is not unreasonable to suppose that the Egyptians may have inherited the practice from their Palaeolithic ancestors, circumcision is known among many peoples which cannot be suspected of communication with Egypt. We meet with it among many of the native tribes of central and southern Africa, especially among the Kaffirs and including the Bechuanas and the Zulus, and likewise among the Bushmen, Hottentots, and Pygmies. It was in use in some form among the ancient civilizations of Central America, and is still practised among some of the primitive tribesfolk of South America. It is found in Madagascar, in many of the islands of the Pacific, including the New Hebrides, New Caledonia, and Fiji, and also among several tribes of aborigines in Australia, especially in New South Wales.

Throughout the world of Islam, circumcision is general, and this notwithstanding it is not a positive precept and is not mentioned in the Koran. It was practised by the Arabs long before Mohammed's time, however, and it may be presumed that the Prophet did not think it necessary to enjoin something which was already so well established. Among Moslems of the present, circumcision is usually performed on boys between their sixth and twelfth years. The other great Semitic people, the Jews, among whom the rite is an absolute obligation, are unique in performing it in infancy.

Since its origins are lost in the mists of prehistory, it is impossible to determine the reasons that first led to the adoption of what is, on the face of it, so strange a form of bodily mutilation. Many reasons have been adduced, but none is beyond dispute, and it may well be that different motives were in operation in different places and at different times.

Some anthropologists have maintained that circumcision was originally instituted on sanitary or hygienic grounds, but while it may not be unreasonable to suppose that Moses and Mohammed were concerned to teach rules of health, it is improbable, to say the least, that the people who performed the operations thousands of years earlier ever gave a thought to such things. From what their midden-heaps have disclosed, Stone Age man lived in squalor and was happy enough in his dirt.

Another explanation that has been advanced is that circumcision may constitute a prophylactic against certain forms of disease. As early as the first century of our era, the Alexandrian Jewish philosopher Philo declared that the practice was undertaken "to prevent a very serious illness that is difficult to cure, to wit, carbuncles". At the present time there may be found doctors who assert that a circumcised male organ is less liable to cancer than one left in the state of nature—but other doctors are not slow to point out that this form of cancer is a rather uncommon occurrence. On the other hand, cancer of the cervix, or mouth of the womb, is not rare among women, and medical advocates of male circumcision have adduced statistics purporting to prove that cancer of the cervix is not usually found among Jewish and Moslem women whose husbands have been circumcised. The belief sometimes expressed, that circumcision removes or at least considerably reduces the risks of venereal infection, is authoritatively stated to be without any foundation in fact. Germs are just not able to discriminate. . . .

On the whole, current medical opinion would seem to discount the sanitary and medical advantages that have been claimed for circumcision, even though the practice may be recommended in certain cases.

Still pursuing the question of origins, a possible answer may lie in the field of magico-religious ideas. Among some primitive peoples, circumcision may have been intended to propitiate the tribal god or spirit by the effusion of blood, so that he or it might be induced by the sacrifice of a part of the body to spare the whole. Perhaps some such idea as this lies behind the archaic tale contained in the fourth chapter of the book of *Exodus*, which relates how Zipporah, Moses's Midianitish wife, "took a sharp stone and cut off the foreskin of her son, and cast it at his feet, and said, Surely a bloody husband art thou to me". Moses (it has been suggested) had not been circumcised and had therefore incurred the anger of

Yahweh (Jehovah), the god of the Israelites; the penalty of his neglect was death, but by circumcising the son in place of her husband Zipporah made a symbolic reparation to the offended deity.

Then there is the very widespread belief that circumcision is an essential preliminary to the successful performance of marital functions, since (so it is held) it not only facilitates intercourse but promotes fertility. This is another of the reasons listed by Philo all those many centuries ago. "Nations with circumcised males teem with fertility," he wrote; "they are the most prolific of the races of mankind."

One more possible explanation is perhaps the most likely. This is that circumcision is to be regarded as a ritual tribal mark or badge. This view is supported by several considerations. In the first place, not only among the Jews but also among the Egyptians and most other circumcising peoples the uncircumcised are regarded by the circumcised with feelings of contempt, as "unclean", i.e., as aliens from the tribe and its worship. As Professor Sollas expressed it, "the Egyptians despised the Jews as an uncircumcised people; and the Jews, when they had acquired the rite, the Philistines; while at the present day, 'uncircumcised dog' is one of the flowers of speech attributed to the Mohammedan in addressing a Christian." Then among peoples who do not practise circumcision we find analogous tribal marks, such as filing and removing the teeth, special tattooings, and in some cases mutilations of the sexual organs even more drastic than circumcision—semi-castration and the like. Finally, with most peoples, circumcision is performed at the age of puberty. By its means the youth becomes a man; he is formally admitted into the ranks of the adult males, receives all the rights and privileges attached to this position, and in particular is given permission to marry. For the first time, he becomes a fully-invested member of the tribe, capable of taking part in its religious and other functions. As such, it is felt that he should wear the distinguishing badge of his tribe and people.

While circumcision has been practised among many peoples, at very various stages of culture, throughout the centuries, its present-day interest and importance largely derives from the fact that it is so distinctive a part of the Jewish faith.

The origin of the rite among the Hebrews or Israelites, the

progenitors of the Jews, is described in the chapter of *Genesis* (xvii) already quoted. Circumcision was instituted as a visible and certain sign of the "covenant" established between Yahweh (Jehovah) and Abraham, the "father" of the Hebrew people. The practice was continued by the "Children of Israel" when they were in Egypt, but it would seem to have fallen into abeyance in the course of the years of wandering in the wilderness after the Exodus, and had to be re-instituted by Joshua. It is expressly enjoined in the Levitical code. Only in one period of Jewish history does there seem to have been something in the nature of a revolt against the obligation, and that was in the 2nd century B.C. when Palestine was under the rule of Antiochus Epiphanes, and such was the prestige and attraction of the Greek culture that he brought with him, that many young Jews fell away from the faith and practice of their fathers and provided themselves with artificial foreskins, so that they would not be so conspicuous when exercising nude in the gymnasia with their Gentile friends. This was shortlived, however, since the reaction against this and other Graecizing ways was so great that the Maccabees were able to launch their eventually successful revolt. Circumcision was reinstituted as an essential rite among Jews, and so it has remained until this day.

When Christianity arose it was a Jewish sect, and it might well have remained nothing more if some of the Apostles had had their way. For years there was a conflict of opinion between the circumcisers led by Peter, and those led by Paul who urged that circumcision should not be insisted upon in the case of Gentile converts. By this relaxation the way was opened for Christianity to develop into a world religion.

The Jewish Torah—the Mosaic Law, contained in the Pentateuch—prescribes that every Jewish male child shall be circumcised on the eighth day after birth. This is the rule even when the eighth day falls on the Sabbath. If it be not possible to perform the rite on the eighth day because the child is sick, it is postponed until the end of the seven days after he is declared cured from his sickness. The obligation of seeing that the act is done, and at the proper time, falls on the father; and if the father wilfully neglects his duty, the Jewish court has the right to step in and order that the rite shall be performed, even though the father should object. A Jew who, for whatever reason, has not been circumcised in infancy, is obliged to have it performed on himself as soon as he reaches maturity.

In Biblical times, the operation was performed by the mother, and it may still be done by a woman, or even a child. Every Jew may perform it, provided he has received the necessary training, but it is usually performed nowadays by a professional circumciser known as a *mohel*. In days past it was carried out in the house of the parents, but it has long been the general rule that the synagogue shall be the place. In addition to the mohel, the actual operator, there is customarily involved another man called the *sandek* or "godfather", and it is considered to be an honour to be selected for this post.

As performed by Mohammedans, circumcision is a fairly simple matter, so simple that it is commonly performed by a barber; only the foreskin is cut off, and the glans remains covered. The Jewish practice is much more radical, since not only is the foreskin removed but the membrane which remains is torn or cut, so as to uncover the glans completely.

When the parties have assembled in the synagogue, the child is carried in, usually in the arms of the sandek's wife, and handed to the mohel, who places it in a chair—"Elijah's Chair"—next to his own. The congregation meanwhile repeats the greeting contained in the 118th Psalm: "Blessed be he that cometh in the name of the Lord." The mohel then recites certain prescribed passages of Scripture, after which, having taken the child in his lap, he pronounces the benediction: "Blessed art Thou, O Lord our God, King of the Universe, Who hast sanctified us by Thy commandments, and hast enjoined us to perform the commandment of circumcision." Now the child is placed upon a pillow resting upon the lap of the sandek, and the mohel exposes the parts by removing the garments, etc., and instructs the sandek how to hold the child during the operation.

This is in three parts. In the first, called the *Milah*, the mohel grasps the prepuce between the thumb and index finger of his left hand, drawing it from the glans, and slips over it a small wooden shield, specially designed for the purpose. Then with a knife, also of special shape, he excises the foreskin with one sweep.

Now is the second stage, known as the *Periah*. The mohel seizes the inner lining of the prepuce with the thumb-nail (which will have been suitably trimmed beforehand) and index finger of each hand, and tears it so that he can roll it fully back over the glans, thus exposing the latter completely. This is done because otherwise a new foreskin might grow in course of time; but another reason is sometimes given, that it is to prevent the adoption of any such disguise as the young Jews in Antiochus Epiphanes's time are said to have adopted.

The third stage is called the *Mezizah*. Traditionally, it consists of the mohel taking some wine in his mouth and applying his lips to the wound, exerting suction, and then expelling the mixture of blood and wine into a bowl made ready for the purpose. But in view of the opposition made against this procedure on hygienic grounds, it is now common practice for the mohel to apply to the spot a specially designed glass cylinder with a compressed mouthpiece, by means of which the suction is effected. In either case, the operation may have to be repeated several times until the bleeding is stopped. Then a dressing is applied, and remains in place for several days, by which time the wound has generally healed up completely.

While among Jews it is rare indeed to find a man who has not been circumcised in infancy as the Torah prescribes, a man who is a Jew by birth is fully a Jew even though the rite has not been performed in his case. There are "reformed" congregations in Jewry, especially in the United States, in which circumcision is no longer insisted upon, and in some quarters its abolition has been urged in the case of adult converts.

One point should be made, that there is nothing sacramental about the Jewish rite of circumcision. Another is, that the Jews are exceptional in that with them it is not an initiation ceremony: all other peoples who practise it in the modern world do so as a puberty rite.

Analogous with male circumcision is that of females, by which is usually meant the removal of the clitoris. Strabo in the first century of our era reported the practice of female circumcision in Arabia and Egypt, and the English Arabic scholar E. W. Lane referred to it in his *Manners and Customs of the Modern Egyptians* (1836) as being performed among Egyptians, both Moslems and Coptic Christians. It has been reported from the sheikhdoms of the Persian Gulf, and in some parts of Africa, more especially along the east coast. A

very full account of female circumcision as practised among
the native people of Kenya will be found in *Facing Mount
Kenya: The Tribal Life of the Gikuyu* (1938), by Mr. Jomo
Kenyatta, who in 1964 became the first President of inde-
pendent Kenya.

Various reasons have been advanced for it. One is that it is
intended to reduce the sexual sensitivity of the woman, so as
to make her more submissive to the rule of one man, her
husband. Another is that it is to match the male mutilation
with a female one. A third would see in it a kind of guaran-
tee of a bride's virginity. We are on much firmer ground when
we recognize that it is an initiation ceremony, through which
a girl becomes a full member of the tribe, just as her brother
is made a full member by the corresponding rite of male
circumcision.

Chapter 18

The Passion Play of the Moslem Martyrs

Mention "Passion Play", and most people will probably think of Oberammergau, where since 1633 a dramatic representation of the Passion of Jesus Christ has been performed by bands of devout peasants. But there is another Passion Play which dates from much farther back in history, and belongs not to Christianity but to the great rival faith of Mohammedanism, or Islam.

This Mohammedan Passion Play—and here we may be reminded that "Passion" comes from the Latin word meaning "to suffer"—is performed each year in India, Persia, and other countries of the East; and while it cannot compare with the ordered and beautiful simplicity of the Oberammergau performances, it is yet deeply impressive and arouses the most heartfelt feelings in those who participate in or behold it.

To trace the origin of the Mohammedan Passion Play we have to go back to the time of the Prophet Mohammed some thirteen centuries ago. When Mohammed died at Medina in

A.D. 632 there was much concern about the appointment of
the man who should succeed him as Caliph or Commander
of the Faithful. Of the possible candidates, the nearest of kin
to Mohammed was his cousin Ali, who was recognized as the
bravest and most faithful of his followers and who was, moreover, the husband of Fatima, the Prophet's favourite daughter.
Mohammed himself had awarded Ali the surname of "the
Lion of God", but it was generally agreed that while valiant
on the field of battle, Ali was mild and forebearing and weak
in counsel. The exigencies of the moment demanded a strong
character at the helm, and in the circumstances Ali was
passed over, and the staunch old veteran Abu Bekr was given
the appointment.

The same thing happened two years later, when Abu Bekr
died, and again in A.D. 644 when Othman became Caliph in
succession to the murdered Omar. Then in A.D. 656 Othman
was assassinated in his turn, and now the claims of Ali were
once again canvassed. By this time, however, he was in middle age and had lost whatever ambition he had once had. He
mournfully shook his head when the notables pressed the
office upon him, but at length his objections were overcome.
Ali ruled for four years only, until A.D. 660, when he was
stabbed to the heart by a Moslem fanatic when he was at
prayers in the mosque at Kufa, near Baghdad. The last words
of the "Bayard of Islam" were a prayer of forgiveness for his
assassin.

Ali left behind him two sons, Hasan and Hosein, who were
now in their middle thirties. The people of Arabia chose
Hasan as their leader, but most of the Moslem world rallied
to Muawiya of Damascus, and after a mere six months of
struggle Hasan retired into private life at Medina, where he
died in A.D. 669—by poison administered by his wife, if the
account given by some writers is to be believed. Hosein remained as pretender to the throne, but Muawiya felt that he
had little to fear from him and treated him with kindness.
Then Muawiya died in the spring of A.D. 680, and his son
Yezid reigned in his stead. Now the opportunity for revolt
seemed to have come, and Hosein boldly laid claim to the
succession, as the indubitable heir of the Prophet. But the
rebellion was carried on in the half-hearted manner characteristic of the family of Ali, and Hosein was overtaken by
Yezid's troops at Kerbela when on the way from Mecca to

join his adherents in Syria, and perished with seventy-two of his followers.

From that time to the present the world of Islam has been divided into two great sects, the Shiahs and the Sunnites. The Shiahs refuse to recognize Ali's predecessors as lawful Caliphs or *Imams*, and pay to him and his sons honours hardly inferior, if at all, to those paid to the memory of the Prophet himself. Their strength lies chiefly in Persia and Afghanistan, but they are strongly represented among the Moslems of Pakistan and India. The Sunnites have been chiefly represented by the Turks, and for hundreds of years the Sultan of Constantinople was recognized as Caliph by the majority of Mohammedans, although his claim was contested by the Shereef of Mecca, the ancestor of the royal house which reigned in Mecca and Damascus up to our own time.

The Mohammedan Passion Play is a distinctively Shiah celebration, in which the tragic events surrounding the fall of Ali's family are recalled and represented in the most striking fashion. It is performed during the first ten days of the first month of the Mohammedan year—the month of Moharram, as it is styled. Since the Mohammedan calendar is a lunar one, this month falls at different seasons of the year, but this makes no difference to the celebration. The ten days are kept as a sacred and solemn festival, during which the Faithful are expected to be particularly liberal in their almsgiving and to concentrate their thoughts as much as possible on the tragic happenings that are commemorated in the scenes of the Passion Play. There are between thirty and forty scenes altogether, and the whole may be performed at least once and perhaps twice on every one of the ten days. The last day, called the Ashura, is the most important of all, since it was on this day that the sainted Hosein was "martyred".

For centuries the text of the Passion Play was handed down by word of mouth, but in 1879 Sir Lewis Pelly published an English version of the text, based on the oral traditions that he had collected in the course of long service in the East. This was prefaced by a lengthy explanation and description by Dr. Birdwood, concerned in the main with the procedure adopted in India.

While many Moslem families keep the Moharram in the privacy of their own homes, in which case the Play is not performed but read aloud in instalments to the assembled mem-

bers by the head of the family, there is set up as a general
rule what is called a *Tazia*. This word signifies "grief", and the
thing itself is a small model, made of every variety of material
according to the wealth and fancy of the family, of the
mausoleum which was erected at Kerbela, in what is now
Iraq, over the remains of Hosein. (To this day Kerbela is
one of the most sacred spots in the world of Islam, hardly
second only to Mecca, and it has been the custom for hundreds of years for pious Shiahs to make pilgrimage to the
place, many of them carrying the bones of their relatives for
burial in the sacred soil.) These tazias may be homemade or
they may be purchased from manufacturers. In the houses of
the wealthier Shiahs they are fixtures, beautifully made of
costly materials, decorated with gold and silver and inlaid
work. The poorer Shiahs will have to content themselves with
tazias specially made for the occasion, constructed out of lath
and plaster, and tricked out in mica and tinsel, or they may
be made only of paper.

A week before the new moon of the Moharram, a space is
enclosed in which the tazia is erected. Then at the first sight
of the moon, a spade is thrust into the ground, marking the
place where shortly after a pit is dug. In this a bonfire is
lighted, which is kept burning throughout the ten days of the
celebration. Those people whose accommodation is too
cramped to allow of an enclosure, or are too poor to afford
even the smallest tazia, still manage to have a Moharram fire,
even though this may be nothing more than a night-light
floating at the bottom of an earthen pot or basin sunk in the
ground. The origin of this custom is obscure, but the "fires"
are regarded by the common people, Hindu as well as
Moslem, with superstitious reverence. All day long, passers-
by stop and make their vows over them, and all night long the
crowds dance round them and leap through the flames, and
scatter about burning brands snatched from them. At the
same time the tazias are also illuminated; and shining through
the dark the richer erections make a splendid showing.

In the cities there are buildings specially designed for the
performance of the Passion Play. These are called in India
"Imambaras", and they may be large enough to hold some
thousands of spectators. Like mosques they are usually square,
with a domed roof, but unlike mosques they are superbly
decorated within. The floor is carpeted, the walls are covered

with mirrors, costly banners are arranged here and there, the reading-desk or pulpit is decorated, and after dark innumerable electric lights are switched on in the elaborate chandeliers that hang from the ceiling.

In the centre of the building is the stage, so everything is done in full view of the audience, who may even help the actors up and down the steps. The performers are men and boys, and as a rule women have no part except as spectators. Stage properties are of the simplest, and there is little attempt to adopt proper costume, though the performers may put on their best clothes and such jewels as they possess, in order to do honour to the distinguished personages they are called upon to represent. "The power of the actors," wrote Count Gobineau in his account of the Persian performances, "is in their genuine sense of the seriousness of the business they are engaged in." This was specially true of the younger members of the cast. "Nothing is more touching," wrote Gobineau, "than to see these little things of three or four years old, dressed in black gauze frocks, with large sleeves, and having on their heads small, round black caps, embroidered with silver and gold, kneeling beside the body of the actor who represents the martyr of the day, embracing him, and with their little hands covering themselves with chopped straw for sand, in sign of grief." They did not consider themselves to be acting; they were not distracted by the audience and were not shy, but went through their prescribed parts with the utmost attention and seriousness, while the beholders watched them with emotions of the liveliest satisfaction and sympathy.

The chief director of the Play is called the Oostad, and this master of the ceremonies is always on the stage, with the "book" in his hand, ready to give the actors their cue, and if needs be to take a part in the performance himself. Sometimes he will turn to the audience and invite them to note some particular point or to let themselves go in expressing their feelings.

The Play takes ten days to perform in its entirety, and whether it is performed in the courtyard of a private house or in the specially constructed hall, it is a most solemn occasion, a deeply moving experience. As the spectators swarm into the "theatre", they will be laughing and talking like a crowd at a fair, but at a signal—the beat of a drum perhaps—the hubbub ceases, the people take their places, and complete silence falls.

Then comes the voice of the director: "O ye Faithful, give ear! Open your hearts to the wrongs and sufferings of His Highness the Imam Ali, the Vicegerent of the Prophet, and let your eyes flow with tears as a river, for the woes that befell their Highnesses the beloved Imams Hasan and Hosein, the foremost of the bright youths of Paradise."

For a while the deep silence is preserved, and the audience sway to and fro and all together. Then suddenly a stifled sob may be heard, or a cry, followed by more sobbing and crying, and the swaying becomes a violent agitation, all the people rising to their feet and smiting their breasts, and then raising the rhythmic wail: "Ya Ali! Ai Hasan! Ai Hosein! Ai Hasan! Ai Hosein, Hosein Shah!" The wailing gathers force, but when it shows signs of becoming ungovernable the performers launch out into a metrical version of the play, and the audience settle themselves to listen.

The first act is introductory, and it must appear somewhat strange that it should be a representation of the Bible story of Joseph and his brethren. But a Mohammedan twist is given to it, for the Angel Gabriel is shown visiting the patriarch Jacob and consoling him for the loss of his son with the intimation that at some time in the future there would be a much more distressing case of bereavement. Jacob is inclined to doubt whether there can ever be a case as sad as his, and in order to convince him otherwise Gabriel calls a troop of angels to perform a Passion Play before the old man, in which the martyrdom of Hasan and Hosein is revealed in all its terrible details.

After this skilful introduction, the scene shifts to Medina, the city of the Prophet, and into the home of Ali and Fatima. Little Hosein is sitting on his mother's knee; she is combing his hair, the comb is caught in a knot, and a hair is pulled out. The little fellow starts, and Fatima soothes him fondly. Whereupon an angel makes his appearance and gently chides her. "A hair falls from the child's head, and you weep! What would you do if you knew what fate awaits him, the countless wounds with which his body will be pierced, the agony that will rend your soul?" Shortly after, the two little boys are shown playing in the garden with their playmates, and then some big bad boys come upon the scene and throw stones, and Hosein is struck on the temples and falls to the ground, senseless. At which the tormentors turn and flee. And who are they? The audience in the Imambara shudder, for they know without being told that the rough boys will grow up to become the actual slayers of Hosein!

The story moves on, as act follows act. Mohammed dies, and is succeeded by Abu Bekr. Fatima dies, and Ali is assassinated. Then Hasan is shown on his death-bed, imploring his brother to take no steps to discover who it is that has wrought his death, since it is incumbent on them to "bear no malice, but to forgive". As Hasan the Good breathes his last, the audience sob and groan.

Now attention is concentrated on the fortunes of Hosein. To his house in Medina come messengers from the partisans of the Ali faction in Kufa, urging him to come to them and raise the banner of Commander of the Faithful. Against the advice of his best friends he agrees, and sets out, accompanied by his wives and children, and a few score of horse and foot. As soon as Yezid at Damascus hears of it, he despatches a force of some four thousand men to intercept the pretender. When he was almost in sight of his destination Hosein is stopped, and although honourable terms of surrender are made to him, he decides to fight it out. A touching act in the play, one that is styled "The Family of the Tent", shows Hosein urging his friends and relatives to make their escape to a place of safety. But not a soul among them will leave him; all insist on sharing his fate, whatever may befall. "Nay, we will die with thee!" they say, and Hosein with tears running down his cheeks murmurs, "May Allah recompense you!" The little band make preparations for defence, and Hosein says: "At any rate, if die we must, then we will die like heroes."

The battle opens, and there is never any doubt of the outcome: when evening is drawing on, scarce one of Hosein's little army remains alive. Gibbon in his *Decline and Fall* has an excellent passage on the battle of Kerbela. "Alone, weary, and wounded, Hosein seated himself at the door of his tent. As he tasted a drop of water, he was pierced in the mouth with a dart; and his son and nephew, two beautiful youths, were killed in his arms. He lifted his hands to heaven; they were full of blood; and he uttered a funeral prayer for the living and the dead. In a transport of despair his sister issued from the tent, and adjured the general of the Cufians, that he would not suffer Hosein to be murdered before his eyes. A tear trickled down his venerable beard, and the boldest of his soldiers fell back on every side as the dying hero threw himself among them. The remorseless Shamer, a name detested by the faithful, reproached their cowardice, and the grandson of Mohammed was slain with three-and-thirty strokes of lances and swords."

At the conclusion of his account, Gibbon writes, "in a distant age and climate the tragic scene of the death of Hosein will awaken the sympathy of the coldest reader". How much more then must be its effect on the crowd gathered in the Imambara? All are in a paroxysm of grief, and when the body of the fallen prince is trampled on by his foes, and still more when the actor goes through the motions of cutting off his head, there are cries of horror, shrieks and groans. So the Passion Play comes to its end, when an aged Mussulman is represented as saying, as the gory trophy is borne past him, "On those lips have I seen the lips of the Apostle of Allah!"

Now the tazias are taken up and carried away to the Moslem cemetery, as representing the "plain of Kerbela", where they are to be solemnly interred. A great funeral procession is formed, in which a number of tazias and their attendants join. The arms and banners of Hasan and Hosein may be carried aloft, and sometimes these are followed by "Hosein's horse". Then may come bands of horsemen carrying lances, and models of Ali's tomb, and of Mohammed's at Medina. Behind stream crowds of excited men, women, and children, shouting, jostling, surging through the streets in a wave of passionate emotion.

In Bombay the "plain of Kerbela" is not the cemetery but the water-front. As Dr. Birdwood described it, the procession at length found its way on to the Esplanade. "The confused uproar of its advance can be heard a mile away, and long before the procession takes definite shape through the clouds of dust and incense which move before it. It moves onward in an endless line of flashing swords, blasoned suns and waving banners, State umbrellas, thrones and canopies, and towering above all the tabuts (or tazias), framed of the most elegant shape of Saracenic architecture, glittering in silver and green and gold, and rocking backwards and forwards in high air, like great ships upon a rolling sea, with the rapid movement of the hurrying crowd, beating drums, chanting hymns, and shrieking, 'Ya Ali! Ai Hasan, Ai Hosein, Hosein Shah!

drowned, drowned in blood, in blood; all three fallen prostrate, dead! Ya Ali! Ai Hasan, Ai Hosein, Hosein Shah!', until the whole welkin seems to ring and pulsate with the terrific wail.

"Ever and anon a band of naked men, drunk with opium or hemp, and painted like tigers or leopards, makes a rush through the ranks of the procession, leaping furiously, and brandishing their swords and spears and clubs in the air. The route, however, is strictly defined by a line of native policemen, and the infuriated zealots are suddenly brought to a halt, wheel round, and retreat back into the body of the procession, howling and shrieking like a flight of baffled fiends.

"So, for a mile in length, the rout advances, against the rays of the now declining sun, until the sea is reached, where it spreads out along the beach in a line at right-angles to the 'sacred way' by which it has come across the Esplanade.

"Nothing can be more picturesque than the arrival and break up of the procession in Back Bay. The temporary tabuts are taken out into the bay as far as they can be carried, and abandoned to the waves, into which all the temporary adornments of the permanent tabuts are also thrown. This operation has a wonderfully cooling effect on the mob. Their frantic clamours suddenly cease. In fact, the mourners of Hasan and Hosein, having buried their tabuts in the sea, seize the opportunity to have a good bath; and a little after the sun has finally dropped below the western horizon, the whole of the vast multitude is seen in the vivid moonlight to be slowly and peacefully regathering itself across the wide Esplanade into its homes again, and the Saturnalia into which the last act of the Mystery of Hasan and Hosein has degenerated in India is closed for another year."

Islam is generally regarded as a hard religion, severe and exacting, but, as Matthew Arnold expressed it in one of his essays, the reverence paid to the martyred Ali and his sons, "these saintly self-deniers, these resigned sufferers, who would not strive nor cry", supplies to the great world-religion a tender and pathetic side. "They might attain to nothing," Arnold goes on, "they were too pure, these great ones of the world as by birth they were; but the people, which itself also can attain to so little, loved them all the better on that account, loved them for their abnegation and mildness, felt that they were dear to God, that God loved them, and that they and their lives filled a void in the severe religion of Mohammed. . . . It is a long way from Kerbela to Calvary; but the sufferers of Kerbela hold aloft to the eyes of millions the lesson so loved by the Sufferer of Calvary: 'Learn of me, for I am meek and lowly in heart, and ye shall find rest unto your souls'."

Chapter 19

The Meaning of the Mummy

WHEN Herodotus visited Egypt in about the middle of the fifth century B.C. there were two things that attracted his special attention—her mummies and her pyramids. And still today the things that aroused the old Greek's wonder have not lost their power to attract and to impress. The first inquiry of innumerable visitors to the British Museum is to be directed to "the room where the mummies are", and the tourist's first excursion in the valley of the Nile is to the Pyramids of Gizeh.

The two things—the mummy and the pyramid—are indissolubly connected, for the one and the other illustrate the pathetic attempts made by the ancient Egyptians to preserve the corpses of their most honoured dead from destruction at the hands of men and of time. The body was mummified because it was believed that its preservation was essential if the spirit of the dead man were to have any sort of after-life; and the pyramid was piled over the tomb in which the mummy of the Pharaoh or some other great one lay, in order to keep it safe. This being so, it will be understood that the mummy is older than the pyramid.

The mummy may be regarded as the end-product of embalming, which is defined as the art of preparing dead bodies by the use of aromatic drugs, etc., with a view to preserving them from disintegration and decay. Both terms come from the names of substances commonly used in the process, for "embalming" is derived from the Greek word for balsam, and "mummy" from *mumia*, which is the Arabic for bitumen.

When the Egyptians first adopted mummification is unknown. In *Genesis*, the oldest book in the Bible and one of the oldest books in the world, we read that when Jacob died, "Joseph commanded his servants the physicians to embalm his father," and in the book's last verse that when Joseph died in his turn, "they embalmed him, and he was put in a coffin in Egypt". Now if we assume that Joseph was vizier to one of the pharaohs of the dynasty known as the Hyksos or "Shepherd Kings", this would make his date about 1700 B.C., but even if he flourished, as some scholars maintain, several hundred years later this still has the sound of a very long time ago. And yet there had been pharaohs reigning in Egypt for two thousand years before this. To put it in other words, when Joseph drove past the Pyramids in his chariot he was looking at structures that were already a thousand years old at least—older than the oldest parts of Westminster Abbey as we see them today. And traces of mummification in Egypt have been discovered that date from before the first stone of the first pyramid was put in position.

All the same, the earliest Egyptians known to us did not mummify their dead. In the latter part of the Neolithic or New Stone Age the natives in the Nile valley—or some of them—were in the habit of cutting the heads off their corpses and dismembering them before laying them in shallow pits in the sand—presumably to prevent the dead man from "walking" and making himself a nuisance to the living. We may actually see one of these Neolithic Egyptians, for there he lies in a glass case in the British Museum—a very ancient Egyptian, a man who died more than five thousand years ago. There he lies in air-conditioned warmth—a slim little fellow, brown-skinned and reddish-haired, resting on his left side with his knees doubled up almost to his chin, and his hands placed in front of his face. Round him are pottery vessels in which he had kept his food, his implements and weapons of flint, etc.

This is an instance of natural mummification, since the body has been preserved in this extraordinarily complete fashion by the hot, dry sand in which it was laid those thousands of years ago, and it may well be that the Egyptians got the idea of artificial mummification from just such instances as this. The practice had begun by the time there were kings in Egypt, and at first only kings were mummified. Doubtless there were many experiments that went wrong, innumerable false starts, mistakes without number that resulted in nothing but an abominable mess, before reliable methods were gradually evolved and made into the general practice.

Among the mummies in the British Museum are the remains of one—the legs and part of the trunk—that have been generally regarded as coming from the mummified corpse of Menkaura, the pharaoh who was the builder of the Third Pyramid at Gizeh. These were found with a wooden coffin and a stone sarcophagus in the mummy-chamber of the pyramid; they were dispatched to England in 1838, but the ship was wrecked off Cartagena and the sarcophagus was lost. The fragments of the mummy and the coffin were recovered, but the romantic story has a depressing postscript, for it is now suspected that the human remnants are those of an Arab robber who had penetrated into the tomb and could not find his way out again.

More authentic was a mummy that was preserved in the museum of the London College of Surgeons, until it was destroyed in the "blitz" in the Second World War; this was held to be the oldest perfect mummy in existence, dating from the 5th Dynasty (about 2700 B.C.). Most of the mummies now in the museums date from much later times.

No details of the methods employed by the Egyptian embalmers have been preserved in the literary texts, and this makes Herodotus's account all the more valuable, apart from the fact that it bears all the marks of being based on personal observation. We are given to understand that a man of some standing in the world has just died, and his relations, after the customary demonstrations of grief, have conveyed the corpse to the Egyptian equivalent of our "funeral parlour", where they have explained to them the various methods of embalming and are shown little wooden models, painted in life-like fashion, of what the corpse will look like on completion. They are given three choices, and naturally the director of the establishment explains the most expensive first; then, if needs be, the second and less expensive; and at length, if he be driven to it, the third and cheapest. We may imagine the relatives discussing the matter over the counter, as it were, until the matter is settled, and the embalmers are left to get on with the job—and a nasty, messy, horribly gruesome job it must have been.

Supposing the most expensive method was chosen. First, the brains were removed through the nostrils, in part by the use of an iron hook and in part by the injection of drugs. Then an incision was made in the left side of the corpse, through which the intestines were withdrawn. This incision was made with what Herodotus calls "a sharp Ethiopian stone", i.e., a stone knife in compliance with the ancient belief that a human body should not be cut with metal. But the Egyptians went further than this, holding it an altogether detestable thing to inflict any wound whatever on the body; and another ancient writer states that there was a special cutter appointed to make the incision in the flank for the removal of the intestines, and that as soon as he had performed his office he was pursued with stones and curses by his mates.

To continue with Herodotus's account, "having taken out all the bowels, they cleanse the abdomen and rinse it with palm-wine, and next sprinkle it with pounded perfumes. Then having filled the belly with pure myrrh pounded, and cassia, and other perfumes, they sew it up again; and when they have done this, they steep it in natron, leaving it under for seventy days, for a longer time than this it is not lawful to steep it. At the expiration of the seventy days they wash the corpse, and wrap the whole body in bandages of flaxen cloth, smearing it with gum, which the Egyptians commonly use instead of glue. After this the relations, having taken the body back again, make a wooden case in the shape of a man, and having made it, they enclose the body; and thus, having fastened it up, they store it in a sepulchral chamber, setting it upright against the wall."

Mummies which have been unrolled and examined prove that Herodotus was very well informed. The "bandages", or mummy swathings, were made of flax, as he states; surviving examples vary in length from a few inches to about 15 feet, and in width from two to ten inches. They were applied separately to each limb, and even to each digit, and then, after the arms had been placed in position, were continued over the whole body. Mummies have also been found wrapped in linen sheets several feet square, however, and those of some of the pharaohs of the Middle Empire were covered with hieroglyphic texts taken from the ancient Egyptian scripture known as the "Book of the Dead". As the swathing proceeded, amulets such as the scarab or sacred beetle were inserted, and sometimes a scroll of papyrus, containing chapters from the "Book of the Dead", or a collection of spells, were placed between the legs. To complete the process, a large sheet or shroud was wrapped round the body and tied at head and heels, then more bandages, then another shroud, and so on. Then as regards the cases or coffins in which the mummies were placed, these were to begin with plain wooden boxes, of rectangular shape, but long before Herodotus's time it had become usual for them to be shaped to the contours of the body, gilded and painted, and bearing a portrait on the front of the dead man—again very much as Herodotus described.

This first and most expensive method of embalming cost, according to Diodorus, a talent of silver, which might be represented as between £750 and £1,000 of our money. The second method cost about twenty minae, or about a quarter as much. In this there was no incision in the flank, but the viscera were dissolved by an injection of oil of cedar made through the anus. Having taken steps to prevent this from escaping, the embalmers steeped the corpse in natron for a certain number of days, "and on the last day they let out from the abdomen the oil of cedar which they had before injected, and it has such power that it brings away the intestines and vitals in a state of dissolution; the natron dissolves the flesh, and nothing remains of the body but the skin and the bones". This done, they returned the body to the relatives for them to dispose of as they thought fit, as likely as not placing it in the family tomb.

The third method of embalming was reserved almost exclusively for the bodies of the poorest classes. First, the abdomen was thoroughly washed out with a substance called "syrmaea", and then the corpse was placed in a bath of natron in which it lay steeped for seventy days, after which "they deliver it to be carried away". Only the first of these methods resulted in a mummy properly so called.

So much for the "when" and the "how" of the mummifying process, and now we come to the "why". This is a question that is much more difficult to answer. A number of suggestions have been put forward from time to time, such as that there was a scarcity of fuel in Egypt for the purpose of cremation, and that it would have been inadvisable and even impossible to bury the dead in a soil that was periodically inundated by the waters of the Nile. Such materialistic considerations as these may have played their part, but the consensus of opinion nowadays is that the real reason is much more likely to have lain in the religious conceptions of the Egyptian people, and in particular those associated with the Osiris cult.

According to the ancient legend, Osiris was a king who reigned in the Delta in the long, long ago, and never was there a better. He ruled his people with benevolence and wisdom, taught them how to worship, persuaded them to abandon cannibalism, showed them how to cultivate the soil and how to make grapes into wine; in a word, he converted them from savages into civilized folk. He married his sister Isis—the marriage of brother and sister was a recognized privilege of the gods and god-kings of Egypt—and she, too, played a most notable part in the civilizing process. But Osiris had a twin-brother named Set, who was as bad as Osiris was good. Set was jealous of his brother's fame and achievements, and he conspired his downfall, hoping thereby to obtain his throne and his queen. And at length Set succeeded in his wicked scheming: by a clever stratagem he managed to imprison the god-king in a chest which, nailed down and sealed, was then flung into the Nile.

When Isis heard what had happened, she spent days and nights wandering up and down amid the swamps of the Delta, mournfully seeking the body of her murdered lord. And one day she found it, where the flood waters had deposited it in the branches of an acacia tree. Fearful of Set's vengeance, she buried it in a secret spot in the mud, and then went off to visit her son Horus at Bouto. While she was away, the wicked Set came across the body one night by accident; he recognized it at once, and, in an effort to destroy it for good and all, tore it into fourteen pieces, which he flung to the winds. But Isis, when she returned to the spot and found what Set had done, sought high and low for the bits and pieces of mangled flesh, and succeeded in recovering them all with the exception of the genitals, which the fishes had eaten.

What happened next is variously described. According to the Greek writers who handled the ancient legend, the queen arranged for each piece of the dead king's corpse to be reverently interred at as many places as there were pieces, and over each a shrine was built and entrusted to a band of priests. But the Egyptian accounts have a different ending. They are inspired by the conviction that Isis was a powerful enchantress, one who was able to transform herself at will into any kind of creature and to travel with equal ease through earth and air, fire and water. She was moreover assisted by other members of the divine company who were dispatched to aid her by the Sun-god Ra. Instructed by his mother, the young Horus performed a series of magical rites and ceremonies which had the effect of raising Osiris from the dead and of establishing him as king in Amenti, the realm in "the West" or the Other World—the world which the Egyptians believed to lie somewhere beyond the western desert of the Sahara. These rites constituted the first embalmment, and the body of Osiris became the first mummy.

Henceforth Osiris was, as the Egyptian texts put it, "King of Eternity, Lord of everlastingness, Prince of gods and men, the God of Gods, King of kings, Lord of lords, Prince of princes, the Governor of the World, whose existence is everlasting". He was the God-Man, who had suffered and died and had risen again, and reigned eternally in heaven. And how had all this come about? Through the ritual of mummification that had preserved his flesh and bones and converted his corruptible body into an incorruptible one!

From this conviction it was no great step for the Egyptian intelligence to argue that similar rites performed with the body of a dead man might well have the same happy result. To the Egyptians, Osiris became the god who "made mortal men and women to be born again", who gave them the assurance of a continued life beyond the grave. As Osiris had risen from the grave, so they, too, would rise—always provided that something of their earthly body was preserved to constitute a refuge and an abiding place for the soul. Some such reasoning as this lay behind and beneath the mummifying process; and although we shall never understand the belief in its full meaning, its strange complexity, we may realize enough to appreciate what the Egyptians felt when they went through the messy procedure which produced the mummified figure standing in the sepulchral chamber or encased in lavishly decorated coffin or noble sarcophagus. To them the mummy was not a bundle of rags enclosing a corpse but the embodiment of one who had become, to use their phrase, a "justified Osiris".

"Homage to thee, O my father Osiris!" runs the text on a coffin in one of the British Museum galleries; "Thy flesh suffered no decay, worms touched thee not, thou didst not moulder away, withering came not upon thee, and thou didst not suffer a corruption; and I shall possess my flesh for ever and ever, I shall not crumble away, I shall not wither, I shall not become corruption."

Mummification was carried on in Egypt for much more than four thousand years, and as the centuries passed it was brought within the reach of ever-larger classes of the population. What had been a royal privilege was extended first to the nobles and the wealthy, then to the middle class, and finally to almost all but the hopelessly indigent. It has been estimated that the number of bodies that were mummified was in excess of seven hundred millions, of which by far the greater number still lie hidden beneath the ground. Even after their conversion to Christianity the Egyptians continued to embalm their dead, and to entomb them with the old, time-hallowed ceremonies. But before the end of the fourth century A.D. the art of embalmment had fallen out of general use, even though it was not altogether extinct for two or three hundred years more. And just as the practice had had its rise—if our surmising is correct—in a religious concept, so its abrogation was likewise owing to a theological dogma. The Christian had a firm belief in the resurrection of the body; why, then, go to the trouble and expense of preserving by artificial means a mortal frame which would be reconstituted in every particle when Christ should come in judgment at the Last Day?

When St. Anthony, the "father of Christian monachism" lay dying in his cell in the desert in A.D. 356, he begged his monks (so St. Athanasius tells us in his "life" of the saint), "not to allow any man to take my body and carry it into Egypt, lest, according to the custom that they have there, they embalm me and lay me up in their houses. But dig a grave and bury me therein, and hide my body under the earth. Let these my words be observed carefully by you, and tell no man where you have laid me, until the Resurrection of the Dead, when I shall receive this body without corruption from the Saviour".

Before leaving the subject, it should be said that mummification has been practised in many other parts of the world besides Egypt. This fact is largely responsible for the theory of the "diffusionist" school of anthropologists who, following the lead and inspiration of Professor Elliot Smith, have concluded that Egypt was the primary parent of civilization. It is hard to believe (so the argument runs) that so bizarre and gruesome a practice should have originated independently in so large a number of widely separated countries of the globe. Far more reasonable, surely, is it that, having originated in Egypt, where the religious and intellectual climate was so suitable for its invention, it spread by stages throughout the inhabited world—along the coastlands of the Mediterranean into Europe and North Africa, thence to the Canary Islands, the regions of the Upper Congo and southern Nigeria—then in the other direction to the Persian Gulf, India, Ceylon, Burma and the Malay Archipelago, and thence to New Guinea and across the Torres Straits into Australia. Another stream of influence is supposed to have moved from the Malay Archipelago to the islands of the Pacific, New Zealand, and Tahiti, and eventually across the South Atlantic to Peru, whence it extended to Central America and the north-west coasts of the American continent.

Chapter 20

An Egg for Easter

ONE of the many happy customs associated with Easter is the giving of Easter eggs to children and even to grownups. These are usually very colourful affairs, made of sugar or chocolate, filled with sweets, and tied round with a bright ribbon, and generally they have attached to them a card bearing a message of affectionate greeting. Few of those who give them or who receive them are inclined to inquire into the origin of so pleasant a practice, and most people would be surprised to be told that this is just one of not a few pagan survivals that have been given a Christian dress.

In the religious philosophy of the ancient world, an egg was regarded as not only emblematical of the universe but as the symbol of fertility and of new life, not least of the return of spring after the long sleep of winter. Such was the underlying meaning of the festival kept by the ancient Egyptians at the occasion of the new moon in April, when the people exchanged eggs that had been brightly painted and gilded, in honour of Osiris, the Great God who had been slain but had risen again and in whose train all his worshippers might hope to share in his joyful resurrection. The Persians, the Greeks and Romans and other peoples of antiquity had similar customs, reflecting the same simple joy in the return of hopeful brightness to a gloomy world.

When Christianity triumphed, all the pagan customs came in for severe scrutiny. Some were prohibited on moral grounds or because they were indissolubly connected with the heathen worships, but whenever possible the Church authorities—being men wise in their generation—decided to adopt those practices which were comparatively harmless and yet were so popular with the masses that it would be impolitic to attempt their suppression. The giving of eggs at the springtime festival was one of these, but they were now presented as a symbol of the Risen Christ, and they were dyed red, as emblematic of the blood that had been shed for man's redemption.

Another pagan custom at the springtime celebrations was the partaking of specially prepared cakes. This custom was likewise given a Christian "face-lift", as it were; henceforth the cakes or buns were to be marked with a cross.

At the present time, eggs play but a small part in the Easter celebrations in the Mediterranean countries. In France, Italy, and Spain they are seldom seen. In France confectioners' shops are filled at Easter-time with representations of fish filled with sweetmeats. It is in the countries of northern Europe, Germany in particular, that the Easter egg plays as important a part as it does in Britain. In England the custom can be traced back for many centuries, although in olden days the egg was not an artificial one but a hen's egg that had been hard-boiled and then dyed a bright colour, generally red. Each part of the country had its own variations on the custom. Thus in Chester the eggs were played with as balls in a game on Easter Monday. Among the dour peasantry of Scotland, too, the children were allowed a quota of hard-boiled dyed eggs, which they might roll about, throw to one another, and finally eat.

But as already indicated, there is very much more in the Easter Egg than a childish practice. It is the expression of an age-old instinct, a relic of a stage of culture and intelligence remote in time and vastly different from our own. To come within a mile of understanding it we should realize that men celebrated "easter" for ages prior to what has come to be styled the "first Easter dawn".

To begin with the word itself, "Easter" is generally believed to have been derived from Eastre, who was the goddess of springtime and the dawn in the pantheon of our Anglo-Saxon forefathers. For this scrap of information we are indebted to the monkish chronicler known as the Venerable Bede, who, writing in the early part of the eighth century, must have known quite a number of people who were still pagans. According to some other writers, however, the word comes from the Old English word meaning "rising", which after all is not so very different. Whatever its exact etymology, the word signifies dawning or rising, and it is not at all surprising that it has come to represent the festival in the Christian calendar that commemorates the resurrection of Christ.

Eastre was the last (so far as this country is concerned) of the long line of divinities who have been associated with festivals of springtime. As might be expected, these festivals were most generally celebrated in those lands where there is a recognizable division between the seasons, in the lands of the Mediterranean and the temperate zone as a whole. Wherever spring comes as a revelation of new life bursting out of what has become withered and decayed, wherever the trees stripped by winter gales show fresh leaves, wherever plants sprout and blossom and the young lambs are seen frisking in the fields—there the springtime is an occasion for rejoicing, for thanking whatever gods may be for the grant of a new supply of the good things of life.

Even in the largely urbanized civilizations of today we know when there is a touch of spring in the air, and we are glad. But we no longer notice something which forced itself upon our ancestors of so long ago, the note of *fear*. We know what to expect. We are absolutely sure that spring will come again at the end of winter. But those who were living in the dawn of human life were not so confident. They had so little experience to go on, and they had no means of storing up that experience for their reassurance. When day by day the sun seemed to get cooler and go farther and farther down the sky, they felt a fear that chilled their hearts—that perhaps the sun would forget to come back again, that he would prefer things in the distant quarter of the heavens to which he had removed, and would stay there and never again bring warmth and light to poor mortals shivering in the chilly gloom of their hovels and caves.

Not until the priest-astronomers of Egypt and Babylonia

had through the centuries accumulated a mass of positive evidence did men feel fairly safe. Until then every springtime was something to be profoundly thankful for, something to be welcomed with the most heartfelt rejoicing.

The discovery that the changes in the seasons can be relied upon, and that they owe nothing to anything that human beings can do, was not made until long after there had arisen on the Mediterranean coasts civilizations of an advanced type. For ages men believed—and the priesthoods encouraged them to believe—that the powers responsible were the gods and goddesses whom they served, and these divine beings might be cajoled and persuaded by gifts and prayers and ceremonial to allow springtime to follow winter, and seed-time to turn into harvest. In some of the principal cultures there were dramatic representations which were supposed to remind the gods of what they ought to do, of what their worshippers expected of them, and among these we may note the real marriage of a man and a woman in the fields which awaited the fructifying breath of spring.

In Phoenicia and the adjoining lands of Western Asia and the Aegean Sea the springtime festival was associated with the tragic figure of Adonis, the handsome young god who was loved by Aphrodite, or Venus, the goddess of Love, but one day when he was out hunting he was slain by a wild boar, and with bitter tears the goddess lamented his cruel death.

In another version of the ancient story, the one which was current in Babylonia for many centuries, the young god bears the name of Tammuz, and his lover is Ishtar, or Astarte, the great Mother Goddess who was the embodiment of the reproductive powers of nature. In this version of the tragic idyll, a copy of which is inscribed on a tablet in the British Museum collection of cuneiform texts, Ishtar follows her lover into the Underworld, into the "land without return, into the region of the dead, whose bread is dust, whose food is mud, who see not the light, who dwell in darkness", and boldly demands of Allatu, the grim Queen of the Underworld, that she return Tammuz to the land of the living. But Allatu is unrelenting, and at her behest the venturesome intruder is stripped of her jewels and ornaments and her clothes, until she stands naked before Allatu's throne. Then the Queen of the Underworld commands that she shall be smitten with "the affliction of the eyes, the affliction of the loins, the affliction of the feet, the affliction of the heart. . . ."

Meanwhile up above, in the world of light and the living they are mourning the prolonged absence of the goddess of love. While she is away there can be no sexual conjugation of man and woman, of the whole animal creation. At last the gods come to fear the extinction of their worshippers, and they bring pressure to bear on Allatu to release Ishtar and her lover. So once again she passes through the gates of the kingdom of the Underworld, mounts higher and higher until she emerges into the light of day, bringing Tammuz with her. And thereupon men and women are at liberty to love and be loved once again.

But every year (so it was felt) the drama must be reenacted. Every year in those lands of Western Asia Tammuz was believed to die and be led away into the land of the shades; every year men and women recalled his slaying by the sharp-tusked boar, and mourned his passing with the music of flutes and the chant of dirges. Every year Ishtar was believed to descend into the Underworld to fetch him back, and while she was absent there was no loving or being loved. Then followed the triumphant return, when Ishtar came back with Tammuz, and with them spring returned to the world, and the very air breathed of love.

Every year when winter was drawing to its close the women of those Mediterranean lands made "gardens of Adonis", baskets or pots filled with earth in which they planted seeds and placed flowers and leafy branches. After eight days, these were taken away and thrown into the sea or a stream, together with little images of Adonis and his goddess; and as they were cast away, the women, with uncombed hair and uncovered bosoms and wearing garments of mourning, wept and wailed. Yet they were not as those without hope, for they were firmly persuaded that Tammuz and the goddess would come back among them, bringing in their train the glorious springtime.

In ancient Egypt, Osiris, the greatest and best-loved of the host of divinities, had likewise a festival of death and resurrection, which suggests that he was considered to have had something to do with the annual return of spring. But the connexion is clearer in the case of Attis, who was to Phrygia in Asia Minor, what Adonis or Tammuz was to Syria. He too, came to a violent end; according to one story he was killed by a wild boar, and according to another he was driven mad by Cybele, his divine spouse, in a fit of jealousy, so that he castrated himself beneath a pine tree and died from loss of blood. Whereupon the now repentant goddess begged Zeus, the King of the Gods, to allow his spirit to pass into a pine tree, and from his blood there sprang up violets.

The two stories are quite inconsistent, but this is often the case in theological myths. There is no doubt that the priests of Attis ceremonially castrated themselves in honour of the god, and that the festival at which this occurred was between the 22nd and the 25th of March. After the orgy of emasculation, indulged in by the new entrants to the priestly order, an image of Attis was ritually entombed. On the third day, as Sir James Frazer has so beautifully expressed it in his great book *The Golden Bough*, "When night had fallen, the sorrow of the worshippers was turned to joy. For suddenly a light shone in the darkness: the tomb was opened: the god had risen from the dead; and as the priest touched the lips of the weeping mourners with balm, he softly whispered in their ears the glad tidings of salvation. The resurrection of the god was hailed by his disciples as a promise that they too would issue triumphant from the corruption of the grave." On the morrow, the 25th of March, which was reckoned as the vernal equinox, the divine resurrection was celebrated with a wild outburst of merrymaking, a springtime festival of joy.

As everyone knows, the Christian Easter is a "movable feast", depending for its date on complicated calculations, so that Easter Day (Sunday) can fall at earliest on 22 March and at latest on 25 April. But it always falls at the season of the year when for untold centuries men and women have celebrated the death and joyful resurrection of the gods of the springtime.

Chapter 21

Christmas Cheer

CHRISTMAS . . . Turkey and plum-pudding and mince-pies; cards dropping through the letter-box by the dozen; letters and packages and parcels, done up in fancy paper with coloured string; the Christmas tree glittering with lights and loaded with toys and sweetmeats; children lying awake, listening for the sounds of Father Christmas driving through the air in his reindeer sledge and coming down the chimney with a bulging sack; crackers being pulled, chestnuts popping on the hob, giggling kisses under the mistletoe; carol-singers grouped round the lamppost in the cold and frosty evening—or, just as likely, the foggy damp.

For most people these are some of the things that spell the magic word, Christmas; and it may be noticed that, although Christmas is one of the great festivals of the Christian Year, there is nothing specifically Christian about any of them. But this is not so surprising as it may appear at first, since Christmas was being celebrated ages before "there was born this day in the city of David a Saviour, which is Christ the Lord".

The word itself is obviously Christian, meaning the day on which a mass or other religious service is celebrated in honour of the Nativity of Christ. The year of Christ's birth is unknown, and we are equally ignorant of the actual day. But the statement in St. Luke's gospel that at the time "there were shepherds abiding in the field, keeping watch over their flock by night", makes it seem most improbable that the Nativity could have occurred on the night of 25 December, for this would have been at the height of the rainy season in Judaea, when man and beast would have been under cover.

Similar uncertainty surrounds the date of the first institution of Christmas as a Christian festival. So far as our evidence goes, the early Christians did not celebrate Christmas, and the first certain traces of it are found about the time of the Emperor Commodus, towards the close of the second century. Nearly a hundred years later, in the reign of Diocletian, when that Roman emperor was keeping court at Nicomedia, it was reported to him that a multitude of Christians were assembled in the city to celebrate the birthday of Jesus, whereupon he gave orders that the doors of the church in which they were gathered together should be shut and the place set on fire, and numbers of the unhappy worshippers perished in the flames. Later still, St. Chrysostom (died A.D. 407) wrote in his *Homilies* that "On this day (i.e., 25 December) the birthday of Christ was lately fixed at Rome, in order that while the heathens were occupied in their profane ceremonies the Christians might perform their holy rites undisturbed."

The "profane ceremonies" referred to were those held in connexion with the worship of Mithras, the Persian Sun-God, whose worship had risen to great prominence and popularity in the Roman world. Mithras's birthday was celebrated on 25 December, which was the winter-solstice festival in the Roman calendar, and the day was given the name of *Dies Natalis Solis invicti*, "Birthday of the Unconquered Sun". St. Chrysostom saw nothing inappropriate in selecting this particular day as the one on which the Nativity of Christ should be celebrated—quite the contrary, in fact, as is shown by the continuation of the quotation just given: "They call this day 'the Birthday of the Invincible One,' but who is so invincible as the Lord that overthrew and vanquished Death? They also style it the 'Birthday of the Sun'—and Christ is the Sun of Righteousness." Thus the date of the Nativity, which the

Gospels say nothing about, was fixed upon by the Christian Church through a reference to mythological analogy.

But long before Mithras conquered so many Roman hearts and minds, this particular week in December was the occasion for much pagan merrymaking. On 17 December fell the festival of Saturn, one of the most important gods of the Romans, but in popular usage the celebrations extended over seven days. The time was one of general jollity and mirth. During the festival all work was suspended, schools were closed, people gave presents to one another, in particular wax tapers or candles and dolls for the children; they entertained one another and amused themselves with social games, such as gambling for nuts, a symbol of fruitfulness. No punishments were inflicted. Every freedom was accorded to slaves, who were given seats at the banquet and were served by their masters, in remembrance of the rule that there were no differences of social rank in that mythical golden age when Saturnus had been the ruler of mankind. Very clearly, it is to the Roman Saturnalia that we must look for the origin of many of the social customs that crowd about our Christmas season.

Another source, equally pagan but nearer home, is the rites and superstitions of the peoples of northern Europe, with whom our Anglo-Saxon forefathers had close racial and cultural and religious ties. The winter solstice was of very special interest and importance to them, since in these northern parts winter is so dark and drear, the cold so bitter, the winds so sharp. And moreover, the season was so long, that there were many among those simple-minded folk who wondered whether it would ever come to an end and the spring come back again. But out of the accumulated experiences of untold generations they had come to realize that about this particular time in December there came a change in the seasonal round. The days which had been getting shorter now began to lengthen. Clearly the sun was winning in his perennial struggle with the powers of darkness, and with that realization they cheered up wonderfully.

For twelve days and nights at this time of the year the heathen peoples of northern Europe feasted and revelled and indulged in every form of licence, rejoicing that the dark days were coming to an end and that erelong the springtime would be back again. The name given to this period in the

Old Norse tongue was *jol*, which became adopted into English as *Yule*. The name is still sometimes applied to the Christmas season, and we may speak of the Yule Log, the massive piece of forest timber that was dragged out of the forest and deposited on the hearth in the great hall to give warmth and sparkle to the wassailing throng. That word, too, comes down to us from Anglo-Saxon times, for *wassail* comes from the Old Norse *ves heill*, meaning "be in health", which was the toast or form of pledge used at the festive board.

Thus it will be seen that Roman paganism and Norse heathenism have both made their contribution to our Christmas usages, furnishing ingredients for the Christmas cake of custom. But there are yet other ingredients which derive from various sources, both religious and secular.

Take "Father Christmas", for instance—the Santa Claus who, so some guileless parents strive to convince their not-so-gullible youngsters, comes down the chimney and fills their stockings with good things. One might have supposed that this jovially rotund figure, dressed in red robes and with white beard descending to his waist and carrying a sack filled to overflowing, has come down to us from the folk-lore of ancient times. Seemingly there *was* a Father Christmas of sorts in the mummers' plays that were performed in the Middle Ages at this season of the year, but he had little in common with our Santa. And Santa Claus did not reach us driving his reindeer-sledge over the snows, but he came across the Atlantic in a grimy, smoke-puffing steamer.

"Santa Claus" is an American corruption of the Dutch Sante Klaas (for Saint Nikolas). And who was this Saint Nicholas? According to Christian legend, he was bishop of Myra, in southern Asia Minor, in the time of the Emperor Diocletian, and some very strange tales are told about him, two in particular. The first tells that there was living in the town of Patara a gentleman who had fallen on evil days, and so was unable to provide his three daughters with suitable marriage-portions. The girls were about to embark upon a life of shame to keep themselves and their father from starving, when their plight came to the knowledge of St. Nicholas, whose father had recently died and left him a large fortune. Filling a bag with gold, Nicholas went to the man's house by night, and surreptitiously dropped it through the window. Next day the father found the gold, thanked God, and provided for one of his daughters. When Nicholas heard how his plan had succeeded, he repeated the performance, and the second daughter was happily married. Now it was the turn of the third girl, and this time the father decided to keep watch and discover if possible who was his benefactor. Just as the saint was about to throw the third bag through the window, the father seized hold of his robe, and with many tears thanked him for his generosity. Nicholas bade him keep the matter secret, but his identity leaked out, and when he was recognized as a saint it was held that young virgins were specially under his protection.

To this incident in the saint's career has been traced the custom of parents on the eve of St. Nicholas's Day (6 December) to place sweets and other small gifts in their children's shoes and stockings, and pretending that these had been brought by St. Nicholas.

The second story is even more remarkable. Two young men who were passing through Myra on their way to pursue their studies in Athens were murdered by the innkeeper, who, after cutting up their bodies, placed the mutilated remains in a pickling-tub along with some pork. But St. Nicholas was informed in a dream of the horrid transaction. Going to the inn in the morning, he confronted the innkeeper and forced him to confess his crime. Then the saint went to the tub in which the bits and pieces of the murdered youths were, made the sign of the cross over it and said a prayer—and, lo and behold, the mangled bodies were made whole again and the two youths were brought back to life and threw themselves at the feet of their benefactor! After this, it was surely not more than his due that St. Nicholas was hailed as the patron saint of children.

In Germany and Holland and elsewhere on the Continent, little children who had been "good" were assembled on his "day" and were rewarded with sweets, nuts, and other small presents. When the Dutch settled in New York (or New Amsterdam, as it was first named) they took this pleasant custom with them, and at some unascertainable date it was transferred to Christmas—very likely, as has been suggested, because parents and friends found it too expensive to give the youngsters presents twice in the same month. And so popular did Santa Claus become that in the early part of the last century he made the trip from New York to England.

The Christmas Tree is another importation from abroad, and not so long ago either. There is a pretty little story told about it, that it was originally "thought up" by Martin Luther in the early years of the sixteenth century. One Christmas Eve he was walking in the country, and the sight of the fir trees sparkling in the moonlight so reminded him of the Shepherds' Watch in the fields at Bethlehem that on returning home he tried to reconstruct the scene with a fir sapling on which he hung little candles to represent the stars. But it is said that the pagan German tribes in the Black Forest had some such custom in their celebrations at the winter solstice, and that this had continued down the centuries right up to Luther's day. From Germany the Christmas Tree spread to other lands, and in England we first meet with it in 1829, when the Princess Lieven, wife of the German ambassador in London, is said to have had one in her country house.

But it was immediately after the marriage of the young Queen Victoria to Prince Albert of Saxe-Coburg in 1840 that the Christmas Tree became established as an essential part of the British Christmas. Albert brought the custom with him from Germany, and every year the newspapers and magazines carried charming accounts and pictures of the Tree at Windsor that was prepared for the children of the prolific "Vicky". As *The Illustrated London News* stated in 1848, "The tree employed for this festive purpose is a young fir of about eight feet high, and has six tiers of branches. On each tier or branch are arranged a dozen wax tapers. Pendant from the branches are elegant trays, baskets, *bonbonnières*, and other receptacles for sweetmeats of the most varied and expensive kind; and of all forms, colours, and degrees of beauty. Fancy cakes, gilt gingerbread and eggs filled with sweetmeats, are also suspended by variously-coloured ribbons from the branches. The tree, which stands upon a table covered with white damask, is supported at the root by piles of sweets of a larger kind, and by toys and dolls of all descriptions. . . ." This Christmas tree, "prepared by her Majesty's command for the Royal children", was the ancestor of the trees which at Christmas-time are to be found in every home, of all classes, and in almost every land.

The Christmas cracker is supposed to have originated in France, although the first *bon-bons* did not crack or bang; they resembled the modern cracker in shape and contents—

sweets, paper-hats, small presents, mottoes, etc.—but they did not "crack": the addition of a small dash of explosive to give the bang was a later development.

Coming now to the custom of sending Christmas-cards, here we have something which has not the slightest connexion with either Christianity or the pagan religions of antiquity. It could not come into widespread use until the introduction of cheap postage in 1840, and it would seem (although there has been much controversy over the point) that the first Christmas-card dates from 1843, when an artist named John Calcott Horseley adopted an idea suggested to him by Henry (later Sir Henry) Cole and designed a card bearing the words, "A Merry Christmas and a Happy New Year to you", surrounded by drawings showing a convivial family party and persons engaged in acts of benevolence to the poor and needy. Copies of this were printed by lithography, coloured by hand, and put on sale at a shilling a time.

The idea was rather slow in catching on, for the second card produced does not seem to have been earlier than 1848, the designer being W. M. Egley. But in 1870 it was decided that Christmas-cards could be sent at half the charge for letters, and before long cards were being put on sale by drapers, toy-shops and tobacconists, as well as by the stationers and booksellers as heretofore. So the Christmas-card was launched on the full tide of success, and nowadays their sales amount to hundreds of millions. Above everything else, the Christmas-card is blamed for that "commercialization of Christmas" which has turned it into "nothing better than a ramp"—a complaint which is echoed by none more loudly or more often than those who have themselves made a not inconsiderable addition to the weight of the postman's bag.

Two other features of Christmas may be mentioned. First, carol-singing. The etymology of "carol" is obscure. The earliest meaning seems to have been a round-dance, a ring-dance; thence it came to mean the song accompanying the dance, and so to the hymn of joy sung at Christmas in honour of Christ's Nativity. The custom of singing carols at Christmas is a very ancient one in the Christian Church. The famous Anglican divine, Jeremy Taylor, maintained "That as soon as these blessed choristers (i.e., the angels on the plains of Bethlehem) had sung their *Christmas Carol,* and taught the Church a hymn to be put in her offices for ever in the anni-

versary of this festivity, the angels returned into Heaven".
Milton, too, in *Paradise Lost,* alludes to the "quire of squad-
roned angels" who heard this "carol sung". In course of time
collections were made of these festive songs or chants intended to be sung at Christmas, and the earliest printed collection was that of Wynkyn de Worde, issued in 1521 from the
printing-house in St. Paul's Churchyard, London, where he
carried on the business that had been founded by his old
master William Caxton.

The Puritans did their best to suppress carol-singing as a
Popish or Pagan superstition, but it came back into full
favour at the Restoration, although it was the general practice to sing carols as often in the open air as within church
walls. In our childhood days it was one of the joys of Christmas to "listen for the waits", these being musicians and
singers who gave carol performances in the evening for two or
three weeks before Christmas up to Christmas Eve. The name
does not derive, as might be supposed, from the "waits" that
they made beneath the lamps by whose light they read their
scores, but from the fact that the name was first given to
watchmen who patrolled the streets at night, sounding their
horns to keep marauders away, and shouting out the hour to
those who had no alarm-clock beside their bed.

Just as clearly as the carol is Christian, kissing under the
mistletoe derives from pagan times. Some authorities trace
the custom to the licentious revels of the Roman Saturnalia,
and others connect it with the practice of the Druids in
ancient Britain. In his account of the kindred tribes in Gaul
(France) the Roman author Pliny the Elder (first century
A.D.) relates that "the Druids, for so they call their wizards,
esteem nothing more sacred than the mistletoe and the tree
on which it grows. It is very rarely met with, but when it is
found, they gather it with solemn ceremony. After due
preparations have been made for a sacrifice and a feast under
the tree, they hail it as the universal healer and bring to the
spot two white bulls, whose horns have never been bound
before. A priest clad in a white robe climbs the tree and with
a golden sickle cuts the mistletoe, which is caught in a white
cloth. Then they sacrifice the victims, praying that God may
make his own gift to prosper with those upon whom he had
bestowed it. They believe that a potion prepared from mistle-

toe will make barren animals to bring forth, and that the plant is a remedy against all poison".

Nothing about hanging up a mistletoe bough, it will be noticed; but it is generally assumed that the kiss under the mistletoe is, like the practice of throwing rice at weddings, a kind of fertility charm. And most people will not be bothering to inquire too closely into the origin of a custom which has such pleasant possibilities. Here is how it is described by Robert Chambers in that delightful miscellany of antique lore, *The Book of Days*. "A branch of the mystic plant is suspended from the wall or ceiling, and any one of the fair sex, who, either from inadvertence, or, as possibly may be insinuated, on purpose, passes beneath the sacred spray, incurs the penalty of being then and there kissed by any lord of the creation who chooses to avail himself of the privilege".

Chapter 22

"Cargo Cults" of the South Pacific

AWAY back in the eighteen-eighties the British administrators of the Fiji islands in the South Pacific were concerned at reports that reached them of strange goings on among the natives in some of the villages along the coast and up the river valleys. Not that there was anything very dreadful about them, at least at first. There was no talk of the revival of that cannibalism which within the memory of living men had been the regular practice, nor of the strangling of widows on their husbands' graves, or the wholesale slaughtering of slaves when the chief built himself a new house or launched a new canoe. There was nothing of this nature, but all the same the British who had taken over the islands only some ten years earlier were worried.

What were the people up to—the people who, according to the tales that drifted down from the hills, had blackened their already dusky faces, garbed themselves in native cloth in place of the trousers for the men and "Mother Hubbards" for the women that the missionaries had insisted upon, and engaged in exercises that seemed to have a suspicious resemblance to military drill?

As the weeks passed, details of the picture were filled in, and it came to have a sombre and even menacing aspect. The natives were said to be quite well organized, in companies of "soldiers" under "sergeants" and "scribes" and (this was what the superior officers were called) "destroying angels". They were armed, and although there were very few guns in their armoury they possessed clubs and spears such as their ancestors had known how to wield with such savage effect. And they had a leader, who seemed to be a man of some capacity as well of powerful imagination. His name was given as Ndugumoi, but it was said that he had assumed the style of Navosavakandua, meaning in the native tongue "he who speaks once", and there seemed to be an ominous significance in this, since it was the title assumed by the Chief Justice in the new administration, symbolizing his power of life and death in the execution of justice. He was putting out the most fantastic claims for himself. He could work "miracles". He was a past-master of all the arts of magic. He could foretell what was going to happen.

And what *was* going to happen? There were no reporters to "take down" what he told the people who assembled in the village squares to hear his harangues, but the gist of it was conveyed to the administrators and missionaries by friendly natives. A good time was coming for the Fijians, and that very soon, and a correspondingly bad time for the Europeans. The position of White and Black would be reversed. The "ancestors" would erelong come back to life, and preparations should be made at once to receive them and make them welcome. The old ways would be restored. A glorious Paradise would come into being, in which the native believers would spend eternity in feasting and sexual indulgence. The old would be made young again, and would be perpetually virile, just as the women and girls whom they enjoyed would be perpetually restored to the virgin state. The storehouses would be crammed with the white man's goods, which the natives would possess without having to submit to the vulgar necessity of paying for them by their daily toil. The supply of tinned foods would never give out, any more than the flow of whisky and beer from the mountainous piles of crates would dry up. There would be yards and yards of calico, enough and more than enough for everybody, and it would all be had just for the asking. . . .

When was this wonderful time to come? In Fiji mythology there is a story of two twin brothers who revolted against their uncle the Snake God and were driven into banishment in consequence. But they would one day come back, and the time of their return was drawing nigh. The White Man knew that well enough: had he not been seen of late, staring out to sea through a strange kind of long tube placed against his eye? He was obviously on the look out for the returning exiles, and hoped to destroy them before they could succeed in reasserting the supremacy of the natives in the land that had been their fathers' and might soon be theirs as in days gone by.

In the meantime, let the Believers eat, drink, and be merry! The leader set the example, and it would seem that his prowess in dancing and drinking and debauchery was such as to prove a bit too much for his supporters. So it was that when the authorities at length decided that the time had come to call a halt to his activities and, on the morning of the anticipated "Day", sent the police to his hut to effect his arrest, they found the job much easier than had been expected. In fact there was no resistance, for Ndugumoi, who turned out to be a "sooty-skinned, hairy little man of middle age, bleary-eyed from excessive drinking", had alienated the sympathies of his followers by his perpetual drunkenness and the way in which he had abused their virgin daughters, thereby reducing the price in pigs that might be asked for them in marriage. The young ladies themselves seem to have been less concerned with their lord and master's amatory requirements than with his insistence that, all day long and often far into the night as well, they should be employed in chewing the roots of the kava plant until they had been sufficiently masticated to constitute the basis of his drink.

Ndugumoi was sent to hard labour for a year, and the lenience of the sentence encouraged him in his boasting that the Governor had been afraid to kill him. When he returned to his village he took up his activities afresh, and was thereupon banished to a distant island for ten years. In his place of exile he got married, and died just as he was about to return home once again. But this did not mean an end to the agitation. There was a revival of the cult from time to time up to the First World War and after, and traces of it are yet apparent.

Clearly there was more in the affair than an isloated instance of native megalomania, and in fact this Tuke movement (as it is called) in Fiji was only about the first of a series of social-religious movements in which similar features may be observed. The name given to these is "cargo cults", from the fact that in all of them "cargo"—the name applied by the South Sea natives to European goods—has a very special place and significance.

As Western civilization—a very materialistic civilization on the whole, notwithstanding the activities of the missionaries of the various Christian churches and sects—has expanded throughout the South Pacific, these cults have spread and have become more frequent. They have appeared in New Caledonia and in the Solomon islands, in the New Hebrides and in New Guinea; and in nearly all there is what may be described as an apocalyptic or messianic element. The arrival of the "cargo" from overseas is to form the prelude to a period of troubles in which the white man is to be made completely subordinate to the native, or he may be driven out altogether, after which the peoples will enter upon an age of peace and plenty and endless joy.

On the whole, the cults are anti-white and anti-missionary, and as such they have given plenty of occasion for Government hostility. In a sense they are also anti-native, since there is not the slightest disinclination to admit that the white man's goods—the cargo—are far superior to anything in the native culture. But there is no proper understanding of the "how and wherefore". So far as the native is able to see, all the white man has to do is to sit in his office and write orders on bits of paper which he puts into the post-bag, or in some completely incomprehensible fashion he conveys his orders from the top of the wireless-mast erected on the hillside or cliff. Surely the native could fill that office chair just as well as the white trader does; while as for "wireless"—he proceeds to raise a pole in imitation and professes to speak by its agency to wherever the cargo is believed to come from.

Reading the accounts of the anthropologists who have witnessed the cargo cults in action, one may be amused at times, and at others saddened, at the exhibition of naïve foolishness. Take, for instance, the "Vailala Madness" that broke out in New Guinea after 1919. An old man named Evara was said to have originated it. He had seen service under Europeans, and had come to appreciate the excellent quality of the goods of the white man. He wanted them for his own people, and now he had a vision of a steamer nearing the shore from somewhere far away. But it was like no steamer that he had ever seen discharging its cargo at Port Moresby. Its passengers were the spirits of deceased Papuans, and its hold was chock-full with bales of goods, each labelled with the name of a village for which it was destined. Flour and rice and tobacco were what it was carrying, and all was for the native and nothing at all for the European.

When the people heard his vision, they were glad, and hastened to make the preparations for the ship's arrival that Evara enjoined. Tables were spread in the villages, and the natives feasted without any thought for the morrow, since they were assured of such bountiful replenishment of their stores. So excited were they at the prospect, that many of them became a little unbalanced, swaying their bodies from side to side, bending from the hips, running and leaping and then standing still in their tracks, gesticulating and mouthing incomprehensible gabbles. An imitation wireless-mast was raised, by means of which they confidently hoped to have an early intimation of the vessel's approach. Watchers were placed in readiness, and there were numerous false alarms, when the sleeping villagers were roused from their beds by shouts of "Sail ahoy!" and rushed from their huts and down to the shore in a frenzy of excitement. Some in their mood of intensely felt happiness discarded their clothes, so as to be quite ready to don the garments which were coming to them in those neatly labelled packages.

The steamer didn't come, at least so far as most of the people were aware. They got tired of waiting; and rather than let the good things they had prepared for the expected ancestors go bad, they ate them themselves. Some there were, however, who made bold to assert that the ship *had* come, but for some reason had gone away again—they hoped for only a short time. They were quite sure of it. They had heard the throbbing of the steamer's engines, they had seen its lights and the wash it made as it moved along, they had heard the rattling of its anchor chain and the splashing of the oars as one of the ship's dinghies had come near to the beach. It had three masts, they alleged, and a red funnel.

Notwithstanding these apparently convincing details, it was soon generally recognized that the mysterious ship had *not* arrived. Nor for that matter did the aeroplane come that Evara spoke about in his more ecstatic ravings. He had never seen an aeroplane, but he knew what one looked like: he had somehow got hold of a copy of an English novelette, on the cover of which an aeroplane was pictured in garish colours.

Among the best-known accounts of the Cargo Cult movement is that given by the eminent American ethnographer, Miss Margaret Mead, of its manifestation in Manus, an island of the Admiralty group to the north of New Guinea. In 1928-29 Miss Mead was one of a group of scientists making a field study of the south-coast region of Manus, and she published in 1930 her book, *Growing Up in New Guinea,* which soon established itself as one of the classics of modern anthropological exploration. In 1953 she went back to Manus, and in *New Lives for Old* (Victor Gollancz, 1956) she describes what she found there, of the "cultural transformation" of Manus between 1928 and 1953.

This was not long after the conclusion of the Second World War, in the course of which the Admiralties had been made one of the largest and most important American bases in the Pacific. Over a million American troops passed through them in those war years, and they left behind them a very different impression of Western civilization than the islanders had gained in the past half-century, during which they had been brought into contact, sometimes but slightly and sometimes profoundly with a touch of violence, with German colonists, Australian soldiers and administrators, and a confusing mixture of missionaries. What the natives noticed most of all was that so many Americans—at one time the majority seem to have been drawn from Negro battalions—had faces as black or blacker than their own! And these black Americans were not downtrodden as the islanders felt themselves to be. They were obviously possessed of all the material goods of their civilization just as surely as their white comrades; they knew how to use them and to derive the maximum of pleasure and profit from them.

When the war was over, the Americans sailed away, but it was thought that before very long they, or others like them, would be arriving, bringing with them a boundless supply of "cargo" for the benefit of the natives.

In sympathetic detail Miss Mead tells of the outbreak of a "cargo cult" in 1946 on Manus and the adjacent islands. "The Noise", as it is styled, was first heard on Rambutjon, where a local prophet suddenly went into trances and ecstatic seizures, and announced that a "cargo" sent by God and the spirits of the ancestors was on its way, and that in preparation for its coming the natives should, without a moment's delay, pitch all their present possessions into the sea. The simple-minded folk did as they were advised; but when some little time passed and there was no sign of a ship, they turned on the unfortunate prophet and slew him.

By now, however, the infection had spread to a number of the neighbouring islands, carried thither by messengers some of whom had deluded themselves into believing that they had actually seen the ships putting in to the shore. Typical of the messages they carried was what one of them, an excitable woman visionary, told the people of Peri. A big ship with many "black men" on board had arrived at Tawi, she declared, and the village was crammed with the "cargo" that had been brought ashore. Other ships had followed, so that there was a ship for every village. Many more were on their way, carrying not only "cargo" but the resurrected ancestors. Why hadn't one of the ships arrived yet at Peri? It was because the people had not made themselves ready for its reception. They clung to their possessions, and these prevented the ship from drawing near. Let them have faith and demonstrate it. Let them throw into the sea everything that belonged to them, and within a very short time they would be repaid a hundredfold. The village would be so filled with the "cargo" that there wouldn't be room to walk in the street, and they wouldn't be able to turn round in their huts. . . .

Many years before the people of Peri had cleared the way for the introduction of Christianity by flinging into the lagoon the skulls of their dead and the other sacred objects of their ancient cults. That was at the behest of the missionaries. Now they had been given a similar injunction, and they hurried to obey. The women and girls tore off their grass skirts, widows their robes of mourning, and cast them into the waters. Men flung away their spears, their vessels of pottery and basket-work, their shell money and dogs'-teeth ornaments. When this was done the people still feared that they had not cleared the way sufficiently for the mysterious "cargo". So they proceeded to cast out many of the things that they had kept from the time of the American occupation—tables and chairs, beds and bedding, clothes that the friendly American servicemen had bestowed on them before their departure. The next morning the priest in charge of the local mission was astounded to see the lagoon choked with the property that his flock had flung away. He hurried down to the beach and argued with the men standing there, but they as good as told him to mind his own business. They knew what they were doing, they assured him; the "cargo" that would shortly arrive would much more than make up for what was being discarded. All they had to do was to wait patiently—and this they did, in their homes or in the church, where the services had been discontinued.

When the excitement had died down somewhat, and the ship did not come, some of the people went down to the shore and (rather shamefacedly) tried to retrieve some of the things that they had flung away in the extremity of their zeal. At length the period of disillusion set in, and the villagers set about restoring their shattered economy. They had had enough of prophets for the time being: now they were prepared to give the comparatively tame and mundane policies of the Australian administrators a chance.

A thousand miles to the east of New Guinea lie the islands of the New Hebrides group. Here, too, there have been displays of the "cargo cult" movement, especially on the little island of Tanna. On the face of it, there would seem to be nothing impossible in the suggestion that news of the outbreaks in New Guinea had reached the island and had provided the inspiration, but in point of fact it would appear that similar causes were at work—jealousy of the white man's ownership of the goods and chattels of civilized society, resentment at his superior position in the world, and resolve to preserve or restore the characteristic features of the native culture.

In Tanna the cult seems to have had its origin in 1940, when the officers of the Anglo-French administration were apprised of the activities of a mysterious personage who went under the name of John Frum (or as the natives usually spelled it, Jonfrum). It seemed that he went about only at night, when he addressed meetings of the headmen in their meeting-places. What did he look like? The informants were not sure, beyond that he was a small man with grey hair and a squeaky voice, who wore a coat with shiny buttons. More important was what he said. Like the other "cargo cult" preachers, he prophesied strange things. A great cataclysm to begin with, in course of which the mountains would be flattened and the valleys filled up. Then would begin a kind of millenarian age. The old people would regain their youth and vigour. The white folk would be made to quit the island, and never come back. The natives would be left in full control, and very shortly ships would be arriving from overseas, ships with their holds filled with "cargo" which would be distributed free and provide everybody with the means for living a full and happy life. For the present, while they were awaiting the coming of the ships, all that the people were required to do was to obey John Frum's orders without question, turn a deaf ear to the exhortations of the missionaries, and revive some of the time-honoured customs that they had been induced to abandon—getting drunk on kava-beer, for instance, and the taking of as many wives as a man thought fit. Forthwith there was an exodus from the churches and schools, and the missionary cause suffered a setback from which it has not fully recovered.

Then in 1941 there was a fresh development. John Frum was said to have announced that the great day was very near now, and that he would be introducing his own currency, stamped with a coconut, which should be used in place of the white man's money. As for the latter, the people should hasten to get rid of it—spend it, throw it away—for since the white man was interested only in money, as soon as it was all gone he would go too, back to the land he had come from. The villagers needed no second bidding. They spent all their cash on whatever took their fancy. They slaughtered all their pigs, and spent the days in feasting and the nights in dancing, in which they threw off their missionary-inspired inhibitions with their clothes. No one went to church.

Before matters had gone too far, John Nicol, the agent of the British in the government, intervened. Several of the leaders of the cult were arrested, put on trial, and sentenced to terms of imprisonment. But "John Frum" escaped capture, and within a year or two he was being spoken of again. By this time American troops had landed on the island in large numbers, and the natives were particularly impressed by a battalion of Negroes. These men had black skins like they had—they had the same kind of fuzzy hair—but they were most certainly not poor! They seemed to have just as much "cargo" as their white comrades. Wild with excitement, the islanders watched the American landings, fully expecting that among the troops who came ashore would be John Frum himself. In vain the Americans told the people that they hadn't the least idea who John Frum was, that they were quite sure that no such name appeared on their rosters.

Not until the war was over and the Americans had all left did the agitation die down. But there was no return to the old ways. The churches were largely deserted, and the school-rooms were nearly empty. Some of the missionary leaders openly admitted that they might have gone too far in con-demning all the native practices, and that the religion that they had preached had been too cold and colourless and repressive. Then the government agreed to tolerate the "cargo cult" manifestations, providing no harm was done to any-body. Perhaps it was hoped that the movement would die a natural death, but in fact it survived, and still survives. The fame of it has reached the outside world, with the happy result that Mr. David Attenborough decided to include Tanna in one of the "Quests" that he has pursued on behalf of the B.B.C. In the pages of his book *Quest in Paradise* (published by the Lutterworth Press in 1960) we may read of the "cargo cult" as a present-day phenomenon.

With a knowledgeable Australian planter as his companion, David Attenborough spent several evenings with the villagers assembled on the *namakal* or ceremonial meeting-ground. He did not try to rush matters. He watched them preparing and drinking kava, and listened to what was being said. At length he found a native who was willing to talk. Sam his name was, and years before he had been a star pupil in the mission school and had taught there until he had fallen under the spell of John Frum.

That was nineteen years ago, Sam told Mr. Attenborough. "Plenty of the big men were having a meeting, drinkin' kava when John 'e come. 'E talk an' 'e say that by an' by he bring plenty cargo. Then men will be happy and get everything they want and it will be good living."

No, he had not seen him, but his brother had. What did he look like? Like a white man, for he was dressed in white man's clothes and had shoes on his feet. He had lived for some time in America. But he did not speak in English but in the tongue of the Tanna people. And what had he told them? That they should leave the mission school because what was taught there was "no good", that they should kill all their cattle because these had been brought by the white man. Then in due course: "By an' by, white man 'e go, plenty cargo 'e come, an' everybody very happy."

But, protested Mr. Attenborough, that was nineteen years ago, and John Frum hasn't come yet, nor the cargo either. Wasn't nineteen years a long time to wait? Then Sam had lifted his eyes from the ground and solemnly rejoined: "If you can wait two thousand years for Jesus Christ to come an' 'e no come, then I can wait more than nineteen years for John."

As he moved about the island, Mr. Attenborough kept on coming across "monuments" of the John Frum cult—gates of solid timber and crosses painted a garish red. One cross stood on the very edge of the crater of the still-active volcano that dominates the eastern side of the island, and he learnt that recently the cult had incorporated into its ideology the ancient myth of a god who has his dwelling in the volcano's heart. Then in a village they passed through on their way back from this expedition they noticed a rough shelter of poles and thatch, encircled by a fence, and beneath the shelter were three exceedingly strange wooden objects. One was of a rat-like creature with wings, enclosed in a cage; another was a crude model of an aeroplane with a white American star painted on its wings and tail—was this supposed to represent the plane which would bring the "cargo"?; and the third was an effigy, standing behind a cross, of what Mr. Attenborough surmised must be John Frum himself. He had white face and hands, and was wearing a scarlet coat and trousers, and his arms were outstretched so as to form a travesty of a Christian crucifix.

Still pursuing his inquiries, Mr. Attenborough was eventually able to interview the man who was reputed to be the high priest of the John Frum cult. This man had been one of the organizers of the Tanna "army" at the time of the troubles years before, and he had spent some time in prison as the result. He was quite ready to talk of his experiences. He knew that Mr. Attenborough was coming to see him, he averred: John Frum had told him so. How? By "radio". Could he see the "radio", enquired Mr. Attenborough. No: "John 'e say that no white man look 'im." Realizing he had pressed the man too far, David Attenborough changed the subject, inquiring if his informant had ever seen John Frum? The man nodded his head vigorously. Where? In the neighbourhood of the volcano, where he had his dwelling. But, Mr. Attenborough demurred, *he* had been to the volcano, and had caught never a glimpse of John Frum. "You no see 'im," retorted the man. "Your eye dark . . . Me see 'im plenty time." And what did he look like? " 'E look like you. 'E got white face. 'E tall man. 'E live 'long South America." And what did he say? " 'E speak, by an' by the world turn. Everything will be different. 'E come from South America and bring plenty cargo. An' every man 'e get every thing 'e want." Would the white man get a share in the cargo? Most certainly not: "Cargo come to native boy. John say he cannot give white man cargo because white man 'e got it already."

"Does John say when he will come?" enquired David Attenborough farther. The man looked at him. Then in a tone of quiet but completest confidence he made reply, " 'E no say *when:* but 'e come. . . ."

Chapter 23

Love and War Among the Redskins

W HEN I was a very small boy August bank holiday was a
red-letter-day, for on that day there used to come to our
old farmhouse—it was in the market-garden belt surrounding
London, and rows and rows of "desirable residences" have
long since covered the fields in which women with skirts
trailing in the mud used to pick strawberries in the rain—an
elderly gentleman of unknown relationship, with grizzled
hair and moustache and side-whiskers which in those days
seemed perfectly natural but nowadays would be referred to
as "so utterly Victorian, don't you know". He was not very
well off, judging from the seediness of his clothes and the
frayed edges of his stiff white collar and protruding cuffs,
and we children were quick to understand that he had seen
better days. But what sort of days! That we found out when,
the tea-things having been cleared away, the magic-lantern
was erected on the dining-room table, and slide after slide

215

was projected on the white sheet draped over the front of the bookcase that served as a screen.

What slides they were, too. The ones I remember best showed Red Indian braves of the middle of the last century, and it was then that our visitor came into his own. Why (so it turned out), he had actually seen them, he had met them, he might even have spoken to them! Red Cloud and Sitting Bull, Little Crow and Crazy Horse and Black Hawk—he had actually seen these men (or men with names like these), and now he could tell us what they had looked like, men with reddish skins, wearing leather trousers with fringes down the sides, and magnificent headdresses of bright-coloured feathers, with tomahawks in their belts and antique guns leaning up against the poles of their wigwams. Not for one moment had I ever dreamt that the world contained such colourful specimens of humanity. They were splendid and commanding, brave and handsome, and their women and girls, hovering somewhere in the background, made no small contribution to the prevailing impression of romantic adventure. No child of the present, who watches, goggle-eyed, the "Westerns" on the screen at the cinema or on a T.V. can have experienced a greater or more lasting thrill.

That is the sort of impression that the Red Man has always made on Western observers, who have come across him, and up against him, in his native plains and rock-bound wastes. Even when he has been feared (and that with very good reason) he has also generally been admired, although the admiration has been grudging. For hundreds of years, ever since his remote ancestors crossed the straits from Asia into Alaska no one knows when, he had the vast open spaces of the North American continent practically to himself. Then the white man put in his appearance, and with gun and the even more deadly weapon of the spade (for the spade holds the territory that the gun has won) drove the Red Man from his hunting-grounds into the least favoured and most inaccessible recesses of the prairies. It was a long struggle, a long war or series of wars, fought with fierceness and horrible cruelty on the one side and the other; and although, looking back, it may seem that the outcome was never in doubt, that was not the opinion of some at least of those who had to do the fighting.

Many a fine piece of descriptive writing was born of the

conflict, and from the accounts of explorers and soldiers and adventurous traders we may picture for ourselves the Red Man in the days when he was in the prime of his splendid vigour and indomitable pride.

Many were the Red Indian tribes, and fine-sounding their names. Iroquois and Mohawks (I was to come across them later when we were told in school about the wars with French and Americans in the eighteenth century), Chippewas and Cheyennes and Cherokees, Senecas and Shawnees, Sioux and Seminoles, Hopis and Natchez and Navajos, Creeks and Blackfeet, and ever so many more, not forgetting the Apaches (whose name, by a deplorable mischance, came to be applied to the lawless hooligans of Paris in the days before the First World War).

"A magnificent wild beast, this Apache," wrote the French ethnographer Elie Reclus, in a book in which our great-grandfathers learnt for perhaps the first time of the "primitive folk" with which their cosy contemporary world was surrounded. Typically (he tells his readers), he is almost always six feet tall, and the women are as full grown as the men. Plenty of muscle, but with dainty hands and feet, large and brilliant black eyes with a really extraordinary power of vision, black hair and a by no means scanty beard—these go to make up a splendid whole. The Apaches (so he informs us, building on the descriptions of a succession of travellers) have often been cited as the finest specimens of the human race.

So thick-skinned is the Redskin that a horse or mule would be covered with blood by cacti that do not even scratch him. For the same reason he is almost insensible to the inclemency of the weather. These Indians usually go about under the most scorching sun with no protection, but sometimes they cover their heads with a mud cap, which is not only agreeably cool but serves to rid them of vermin. For like reason, they coat their bodies with a layer of mud. As for clothing, "they dress themselves up to a ridiculous extent, not for the sake of hygiene, still less for that of modesty, but out of vanity and coquetry, to attract attention—the men by some trophy of murder and rapine, the young women by some coloured rag, by a bark petticoat or by a sheep-skin, which they have adorned with lines and stripes, and made flexible by industriously rubbing it with brains. Some tattoo their chin; but the pink of fashion is to be smeared with gaudy colours. This painting runs no danger from their ablutions, for they only bathe for pleasure, and there is very little water. . . ."

With no agriculture worthy of the name, and no domestic animals, other of course than the horse, the larder of these unfortunate folk is often empty. They sow a little maize, but for the rest they subsist almost entirely on what they can kill in the chase. In small bands they set out in pursuit of prey, often covering enormous distances on their wiry steeds, happy when they may light upon some scanty herbage, or find grasshoppers, a lizard, or a chance bird. Meanwhile they nibble at the strips of dried meat that hang from their saddles.

Sometimes they are driven in desperation to attack human prey. "They lie in ambush like a wolf; they cower down and hide for days, disguised as bushes, rocks, and logs of wood; then, when the fitting moment arrives, they rush upon their victims, killing the men, sometimes carrying off the women as slaves, and the children for the sake of ransom, or to make brigands of them; but first and foremost they seize upon the horses and mules, which they drive before them. Before any one can set out in pursuit, they have fled like the wind into the labyrinth of gorges and canyons, into those deserts of burning sands, which are real lakes of fire. . . . The ravishers are at home on desert and mountain; they double and triple the stages, until covered with bruises and wounds, exhausted and footsore, the captured beasts fall dying before the den of the human-visaged wolves, male and female, who greet them with yells of joy." After this there is an orgy of feasting: "flinging themselves on the prey, they devour it while still alive, some cutting and carving, others tearing off the limbs and mangling them by main force. . . . When the first fury of hunger is appeased, they spit some pieces over a fire, but it is a very little while before these too are swallowed, still smoking and burning, partly raw, partly charred. The entrails are looked upon as tit-bits, and bestowed as a special honour."

Not a pleasant picture, but probably not too highly coloured. The Redskins were cruel and rapacious and fierce in their appeasements of the demands of their sinewy flesh. Their women likewise were hardy and stoical where the women of other races might be weak and deserving of every consideration. Here is another example of simple animal procedure, this time taken from the journal of the account of the expedition made by Meriwether Lewis and William Clark through the Rockies to the source of the Missouri at the beginning of the last century. "One of the women, who had been leading two of our pack horses, halted at a rivulet about a mile behind and sent on the two horses by a female friend. On inquiring of Cameahwait the cause of her detention, he answered, with great apparent unconcern, that she had just stopped to lie in, but would soon overtake us. In fact, we were astonished to see her in about an hour's time come on with her newborn infant, and pass us on her way to the camp, seemingly in perfect health."

Such an incident was bound to create a powerful impression on the European observer, and from the first a great deal of interest was shown in the behaviour and status of the Indian women. The results of the inquiry were often at variance. H. H. Bancroft, who made a pioneering study of the Indians of the West Coast from California northwards, was told that the Apaches were distinguished from their more civilized white neighbours by the chastity that they imposed on their women, both before and after marriage. Other writers, possibly with other tribes in mind, declared that marriage as the white man understood it was unknown among the Indians, that Indian men and women paired just as and when the spirit moved them, and even that on certain special occasions they indulged in orgies of promiscuity.

The Chippewas countenanced pre-nuptial intercourse, which took place in the course of nocturnal visitings; this might lead to marriage or a more or less permanent connection, after formal negotiations had been entered into by the families concerned. The same thing is reported of other tribes, and it is noteworthy that among those following this custom the women were stated to be in "no hurry to get married". Furthermore, they were said to be well acquainted with methods of birth prevention, so that they were in a position to postpone entering upon the married state until such time as it suited them.

Two hundred years ago the Franciscan fathers who were so zealous in establishing Catholic missions throughout the South-West noted that virginity was very lightly regarded among the Navajos whom they sought to convert, and that celibacy was at a most decided discount. This attitude, it may be noted, would seem to have been perpetuated, for among the Navajo Indians of the present time it is stated that not more than one in four of the girls retain their virginity after they are twenty, while as for the young males the great majority have indulged in a good deal of sexual experimentation before deciding to "settle down".

In the light of these reports it is rather surprising to learn that the Navajos are quite prudish in all matters of decorum between the sexes. Almost from infancy, little girls and boys are taught to conceal their persons, and grown-up men drape themselves in their blankets when in the "sweat bath".

Among the Indian tribes in general, it was the custom for a young "brave", when he set out on a hunting expedition, to take with him a young woman, who would serve him as a sexual partner and also give him a hand in cooking and the carrying of his impedimenta. If the trip was a successful one, the girl was awarded a share in the profits and then went back to her home none the worse in reputation for her adventure.

To see an Indian squaw trudging along behind her husband and carrying on her bent back most of the heavy baggage, may give the impression that Indian women are very much the subordinate sex. This is very far from being so, however. On the contrary, the Indian tribes afford one of the most effective examples of that form of social organization that is known as "matriarchy".

This fact was first established by Lewis Henry Morgan, the "Father of American Anthropology" as he has been styled, who in the middle years of the last century made a long and detailed study of the Indian tribes, the Iroquois in particular. At a time when the white settler's wife, however capable and courageous and fine-spirited, was still in the eyes of the law the chattel of her husband, the Iroquois squaw enjoyed a position far superior to that of her spouse. The fields and crops and hutments were deemed to be hers. Descent was traced along the female line. Any children born were considered as belonging to their mother's tribe or clan, and if the marriage broke up they remained in her charge as a matter of course. Men went to live with their wives, and not the other way round. Divorce among the Indians was an easy matter enough, but it is significant that when it occurred it was the wife who showed her husband the door.

As with other barbarian peoples all the world over, the onset of puberty—the period when girl becomes woman, and boy becomes man—was celebrated among the Indian tribes with special rituals. Indeed, where the native traditions are still living and powerful, the age-old custom is still carried out. Thus among the Navajos there is a puberty ceremony extending over four days, starting from the first appearance of the menses. During the first three days the girl is kept in seclusion, and she is enjoined not to wash herself, to drink water only through a tube, not to sleep for any length of time on her back, not to scratch herself, and to see that her face is always partly hidden by her hair. There are also some dietary rules that she must observe. Then follows the "kneading" ceremony, when she is stretched face downwards in a blanket and the women of her family knead or massage her body with their hands, with a view to shaping it into a womanly maturity. The ceremony concludes with the girl baking a special kind of cake, and then distributing it among the assembled company. The way in which she does this is carefully watched, for it may provide a clue to a favoured suitor.

Women accompanied their menfolk on the warpath, although they did not as a rule join in the actual fighting. But they encouraged the warriors with their shrill shouts and cries, and after the battle they helped to gather up the plunder and despoil and dispose of the slain.

Boys were trained for war from their earliest days, for war was considered to be man's most natural and honourable occupation. They were toughened by exposure to all weathers, hardened by bodily exercises and arms drill. In the heat of the day they were told to take a mouthful of water and then run at full speed for two or three miles—and if they could spit out the water at the end of it they were deemed to have done well. Sometimes they were made to stand with their backs to a tree and remain unflinching as arrows were discharged to hit the trunk with only an inch or so to spare. Juvenile boasting was encouraged, and as soon as they were able the boys joined in the ceremonial dancings that preluded departure on a raid or full-scale campaign. With tomahawks brandished above their heads, they mimicked the tracking down of the foe, the slow approach, the attack, the parry, the assumed flight, the sudden return, the crashing blow and the death-dealing stroke. There was no formal collecting of human scalps as among the head-hunters of the Amazon, but a youth would be quick to learn that there was no surer way to win a girl's favours than the present of a scalp taken in a fight that had been fierce if not always fair.

For Apaches and Navajos and many another tribe, war was a matter of business, in which the aim was plunder and rapine. Horses, arms and equipment, domestic gear, and women and children to serve as slaves—these were the objectives that sent them on the warpath, nerved their endurance and inspired their courage. But with others of the American Indians—the Iroquois in particular—it was a case of war for war's sake. This is what made them specially dreaded, and specially hated, and it was hardly surprising that it became a common saying with the embattled farmers who were bent on submitting the prairies to their ploughing, that "the only good Injun is a dead one".

There was also something else, their reputation for cruelty, and their unfeigned delight in the infliction of pain on those who were so unfortunate as to fall into their clutches. Torture with them was developed into a fine art. But it should be recognized that they looked on torture with very different eyes from the white man's. They saw nothing wrong in it. It was one of the facts of life: a man who went to war might expect to be tortured if he were captured, and he must endeavour to meet it with unflinching heroism. Surrounded by his gloating captors, the brave tried to smile in the midst of his agonies—the knife prickings, the thorns thrust into his tenderest parts, the burns inflicted with flaming brands, the slow strangling with cords, the arrows that wounded but did not kill—and like a player on the stage he hoped to arouse the admiration of the men who were striving so hard to break his body and spirit.

Those days are past: the "Indian Wars" have passed into the history-books and on to the celluloid screen; no longer do the braves go on the warpath as their ancestors did from time immemorial. But the Red Man can still fight: the records of gallantry in the World Wars have put that beyond the shadow of a doubt.

According to the last Census, there are about half a million

"Indians" in the population of the United States, and of these more than half live in the Reservation Areas allotted to them in Arizona, Oklahoma, New Mexico, South Dakota, and Montana. But in the rest of the country are a great number of persons with Indian blood in their veins, perhaps without knowing it.

A man who is not only an Indian but looks like one, has, it is said, a pretty tough time when looking for a job or trying to take a step up the social ladder. Most of them are poor, by customary American standards, but some are very well off—the Navajos, for instance, who have been granted large sums in late years in respect of mineral rights in their territory. Only too often, Indian culture, where it still exists and is allowed to flourish, is looked upon as something "quaint", a matter of painted baskets and brightly coloured blankets and jewelry which may be exquisite or just the sort of stuff that may be expected to catch the tourist's eye.

In their long history the Redskins have been responsible for many strange contributions to the life and material expression of human society. We think of the wigwam and the tomahawk and the barbaric splendour of their dress, their fierce delight in war and their enjoyment of the "pipe of peace" beside the camp fire, their matriarchal system of family descent, their development of a satisfactory amatory life for both men and women, and the fundamental democracy of their tribal gatherings which (so it has been suggested) percolated by way of English explorers and French philosophers to the "Founding Fathers" of the great American Nation. There are some fine things here, and some that are fearsome, and there is an abundance of strangeness in them all.

Hundreds of years have passed since their ancestors crossed the Bering Strait into Alaska, and from there moved on in slow progress to possess a continent of superlative extent. Then after untold centuries they met their match, and after a hard-fought struggle went down at last before the bullet and axe and puffing locomotive of the white invader. And yet their glory has not departed. For—and this is surely the strangest thing about them—in defeat they have taken their conquerors captive. At the end of the long, long trail (which is also the end of this book), let us not be slow to acknowledge that the Red Man—that bronzed figure sitting motionless on his horse, staring with penetrating gaze into the far distances of plain and range and canyon—has come to dominate the imaginations of our city-prisoned millions, giving them a vision of a life that was Wild and Western, savage and free.

Index

The Moon and Sixpence

W. SOMERSET MAUGHAM

THE CLASSIC STORY OF A REBELLIOUS GENIUS
WHO SACRIFICED FAMILY AND FRIENDS
TO PURSUE HIS ARTISTIC DREAM

75198/75¢

CAKES AND ALE . . . . 50029/50¢

If your bookseller does not have these titles, you may order them by sending retail price, plus 15¢ for mailing and handling to: MAIL SERVICE DEPARTMENT, Simon & Schuster of Canada, Ltd., 225 Yonge Street North, Richmond Hill, Ont., Canada. Not responsible for orders containing cash. Please send check or money order.

PUBLISHED BY
POCKET BOOKS

Margaret Mitchell

————— ☆ —————

GONE WITH
THE WIND

————— ☆ —————

*Winner of the Pulitzer Prize,
inspiration for the most popular motion picture
ever made, this flaming epic of Civil War
and Reconstruction is the most widely
read American novel ever written.*

12511/$1.25

PUBLISHED BY
POCKET BOOKS